Scientific Guide to Hop Aroma and Flavor

Scott Janish

Foreword by Stan Hieronymus

ISBN: 978-0-578-47786-2

Publisher: ScottJanish.com
Editor: Bryan Roth
Cover: Keith Hartwig

v.1.2

Table of Contents

Acknowledgments

I've always heard that the brewing community was friendly, open, and helpful, but until I started writing this book, I didn't fully appreciate the truth of it. Homebrewers reached out to me over the internet to offer advice, support, and encouragement. Professional brewers, whom I've never met, spent hours with me answering every question I'd throw at them. Hop chemists would walk me through their experiments, answer countless emails, and proofread my attempts to explain their excellent work.

I want to thank all of the homebrewers who have read and interacted with my writings over the years. The confidence to even begin this project began with the success of a blog I started with no sense of where it would take me. I'm amazed at the willingness of homebrewers to help out with this project, especially in areas where they have expertise, and I do not! I particularly want to thank Keith Hartwig for designing such a great book cover and Jesse Ewing for advice on self-publishing.

I'm incredibly grateful to all of the brewers who sat down with me and walked me through their hazy beer making process. The transparency in this profession helps us all become better brewers, and I hope to pay that favor forward in the future. In no particular order, I want to thank Noah Bissell, Brandon Tarr, Josh Hare, Joe Mohrfeld, James Dugan, Andy Miller, Ben Edmunds, Adam Robbings, Sam Richardson, and Ben Maeso.

It was Stan Hieronymus's book, *For the Love of Hops: The Practical Guide to Aroma, Bitterness, and the Culture of Hops,* that shifted my view of hops from an ingredient in beer to something I'd research and write about over a span of two years. I can't thank Stan enough for writing the foreword to this book and being such a big inspiration to me as researcher and writer of all things hops.

This book wouldn't be possible if it weren't for all of the incredible work done (and is being done) in the area of hop science. I want to thank everyone who devotes their career to helping us understand the fascinating world of hops and beer. I especially want to thank Dr. John Paul Maye for focusing his research on hazy IPAs, reading sections of this book, and even running some of my beers through his lab!

When I realized I would be self-publishing, I immediately knew who I wanted as an editor. Bryan Roth has long been one of my favorite beer writers; his seriousness and professionalism in print is matched only by his goofiness on Twitter (@BryanDRoth). I appreciate Bryan's willingness to read through my early rough draft chapters and somehow, is still willing to sit down and have a beer with me today.

Some of my best friends today are ones I've met through homebrewing, and a couple of them have been a big part of this book. I want to thank Sean Gugger for traveling the country (and world) with me on various beer adventures and for always listening as I excitedly blurt out new hop research I'm dying to share with anyone that will listen. I also want to thank Trevor Fisher for not only proofreading the book (somebody had to tell me I had two Chapter 10's) but for also lending his palate to my experiments, listening to me go on and on about thiols, and even brewing an experiment for the book.

I also want to thank my good friend and now business partner Michael Tonsmeire for reading the book with a skeptical set of eyes. Michael has been a big inspiration to me as an early brewer, blogger, and now author. In part, it was early conversations about this very book that got us together and sparked the first talks of Sapwood Cellars. Michael's brewing knowledge and creativity amazes me every day, but so too does his dedication to the craft and his willingness to be a source of information for both homebrewers and professional brewers alike.

Lastly, I want to thank my parents, who have watched me jump 100% into new hobbies and interests my entire life, always encouraging me and never cautioning. Seeing them follow their passions and take risks has been a big inspiration to me as I stepped outside the comfort of a desk job, PTO, and health insurance to start a brewery and write a book!

Foreword

In 2010, scientists working for Japanese brewery Sapporo reported on their research into how geraniol metabolism might add to the citrus flavor of beer. They brewed two beers, using Citra hops in one and coriander seeds in the other because both are rich in the compounds geraniol and linalool. The finished Citra beer contained not only linalool and geraniol but also citronellol, which had been converted from geraniol during fermentation.

The same transformation from geraniol into citronellol occurred during fermentation of the beer made with coriander. Taste panels perceived the beers as relatively similar. The concentration of geraniol and citronellol in both increased depending on the initial concentration of geraniol. The results suggested the importance of citronellol and an excess of linalool in the hop-derived citrus flavor of beer, but because there was little citronellol in raw hops the generation of citronellol depended on geraniol metabolism by yeast.

In 2012, these researchers – whose work you'll find documented in this book—followed up that study by comparing the composition of monoterpene alcohols in various hops. They examined the behavior of geraniol and citronellol under different hopping conditions as well as hop blending conditions influencing the citrus flavor of hopped beer. In the process, they found many U.S. varieties contained relatively high amounts of geraniol, but that European hop varieties did not.

They concluded that a blend of geraniol-rich hops could enrich the levels of geraniol and citronellol in finished beer. They also suggested that citrus character in beer could be enhanced by blend-hopping of geraniol-rich hops; and composition of monoterpene alcohols and flavor character in beer could be controlled by blending two hops having different flavor characteristics. They also provided a chart that showed levels of various compounds in several hop varieties.

Adventurous brewers making hop-forward beers used varieties listed on that chart or information from other sources to find hops rich in geraniol and linalool that might be substituted for hard-to-get varieties. They reported brewing beers that had more citrus-like aromas and flavors, sometimes "tropical" if not as "juicy" as beers made with more expensive New World hops.

Those brewers found a method that worked, but it turns out linalool and geraniol were not totally responsible for the results.

The team from Sapporo, headed by Kiyoshi Takoi, continued to follow up, reporting in 2016 on their discoveries in an appropriately named paper titled, "Control of Hop Aroma Impression of Beer with Blend-Hopping using Geraniol-rich Hop and New Hypothesis of Synergy among Hop-derived Flavour Compounds." The new hypothesis added thiols—sulfur compounds that, like linalool and geraniol, may be contained in the essential oil of hops—to the equation.

They examined the impact of a volatile thiol, in this case one known as 4MSP or 4MMP, in a model solution with a blend of linalool, geraniol and citronellol. The solution with 4MSP was perceived moderately tropical, while the LGC mix was not tropical but more citrus-like and fruitier. A solution containing both the LGC mix and 4MSP had distinctly tropical character.

Brewers who sought out hops with high levels of geraniol and also picked ones, such as Chinook, containing 4SMP are the ones who reported more tropical aroma and flavor. Those who chose hops with high levels of geraniol but a lower level of 4MSP, such as Bravo, did not.

Is this the final piece in the puzzle? Likely not. The ongoing quest to pack more intense, unique aromas and flavors into beer continues. Brewers keep experimenting, discovering new methods to produce bolder flavors. Scientists keep looking for answers to explain why, and in the process illuminate new pathways to innovation. They will be building on the research documented here.

I've read hundreds of papers like the ones that Scott Janish has leaned on to write this book. What they often lack is the perspective that only a brewer can provide. As well as digging through thousands of pages to collect the information within, Janish looks at what he has found through the eyes of a brewer, and he provides other brewers an opportunity to do the same.

He has gone down the rabbit hole, and he's invited readers to follow.

Stan Hieronymus
Author
Brewing Local (2016), For the Love of Hops: The Practical Guide to Aroma, Bitterness and the Culture of Hops (2012), Brewing with Wheat (2010), and Brew like a Monk (2005)

Introduction

In late January 2016, a snowstorm shut down the Federal Government and I found myself stuck at home fascinated with a study I came across on extraction during dry hopping. Previously, I had spent more time than I care to admit reading through homebrew forums and blogs trying to find answers to processes-related brewing questions that intrigued me. With that first study that caught my attention authored by Peter Wolfe, I finally had a source that wasn't online anecdotal experiences and opinions, but actual tested data with sensory results. I was hooked and spent the remainder of that snow day scouring the internet for similar hop studies, eventually writing my first scientific blog post summarizing what I learned titled, "Examination of Studies: Hopping Methods and Concepts for Achieving Maximum Hop Aroma and Flavor." From that day forward, I created alerts for brewing studies, signed up for the various academic organizations that publish journals and stashed every brewing study I collected into a searchable cloud database, which would become the ultimate source for this book.

The snow day was a blessing in that I found my niche as a blogger, which to me, was somebody willing to spend countless hours digging through research (not always knowing what I was looking for) and testing out the findings that excited me the most with 5-gallon experimental batches on my stove. This book is the organic extension of that passion to learn and put into practice the great work of brewing researchers around the world. Over the span of two years, I spent my free time reading over 1,000 academic studies (citing over 300 of them in the pages ahead) focusing the direction of the research on information that could help explain the mystery of hop aroma and flavor.

This isn't a book promising the absolute best methods to brew world class hazy IPAs (it should help with that, however). Rather, it's a book exploring the science of the various factors that contribute to brewing intensely aromatic and flavorful hoppy beers, with the hope of getting brewers to think differently about how to approach the style. My goal for the book is to inspire brewers to use the research to experiment and disrupt ingrained brewing habits and commonly held beliefs. I often think I'm onto something when my brewing friends and colleagues think my next planned experiment is crazy. It's this outside the box thinking, driven by scientific data, that can produce amazing (and horrible) results.

Brewing amazing beer isn't always the goal of experimentation. For example, research related to dry hopping and bitterness inspired me to brew a hazy IPA with zero hot-side hopping, choosing to only dry hop the beer at high levels. The resulting beer wasn't very good, it was extremely bitter in a polyphenol-vegetal way and was void of any fruity hop saturated flavor. Despite the taste, I considered the experiment a success. It taught me that hot-side hopping was a valuable part of making a great IPA and the research portion of the experiment (authored by John Paul Maye Ph.D.) gave me a new understanding of how dry hops contribute to bitterness and flavor.

The decision to self-publish this book was one I approached cautiously. A publisher would help polish the contents with a professional staff dedicated to the craft. Their reach in promoting the book would be another obvious upside. The downside of self-publishing is that all the work is on me, somebody with zero experience in book production. So, should I go with a publisher or self-publish? Luckily for me, none of the major publishers seemed that interested in a book focused solely on hop science, so the decision to go at it alone became an easy one!

I'm excited about the benefits of self-publishing, however. The ability to focus on the topics that I'm most interested in is extremely rewarding. Working on this project on my own timeline was also a huge bonus as starting up a brewery at the same time really slowed its progress. I'm also excited to have the rights to the content so I can use it on my blog or in other publications as I wish. Another big bonus to self-publishing is the ability to put out updates to the book as often as I wish (including small updates to address inevitable typos and formatting issues). As the science evolves and I continue to talk with other brewers, there should be plenty of future findings to write about!

About the Book

I start the book out in Chapter one exploring the history of hop research and build a foundation of basic hop compound knowledge to use as a guide throughout the book. I also look closely at the differences between hop pellets, cones, and various extract products.

Chapter two is all about hot-side hopping, which includes science on early addition bittering hops and late whirlpool hops. I look at research into the importance of whirlpool hopping for enhanced hop flavoring. How the temperatures and durations of whirlpool hopping can impact hop compounds. Also, how certain hop varieties can have higher extraction efficiency than others.

Chapter three takes a close look at the importance of proper hop storage and how aging hops can impact their compounds and ultimately the flavor of the beer. Surprisingly, some of the research may inspire experiments using slightly aged hops on the hot-side!

Chapter four focuses on one of the most important characteristics of a great hazy IPA, a soft and approachable mouthfeel. Water chemistry (sulfate-chloride ratios), additions of minerals from malts, how minerals can impact hop flavors, and personal experiments help to appreciate the keys to great mouthfeel.

Chapter five examines how grist selection can impact flavor perceptions in hoppy beers. In particular, how the concentrations of proteins, carbohydrates, and viscosity can alter flavor and aroma perceptions. Even certain base malts may contribute more fruity flavors than others! Yeast pitching rates is also looked at as another factor in the retention or elimination of volatile hop compounds.

In Chapter six, I break down esters and fusel alcohol production during fermentation, both of which can play large roles in the final taste and aroma of beer. A little bit of fruity ester production with the right yeast strain can play a positive role in making a hoppy beer more complex and aromatic, while too much can compete and potentially dominate the hop flavors you might be seeking. This Chapter looks closely at what brewing variables may increase or decrease esters and alcohol production so brewers can make changes to their processes to get closer to their desired goals.

Chapter seven covers one of my favorite aspects of brewing hazy hoppy beers, dry hopping! I look at research on the importance of keeping oxygen out during dry hopping, how different dry hopping durations and amounts can impact hop compound extraction, and the some of the potential negative aspects of dry hopping (like too much polyphenol extraction).

In Chapter eight, I continue looking at dry hopping research focusing on how processes can impact the bitterness of beer. It's commonly believed that the only way to get hop bitterness into beer is with hot-side additions, but recent research sheds light on the importance of different hop bittering acids and their extraction during dry hopping. In addition to bitterness, this Chapter looks at the impact dry hopping can have on the final pH of beer, which can impact perceived bitterness.

Chapter nine explores research surrounding dry hopping and enzymatic activity which can lead to refermentation. Often referred to as hop creep, the enzymatic activity from dry hops can be put in check with various processes maneuvers like controlling dry hop temperatures and contact time.

Chapter ten gets into another one of my favorite topics, biotransformation of hop compounds. The term biotransformation is often thrown around as a key to hazy hoppy beers but is largely misunderstood and mystic. This Chapter gathers together the relevant papers on the subject to give brewers a better understanding of what biotransformation is as well as factors that favor its production.

In Chapter eleven, I stay with the topic of biotransformation focusing on hop thiols, which despite having low concentrations in hops, have the potential to enhance hop flavor. This Chapter also explores research from the wine industry on important thiols contributing to fruity flavors in wine (many of which are found in hops) and methods used to increase their presence in beer via biotransformation. I also share my experience using wine strains in hoppy beers inspired by the research.

Chapter twelve looks at a new and popular product called lupulin powder, developed by Yakima Chief, Hopunion Cryo Hops® (as they are called) are advertised as the concentrated lupulin of whole leaf hops which contain aromatic hop oils but less of the vegetative material of traditional hop pellets. I talk to commercial brewers about their experience with lupulin powder and look at tested data on IBU and polyphenol contributions from cryo hops.

Chapter thirteen looks closely at the science of why hazy IPAs are in fact hazy. Various factors have been studied like mid-fermentation dry hopping, pH and ABV levels, grist and hop selections, all of which can help brewers obtain different haze levels.

Chapter fourteen examines the fragile nature of hazy IPAs by exploring some of the research surrounding beer oxidation and ways to increase shelf-life. Grist selection, dry hop varieties, and early hot-side hopping can all impact the stability of hazy beers.

Chapter fifteen was one of my favorite Chapters to write. I was lucky enough to travel around the country interviewing brewers I respect the most (not only for their established haze credentials, but for being open to sharing their secrets and lessons learned over the years). There is no question that the early success of brewing hazy hoppy beers at Sapwood Cellars is a direct result of these honest brewing conversations. In this Chapter, you will learn from the best, including Other Half Brewing, Prison City Pub and Brewery,

Reuben's Brews, Breakside Brewery, Bissel Brothers, and Great Notion!

Chapter 1: Introduction to Hop Compounds

Chaston Chapman (1869-1932) was one of the original hop chemist pioneers authoring the first works on hops and their specific compounds dating back to 1895. Chapman's research was awe-inspiring considering his era and matched only by his confidence in the totality of his work, writing in 1928:

> For some years, as opportunity offered, the investigation of this oil was continued in my laboratory, and several Chapters were added to the story, but with the publication in 1903 of a paper dealing more fully with the chemistry of some constituents of the oil, I felt that the last Chapter had been written. Only a year or two ago, however, some high boiling fractions of hop oil came into my hands through the kindness of Messrs. White, Tomkins & Courage, Ltd., and I took the opportunity of submitting these to an examination with the object of ascertaining whether other compounds than those I had already discovered existed in this oil, and if so, what their nature was. This investigation, in turn, has been brought to a conclusion, and the results were communicated to the Chemical Society in May of this year. It resulted in the discovery of several new and unsuspected compounds, and I believe that the last Chapter has now in reality been written—at any rate, by me, and that something very near the full story has been told.[1]

This book will show that the full story hasn't been told and the last chapter wasn't written as Chapman boasted. Thankfully, hop research continued to advance and fifteen more chapters could be written!

History of Hop Oil Research

It's important to look at the history of hop research to not only appreciate where our current state of science stands, but to honor the work done by people like Chapman. Their studies have helped lay the groundwork for current hop investigation, analysis, and examination.

Chapman, for example, discovered and named the oil humulene in 1893,[2] but also went on to reveal additional hop compounds, which he would name luparone, lupaenol, and luparol.[3] Further research has shown how incredibly complex hops are and new tools like gas chromatography (GC) have proven to be pivotal in advancing knowledge and confirming some of the early discoveries.

The first use of GC with hop oils was by G.A. Howard, M.SC., Ph.D. in 1956, where Howard used GC to discover the separation of 18 components of hop oils obtained from Fuggle hops including myrcene, methyinonylketone, caryophyllene, and humulene.[4] It was Howard's goal to establish both the makeup of oils in hops and the proportions in which they occur, because different hop varieties had different oil compositions, and presumably, different aromas.

In 1963, V.J. Jahnsen, Ph.D., furthered the new and exciting research into hop oils by enhanced temperature-programmed gas chromatography analysis. Using this method, Jahnsen tested the Bullion hop variety and found approximately 200 components, which made it very clear just how complex hops were becoming to researchers and brewers.[5]

Fifteen years later, Roland Tressl studied the Spalter hop variety using distillation-extraction, liquid-solid chromatography, and capillary gas chromatography-mass spectrometry, to (semi) quantify more than 120 volatile constituents. Tressl tested the hops after a storage period of three years, which showed the potential downside of aging hops. Components typically considered off-flavors in beer were found in older hops, including aldehydes and fatty acids.[6]

Fast forward a few more years, Martin Steinhaus tested dried cones of the Spalter hop variety grown in the German area of Hallertau in 2000, finding 23 ordants with aroma extract dilution analysis (AEDA). Of the 23 odorants, ten of the "high-impact" hop aroma compounds had previously not been identified.[7]

Two years later in 2002, the total count hop compound count had grown to 440. Then Mark T. Roberts published a study in 2004 looking at hop oil compounds through a more advanced method called comprehensive multidimensional capillary gas chromatography (GCxGC). Roberts discovered 45 additional compounds that had not been previously reported and suggested that it's possible there may be over 1,000 compounds in hop oil to be found with additional testing![8]

Hop Bittering Acids

There are three major components of hops that reside in the lupulin gland of the hop. These are 1) α-acids (humulones), 2) β-acids (lupulones), and 3) essential hop oils. The bittering component of hops comes from α-acids and β-acids (β-acids less so than α-acids). The three major α-acids are humulone, adhumulone, and cohumulone. Humulone and cohumulone percentages depend on the hop variety but are typically around 20-50%, and the adhumulone is around 15% of the α-acids in the lupulin glands. When these α-acids are boiled, they isomerize into iso-α-acids via a chemical reaction. For example, humulone isomerizes into cis-isohumulone and adhumulone isomerizes into cis-isoadhumulone.[9]

Cohumulone has been shown to isomerize more efficiently than humulone and adhumulone. Specifically, a utilization rate of 60% was found for cohumulone when boiled, where a yield of 55% was found for the total α-acids.[10] Many brewers believe that beer brewed with isomerized cohumulone (cis-isocohumulone) lends an undesirable bitterness to beer, however, this claim doesn't appear to be scientifically substantiated. This belief started in a 1972 article titled, *A Theory on the Hop Flavor in Beer*. In the paper, beers were brewed with humulone and cohumulone and compared for bitterness intensities.

Although the bitterness of the cohumulone beer was rated stronger and harsher, it also had more iso-α-acids, which of course would make it more bitter! The beer brewed using cohumulone had 34 mg/L of iso-α-acids, and the beer using humulone had only 21 mg/L of iso-α-acids, which the author suggested was enough to not properly compare the two beers. The cohumulone public opinion damage appeared to be done, however, as the article had significant consequences for hops and the brewing industry as brewers demanded hops low in cohumulone and breeders started to select for low-cohumulone varieties.[11] As a general rule for bittering potential of hop acids, the more polar the hop bittering acid the more likely the impact is a smoother bitterness.

The isomerization of hop α-acids into iso-α-acids is dependent on the time and temperature of the boil. When the boil duration is short or low kettle temperatures are utilized, the isomerization yields are significantly reduced.[12] Other factors like wort pH and minerals can also enhance isomerization. The addition of calcium or magnesium to the wort also increased the isomerization rate.[13]

Subsequent testing of isomerization yields after 60-minute wort boils with the addition of metal ions at the start of the boil also showed higher rates. For example, the addition of magnesium enhanced the utilization rate an average of 24%.[14] I would be very interested in further studies on how adding magnesium during the whirlpool may or may not also enhance the extraction of desirable fruity hop compounds from whirlpool hop additions.

Hops do not have to be boiled to isomerize as one study found that even at 194°F (90°C) substantial amounts of iso-α-acids were produced. This means when beer is waiting to be chilled or during a whirlpool, you are still getting bitterness from hops.[15] I've even had very small amounts of tested isomerization from dry hopping, but this is a more complex topic covered later in Chapter eight.

Back in 1956, it was determined that approximately 38% of bitter acids are lost to trub, 35% to spent hops, and 10% to yeast.[16] However, more recent work suggests that the distribution percentages of bitter substances from whole hops lost during the brewing processes are 50% from trub, 20% from spent hops, 10% from evaporation and yeast, and 20% remaining in the final beer.[17]

Aaron Justus, Director of R&D and Specialty Brewing at Ballast Point Brewing authored a paper in 2019 examining IBUs throughout the brewing process.[18] Starting with mash hopping (which Chapter fourteen suggests may help improve beer stability) Justus used Palisade (7.5% α-acid) and Calypso (14.1% α-acid) each mash hopped at two different levels (0.25 and 0.50 lbs./bbl). Measuring the wort of the beers prior to the start of the boil resulted in an average utilization rate of 9% from mash hopping. The overall rate decreased when the level of hops used increased. In addition, despite different IBUs measured at the start of the boil with the different hop varieties and amounts, the knockout IBUs (tested after boiling and chilling) was about the same. The author suggests this pullback in IBUs during the boil may be from thermal degradation of iso-α-acids. This finding could mean that high levels of mash hopping might not necessarily translate to higher IBUs.

Next, Justus looked at 60-minute hop bittering additions across twelve different brews and found, on average, a utilization rate of 44%. As hop rate and gravity increased in the test beers, utilization steadily declined which may be why many brewers believe higher ABV hoppy beers can handle a higher volume of hops thrown at it. For example, a double IPA high in wort gravity could see lower IBU pickup than expected from a large hot-side addition.

Moving towards whirlpool hop additions and IBU pickup, Justus found over 19 test brews an average utilization rate of 29.9%.

Interestingly, IBUs seemed to peak after just 10 minutes in the whirlpool (only seeing an increase utilization rate of 2% with a full 70-minute whirlpool). This finding suggests long whirlpool times may not be contributing as much bitterness as many might assume.

Tracking IBU losses during fermentation across fourteen brews, Justus found an average rate of IBU losses of 33.7%. Interestingly, beers that relied on whirlpool hops for most of the bitterness (think hazy IPAs) tended to lose more IBUs during fermentation. Also, high gravity beers lost more IBUs than lower gravity beers.

Taking a step back from the science and speaking from my experience brewing both commercially and at home, I've become convinced that hot-side hop additions (including whirlpool hops) are essential to achieving hop saturated flavor in beer. I'm often shocked by how few hops brewers are adding to their beer on the hot-side in fear of picking up too many IBUs. The work from Justus can put some at ease in that large whirlpool additions (especially in high gravity beers) will result in lower IBU extraction. In addition, fermentation will also strip IBUs. Combine this knowledge with information we learn in detail later in the book that dry hopping will also strip iso-α-acids in beer. This is all to say don't be afraid to experiment with large hot-side whirlpool hop additions!

Hop Aroma Compounds

Essential oils in hops, which make up their aroma and flavor profile, are about 0.1-2.0% by dry weight of the hop depending on the variety.[19] Certain hops like Polaris and Galaxy, for example, can be much higher (3-5%) and varieties like Czech Saaz and East Kent Goldings are much lower (0.4-0.8%). Below is a list of some of the hops with the highest total oil amounts. Keep in mind different lots will include hops with different oil percentages as growing conditions (like temperature, rainfall amounts, and harvest timing) are a few variables that can alter hop oil percentages.

Hop Variety	Total Oil (mL/100g)[20]
Polaris	4 - 5
Super Pride	3.4 - 4
Galaxy	3 - 5
Columbus	2.5 - 4.5
Tomahawk® Brand F10 cv	2.5 - 4.5
Zeus	2.5 - 4.5
Ekuanot™ Brand HBC 366	2.5 - 4
Ella	2.4 - 3.4
Bravo	2.3 - 3.5
Rakau	2.2 - 2.2
Mandarina Bavaria	2.1 - 2.3
Magnum (United States)	2 - 3
Merkur	2 - 3
Waimea	2 - 2.2

Flavor and aroma come from the essential oil fraction of the hop and can be divided into three groups: 1) hydrocarbon components, 2) oxygenated components, and 3) sulfur-containing components.

Although each individual hop will show different results, a study looking at Brewers Gold sheds some light into the makeup of the oils as it relates to the three main groups mentioned above. The researchers found that hydrocarbons make up 40-80% of the total oil, of which, myrcene, humulene, and caryophyllene make up most of this fraction.

The oxygenated fraction is only about 14% of the total oil but can contribute up to 34% to the hop's aroma. This oxygenated fraction was more complex as about 20 components made up about 47% of the total. This study shows that in the Brewers Gold variety, the hydrocarbon fraction was up to six times greater than the oxygenation fraction, but only contributed twice as much to the total aroma profile of the hop.[21]

Because hops contain numerous aromatic components, it's difficult to say with certainty which compounds are solely responsible for contributing directly to specific aroma characteristics of a variety, particularly when different compounds have different sensory thresholds and compounds can also work together to form a synergistic effect on flavor and aroma. It does appear, however, that even though many compounds make up this oxygenated fraction, a much smaller number are likely contributing to overall aroma. To help focus hop research, myrcene (hydrocarbon fraction), and linalool (oxygenated fraction) are often thought to be good indicators of hop aroma and flavor intensity and are often the compounds focused on in the research throughout the book.

The following chart of the chemical composition of hop oils should help serve as a reference as many of these compounds are mentioned and put to the test in various brewing conditions in the pages ahead.

CHEMICAL COMPOSITIONS OF THE ESSENTIAL OILS OF HOPS

Based on general averages, actual percentages vary depending on hop variety and other factors.

HYDROCARBONS

Approx. 40 - 80%

EXTREMELY VOLATILE

Sesquiterpenes	Monoterpenes	Other Aliphatic Compounds
EXAMPLES β-farnesene α-humulene β-caryophyllene	**EXAMPLES** myrcene α-pinene β-pinene	**EXAMPLES** pentadcane
(spicy)	(spicy, herbal)	

OXYGEN CONTAINING COMPOUNDS

Approx. 30%

Hemiterpenes Alcohols	Monoterpenes Alcohols	Sesquiterpenes Alcohols	Other Oxygen Containing Compounds
EXAMPLES 3-methyl-2-butene-1-ol	**EXAMPLES** linalool geraniol β-citronellol	**EXAMPLES** humulenol farnesol	**EXAMPLES** aldehydes ketones esters epoxides
(fruity, citrus)	(floral, fruity, citrus)	(herbal)	(fusel, fruity, sweet)

SULFUR CONTAINING COMPOUNDS

<1% Low Sensory Threshold

Thiols and Other Sulphur Containing Compounds	Sulphides	Thioesters
EXAMPLES 3SHOL 3SH (3MH) 3MHA 4MSP (4MMP)	**EXAMPLES** dimethyl sulphide dimethyl disulphide	**EXAMPLES** S-methyl-thio-hexanoate
Desirable: fruity, passionfruit, exotic	Undesirable: cooked corn, cheesy	Undesirable: cooked cabbage, garlic, onion

To help put flavor and aroma descriptors to many of these same hop compounds listed in the previous image, below is a chart presented by Victor Algazzali at the American Society of Brewing Chemists Meeting at Brewing Summit in 2018. The chart is a fantastic reference as new compounds are introduced in the various studies throughout the book.

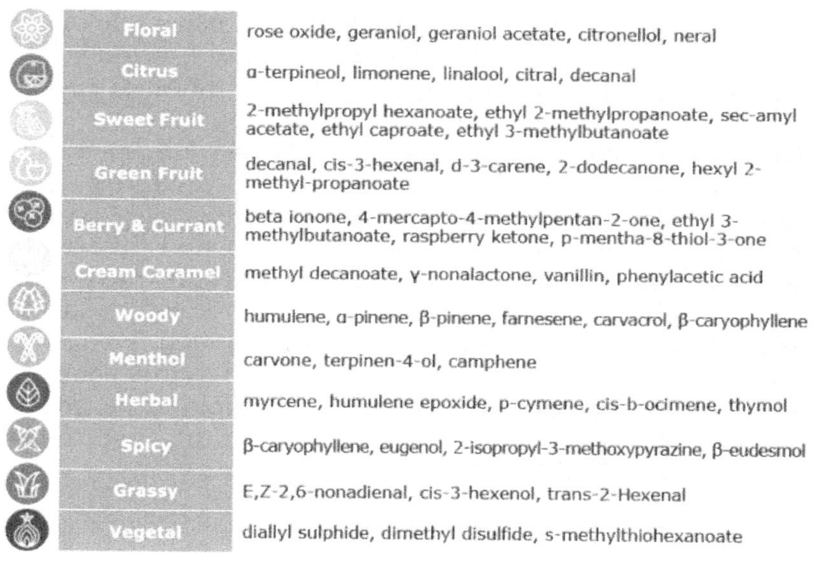

Descriptor	Compounds
Floral	rose oxide, geraniol, geraniol acetate, citronellol, neral
Citrus	α-terpineol, limonene, linalool, citral, decanal
Sweet Fruit	2-methylpropyl hexanoate, ethyl 2-methylpropanoate, sec-amyl acetate, ethyl caproate, ethyl 3-methylbutanoate
Green Fruit	decanal, cis-3-hexenal, d-3-carene, 2-dodecanone, hexyl 2-methyl-propanoate
Berry & Currant	beta ionone, 4-mercapto-4-methylpentan-2-one, ethyl 3-methylbutanoate, raspberry ketone, p-mentha-8-thiol-3-one
Cream Caramel	methyl decanoate, γ-nonalactone, vanillin, phenylacetic acid
Woody	humulene, α-pinene, β-pinene, farnesene, carvacrol, β-caryophyllene
Menthol	carvone, terpinen-4-ol, camphene
Herbal	myrcene, humulene epoxide, p-cymene, cis-b-ocimene, thymol
Spicy	β-caryophyllene, eugenol, 2-isopropyl-3-methoxypyrazine, β-eudesmol
Grassy	E,Z-2,6-nonadienal, cis-3-hexenol, trans-2-Hexenal
Vegetal	diallyl sulphide, dimethyl disulfide, s-methylthiohexanoate

[22]

Diving a little deeper into the three hop compound classes, hydrocarbons represent approximately 40-80% of a hop's oils and can be divided into three groups: 1) aliphatic, 2) monoterpenes, and 3) sesquiterpenes. The latter two are the most studied and referenced. The monoterpenes are spicy, herbal, and green, and consist of compounds like myrcene, α-pinene, and β-pinene. Sesquiterpenes, like β-farnesene, α-humulene, and β-caryophyllene lend more of a woody characteristic.

The oxygenated fraction, which represent about 30% of the total oil, is a very complex mixture of alcohols, aldehydes, acids, ketones, epoxides, and esters. Most important to brewers looking for intense fruit-forward IPAs are the terpene alcohols located in the oxygenated fraction of hops (examples: linalool, nerol, geraniol). Despite representing a small fraction of the hop, these compounds are more likely to remain in beer throughout the brewing process and are less volatile than terpene hydrocarbons such as myrcene.[23]

Most of the research in this book related to increasing "hoppiness" of beer is focused on these oxygenated alcohols.

Turning to a paper titled, *Just How Insoluble are Monoterpenes?*, we can get a better sense of how less-soluble hydrocarbons are from oxygenated monoterpene alcohols. The paper found that hydrocarbons (woody, spicy, resinous-like) have very low solubility compared to oxygenated monoterpenes (fruity, floral, and citrus-like). Specifically, the paper found that monoterpenes containing oxygen in the form of a ketone, alcohol, ether, or aldehyde had solubilities 10-100 times greater than hydrocarbons.[24]

The sulfur-containing compounds of the hop oil fraction are a very small percentage of the hop oils but can play a role in flavor development because of their low sensory thresholds (silent but deadly). They contain some organosulfur compounds like hydrogen sulfide, methional, methanethiol, diethyl sulfide, dimethyl sulphide, dimethyl disulfide, and methyldithioatcetate.[25] Many of the sulfur compounds would be considered negative in hop-forward beers except for hop thiols, which are fruit-forward sulfur compounds. Researchers are finding these hop-derived thiols to be important compounds in modern fruity IPAs. Because of this, hop thiols are covered in more detail in Chapter 11.

Hop Pellet Blends and Oil Testing

Pellets are typically blends of a few different hop lots selected to balance out variability because different factors like growers, growing regions, the age of hops, and harvest date can have an impact on final hop oil figures. In general, hop pellet blends are carefully created to achieve a "standard" mix that's representative of the variety. Therefore, when we brew with a bag of Citra hops we can be confident (hopefully) that the result won't be a surprise.

Not all harvested lots are included in pellet blends because some lots are extreme outliers when it comes to measured oil concentrations. The wide gap between tested oils from different lots can increase the difficulty of getting a homogeneous mix. In other words, if one lot of Citra is drastically different (both in aroma and measured oils) than another, it may not be worth including the outlier lot in the blend because it could alter the standard Citra flavor we are expecting.

Another reason not to include too many hop
the importance of hop traceability. It's crucia
traceability from the field to the brewery becaus
happen, for example, having fewer lots in eac
narrow down the problem lot and affected packa

How different can hops of the same variety
Data provided by Hopunion LLC in 2015 shows swing
and 2014 for all the Simcoe lots tested (Simcoe is known for being a high variability hop). Looking at myrcene, the data shows that the lowest recorded myrcene lot in 2014 was around 40% of the total oil while another grower had myrcene levels over 70%. Looking at the average myrcene levels across all the hops lots tested, this particular hop variety averaged around 57%, making these two hop lots outliers to the average.

Outlier hop lots don't go to waste however, they can be used for a generic bittering extract or to brew beer with unique flavors and aromas that you cannot achieve with a standard blend. As an example of how the different lots can alter flavors, going back to the lot-to-lot data mentioned above, the average geraniol (floral, sweet, rose-like characteristic) content across lots was less than 0.1%. But some growers had lots with geraniol coming in slightly over 0.5% (this is like a Fuggle to Mosaic swing in geraniol).

Hops, just like grapes from the wine industry, can vary quite a bit within a variety. As much as brewers appreciate the stable flavors they can get from blends of single hop varieties, many would also likely enjoy brewing with hops directly from growers and experiment with the same hop varieties from different lots. Just like we have famous breweries, maybe we could start to see renowned hop yards! I should note that these differences in single varieties across hop yards aren't as much of an issue with the newer fields and "trademark" varieties, but it can be more prevalent in older yards like a 15-year-old Cascade yard.

Not all pelleted hops are blends, however. For example, if a purchasing brewery has a large enough order, they have the luxury of being able to receive non-blended pellets if they want to enjoy the characters of a grower's variety over the blend. This is something Sam Richardson from Other Half Brewing describes as an advantage to his brewery. These customer-selected lots mean a brewery has purchased bales from a single lot and likely met the minimum volume required for pelleting. During hop selection, brewers can purchase individual lots containing as much as 1,000 pounds of me brewers buy several lots and don't necessarily blend but some might.

Sometimes these unblended pellets find their way into the general market. For example, if a brewery finds that they are over-contracted they could choose to release some of their inventory to the public. These hops are no better or worse than the blended lots, but they may have some subtly unique characteristics that caught the attention of the commercial brewer. It would be nice to see special sales of these individual lots by the biggest hop suppliers advertised and sold to homebrewers and small breweries when and if they become available.

Even hops from the same lots can vary in measured oil concentrations from year-to-year. Variables like growing practices and different weather conditions can alter hop oil averages, but generally the change is minor. To look at how different lots can be year-to-year, I looked at data from the 2013-2014 hop crop and found there was very little change in measured hop oils. I also looked at the variance between all the oils for each variety to see what hop had the most significant fluctuation in the two crop years. Glacier had the most significant variation, with the largest jumps coming from a reduction of 15% in myrcene and a 10% addition in humulene. The most stable hop was Palisade, which showed virtually no change from the two hop crop years.

Hop blending of different lots helps to maintain a steady year-to-year profile across the varieties. This is particularly true when there is an abundance of a certain hop. Popular varieties are grown in greater numbers to keep up with demand, so there are more choices available when blending. The larger sample size tends to converge around the true mean. The opposite is true if there are only a handful of lots grown for a variety. For example, one pest outbreak or one thunderstorm can affect the mean for the entire variety. Mother Nature, please be kind to the hops.

Whole Hop Cones

Whole cone hops are unblended, which is why some brewers may choose to use them over pellets. One reason they aren't blended is because doing so would introduce oxygen when breaking up the bales, leading to accelerated deterioration. Brewing with cones from different hop lots could result in more hop oil variation (both good and bad), which could be why some brewers seek them out. Other brewers may choose to use whole cones for the aesthetic of using a "pure," unadulterated product. For example, Sierra Nevada Brewing Co. famously brews with whole cone hops.

Because whole cone hops represent the terroir (the natural environment where the hops are grown) the choice between whole hops and pellets is one of local character vs. consistency. However, most of the hops that are sold in whole cone form are from low variability lots, so it's rare to find anything too unexpected when brewing with them but is still more likely than when using pellets. The ease of storage and use of pellets over cones is also a big reason more brewers use pellets as using cones in large amounts can be problematic. However, don't forget that individual hop lots can also be made into pellets to get ease of use for brewers as well as potentially unique flavors from not being part of a blend.

Other than terroir having an impact on differences in hop cones between different lots, something as simple as hop harvesting can impact flavor. Research looking at different harvesting times in the Czech Republic's Saaz region (August-September) found interesting results when studying harvest dates paired with testing for hop oil compounds and sensory tests. For example, linalool increased in all four hop lots tested the further from August they were picked, only slightly dipping in late September. So, the timeframe for fruity late harvest hops, according to this study, would be late August into early September.

When the Czech Republic's Saaz region hops were put to the test in hop teas, the sensory results largely mirrored the linalool results. In other words, the later the harvest date, the higher the hoppy aroma intensity. The results don't appear to be a fluke either, as the same thing was done over a three-year period and each year, the later the harvest date, the more linalool increased (2010-2012). Boston Beer Company is a commercial example of this, they prefer to brew with hops harvested about seven days later than what is considered the ideal date.[26]

In the study above, the authors found that individual compounds increase at different rates throughout the growing year. For example, in six compounds tested (linalool, geraniol, myrcene, ocimene, β-pinene, D-limonene) measured increases were found as the crop year went on. On the other hand, other compounds (β-farnesene, bergamotene, α-humulene , and β-caryophyllene) were produced early in the harvest year. It appears then that some of the more fruity, citrus, and floral characters develop later, and more traditional woody tones develop early.[27]

Hop Oil Testing

The American Society of Brewing Chemists has an approved standard for quantifying hop oils, which involves performing a four-hour boil of hops in a distillation apparatus to collect and measure oils. You can see how this varies to how brewers use hops with a traditional 60-minute boil. One reason for the long boil is to be sure that all the oil has been extracted. The distillation is primarily used to determine the oil content (mL oil/100g hops), so it's important to be sure that all the oil has been collected. The compounds that boil off aren't lost, however, because the vapor is condensed and collected.

In testing, as the hops boil, the oils are separated from the plant material. This long boil standard is used (as opposed to a process that more closely resembles brewing) because results are then comparable with all other labs. It's important to have consistent measuring processes across all labs to help make sense of the data. The major problem of this type of testing is that some of the compounds are not heat tolerant, meaning they degrade when exposed to boiling temps for that long. There are alternatives to steam distillation, but they involve nasty chemical extractions which are also not analogous to brewing. In an ideal world, hop oils would be tested after being extracted into wort, but then you run into other variables. How do you choose the standard wort gravity and pH? What should the wort grist be comprised of? Should hops be added early or late during the boil?

Hop Extracts

There are two main types of hop extracts, those made from carbon dioxide supercritical fluid extraction (SFE) and ethanolic extracts. The carbon dioxide extracts contain the more nonpolar components, including the essential oils and acids. The ethanol extracts generally contain the more polar components including polyphenols.

Some breweries use hop extracts primarily for bittering their beers. Because the α-acids in hops can degrade with age, storage conditions, and across different hop lots, extracts may give brewers more consistent control over their bittering targets. The use of extracts also means less hop material finds its way into the kettle, which can result in increased yields. This is especially true when big whirlpool additions are swapped or partially substituted with hop extracts vs. pellets. Extracts used early in the boil can also reduce the hot-side foam formation during the boil, which can help with boil overs.[28]

Hot-side hop additions are required for bittering when using CO2 hop extract because it's not isomerized until it's boiled. Boiling CO2 extract for 60-90 minutes will result in about 35% isomerization of the α-acids, according to YCH hops. Just like pellets, CO2 extract can be used late in the hot-side process (whirlpool) for flavor and aroma. When using hop oils for aroma and flavor, extracts are typically added after fermentation is completed. These hop oil extracts are available in a generic form or by specific hop varieties.

One study found that using hop extracts for dry hopping closely compared to the aroma you can get from traditional dry hopping. The aroma matches were closer when using extract made from low temperature, steam-distilled hops. The authors found that when adding hop extracts with yeast present (prior to filtration) resulted in a reduction in hop aroma intensity compared to adding the extract directly to filtered (brite) beer. Adding the extract to brite beer ultimately caused haze formation, but some might not complain with that result. This study also showed that hop oil extracts are more storage stable than whole cones or pellets. In this case, very little oil loss was found after 11 months of refrigeration storage of the extract.[29]

In addition to flavor and bitterness control from extracts, another benefit is the potential for foam stability as one study found when using pre-isomerized α-acid hop extracts.[30] Another study found that extracts (specifically SFE) significantly increased mouthfeel and fullness of body.[31] Because of these post-fermentation benefits, certain extracts can be used to enhance a beer where it needs the help in the brite tank (increase bitterness, mouthfeel, and even head retention).

Hop extracts used for bittering may have a downside in that they aren't as effective as pure hops to prevent beer staling. A study looking into this area measured staling by "reducing power," and found that despite adding five times more α-acids with the CO2 extract compared to the pure hop beers, the reducing power was almost nothing. Interestingly, the lower the α-acid content of the hop, the higher the reducing power.[32] Slightly higher reducing power when bittering with pure hops could be an argument to use them as bittering additions in shelf sensitive beers.

Another option for bittering is isomerized pellets (iso-pellets) which are similar to typical pelletized hops in physical appearance, but instead of being stored cold, they are initially stored at 122°F (50°C) for 8-12 days to isomerize. One benefit to iso-pellets is the bitterness yield is increased compared to standard pellets. One study found a yield of 65% compared to just 37% with conventional pellets and was independent of the time of the addition.[33]

Pre-isomerized extracts are made by isomerizing conventional carbon dioxide extracts and can be added directly to wort during the boiling process. The two different forms of pre-isomerized extracts are isomerized kettle extract (IKE) and potassium-form isomerized kettle extract (PIKE). Of the two, PIKE has better solubility and better for last minute hop additions. Both IKE and PIKE achieve approximately a 70% bitterness yield, where PIKE got as high as 75.7% when it was added after the end of boiling and before a whirlpool rest.[34] In addition to iso-α-acids, both IKE and PIKE also contain β-acids, resins, hop waxes, and hop oils.

Another class of hop extract intended for use post fermentation, but can also be used in the kettle, is Rho-iso-α-acids (RHO). RHO is made by reducing iso-α-acids with sodium borohydride and is light stable and has a smooth bitterness. Approximately 1 ppm of RHO contributes about 0.7 IBUs of bitterness. RHO can prevent lightstruck flavor, but RHO cannot prevent lightstruck flavor if the beer is also brewed with regular hops or contains iso-α-acids.

Lightstruck flavor is the photo-oxidation of isohumulones from hops and can produce a skunky "lightstruck" (3-Methyl-2-butene-1-thiol) aroma in beer.[35] Unfortunately, the threshold for tasting this skunky flavor in beer is relatively low at just 4.4–35 ng/L.[36]

The creation of lightstruck flavor can take place even in cans kept cold and accelerated formation can occur at warmer temperatures. One paper found that a can of lager bittered with iso-α-acids stored at 86°F (30°C) developed the lightstruck thiol well above threshold after just four weeks, but was also detected in a control can kept at 35°F (1.6°C). If you are finding this type of skunky flavor in your beer, RHO may be a good option to try post fermentation.

Another post-fermentation extract (it can also be used in the boil if desired) is called tetrahydro-iso-α-acids (Tetra). Tetra is made by palladium hydrogen reduction of iso-α-acids. It is light stable, foam enhancing, and has a sharp non-lingering bitterness. Tetra is a relatively non-polar iso-α-acid and is primarily used for its foam stability benefits and prevention of lightstruck flavor. Tetra is thought to be more astringent than Hexa described below.

Hexahydro-iso-α-acids (Hexa), is yet another post-fermentation extract. Hexa is made by performing the sodium borohydride reduction on Tetra. Hexa, like Tetra is light stable, foam enhancing, and 1 ppm contributes 1 IBU of bitterness with a harsh lingering bitterness profile like iso-α-acids. Kalsec, a supplier of Hexa, advertises that 1 ppm can improve the NIBEM (foam stability measurement) value 10-12 seconds.[37]

Hexa can be used downstream as it only contains iso-α-acids. Hexa can help with lightstruck flavor but may also cause haze. Hexa can also increase the creamy mouthfeel of beer. Because Hexa is also relatively non-polar, it's not recommended to use it in the brew kettle.[38]

I've tried dosing Hexa (from Kalsec) in a few hazy IPAs with some success. For a 5-gallon batch, I experimented by adding 1 mL into the serving keg prior to transferring. The beers had a nice smooth mouthfeel and the head retention and cling was decent, but without testing the variable alone, it's difficult to say how much the Hexa was responsible for either the foam retention or body. Both beers were made with a healthy dose of chit malt and malted wheat, so other factors could have contributed. If your hazy IPAs are lacking in head retention, it does seem worth experimenting with dosing Hexa into either the serving tank or keg. Be sure to follow the recommended dosage rates so there isn't a big increase in bitterness, which could negatively impact the beer.

Typically, 4-5 ppm of Tetra or Hexa (or a 1:1 blend) is required for foam enhancement and that will add 4-5 IBUs of bitterness. Brewers could compensate for the increase in IBUs by reducing kettle hopping if noticeable differences are detected with the addition of Tetra or Hexa. At Sapwood Cellars, we have used both in a handful of beers (particularly hoppy sour beers where head retention can be lacking) and we haven't found the bitterness increases to be noticeable in a negative way.

Key Findings

- Hops are extremely complicated plants; the total hop compound count is at least 440 and could be as high as 1,000 with further testing.
- The isomerization of hop α-acids into iso-α-acids is dependent on the time and temperature of the boil, wort pH, and minerals (addition of calcium or magnesium to the wort also increases the isomerization rate).
- Hydrocarbons make up 40-80% of the total oil of hops and are the most volatile (harder to keep in the beer). They are generally described as spicy, woody, and earthy compounds.
- The more fruit-forward oxygenated fraction is only about 14% of the hops total oil but can contribute up to 34% of the hops flavor, in part because they are more soluble than hydrocarbons.
- Hop pellets are generally blends of different lots to achieve a more consistent product, where whole cones can be more unique and truer to the hop lot and harvest date. Many professional brewers that pick their hop lots feel they have an advantage achieving great hop flavor and aroma over using standard pellet blends.
- Hop extracts can be used to increase yield, improve bitterness precision, mouthfeel, head retention, and prevent lightstruck flavor.

Chapter 2: Benefits and Drawbacks of Hot-Side-Hopping

To achieve big hop aroma and flavor, many brewers are moving more of their total hops used to the cold side via dry hopping and pushing hot-side additions late in the boil. While this book covers research on why late hopping is important, it's also valuable to look at what happens to hop compounds when they are added early in the boil. This chapter discusses the importance of hot-side hop timing, and how the hop variety, age of the hops, temperature of late-hopping, and other factors influences beer flavors.

Kettle Aroma

Traditional kettle aroma in beer (described as being spicy, woody, and herbal) is complex because hops used to achieve this flavor are added at the start of the boil, causing a gambit of potential changes along the way. These changes can occur from compounds evaporating, the oxidation of terpenes into oxygenated derivatives, and biotransformation of oxygenated derivatives during fermentation.

In general, kettle aroma is associated with hops that are rich in sesquiterpene hydrocarbons, which tend to have descriptors like earthy, herbal, woody, and spicy.[39] In 2016, researchers showed that several sesquiterpene oxidation products are newly formed upon boiling and can influence the spicy and hoppy notes of beer. The increases in oxygenated sesquiterpenes when boiled in water (not wort) were attributed to increased levels of α-humulene and β-caryophyllene derivatives. Some of these newly-formed compounds were detected in some commercial kettle-hopped lagers.[40] In other words, there are earthy and woody compounds found in packaged commercial beers that were not present in the hops themselves until boiled. So, not only are these newly formed oxygenated sesquiterpenes created during the boil, they have staying power finding their way into the package product.

The same researchers did a follow-up study shortly after to further examine how boiling hop essential oils may contribute to hop aroma in beer. [41] This time the testing was done by boiling essential oil from Saaz, Hallertau Tradition, and Hallertau Perle in wort (experimental group) and water (control group). When the level of hop oils used was low, they didn't find much of an increase in hop essential oil and sesquiterpene and monoterpene hydrocarbons. However, a "remarkable" increase was found upon boiling with high hop oil concentrations for the spicy compounds.

Results above suggest that as hop oils increase in the boil (more hops) higher yields of oxygenated sesquiterpenes may be reached because of chemical oxidation of the sesquiterpene hydrocarbons. The results were comparable when testing in both water and wort. This isn't too terribly surprising: the more hop compounds you put into the boil, the more potential to increase these newly formed oxygenated compounds. Practically speaking, the experiment shows that as brewers increase early-boil hop additions, they may experience spicier and earthier hop flavor in the beer which can more closely resemble traditional kettle aroma.

Taking the above results a step further, the authors suggested that if you want higher levels of these oxidation products leading to increased "hoppiness" potential (hoppiness here means spicy and earthy not fruity), it might be worth selecting hop varieties for the boil with high levels of α-humulene and β-caryophyllene. If you want to bump up the oxidation products even more, consider mildly aging these hops before brewing. Aging of the hops will increase these oxidized products, which can lead to even more formation during the boil.

Kiyoshi Takoi, Ph.D. senior research brewer at Sapporo Breweries Ltd., told me the formation of these sesquiterpene oxidation products discussed above is less important as it relates to newly bred aroma hops (like Citra) where volatile thiols and monoterpene alcohols contribute more. However, in beers made with traditional aroma hops, the flavor of sesquiterpene oxidation could contribute to the total beer flavor. Whether having this kettle hop flavor in beer is good or bad is up to the preference of the brewer but understanding why certain hops and hop timing can impart the flavor at higher levels is helpful knowledge to have. Takoi concludes that not only late-hopping, but also kettle-hopping, are important for total hopped beer flavor in the case of traditional aroma hops because you can get both the spicy and earthy flavors, but also the floral and citrus notes traditional kettle hops can impart when used late in the boil, as the research below shows.[42]

Hop Timing and Kettle Aroma

So how can the timing of using these hops play a role in kettle flavor? A 2015 BrewingScience paper experimented by brewing separate batches of beer using Saaz for each, but with the timing of the boil additions altered. The question was to see how early kettle hopping, early and late hopping, late hopping (10 minutes left in boil), or whirlpool-only hopping affected overall hop flavor in the beers. The researchers found that most of the floral compounds were reduced with extended time in the boil because these compounds tend to be more volatile. The spicy compounds showed low levels to start, but significant increases were found during the boil, especially after 20 minutes (agreeing with the research described above).

Specifically, the study found that the α-humulene and β-caryophyllene oxidation products showed a recovery higher than 100%, again showing these compounds were formed by the oxidation of their sesquiterpene hydrocarbons during the boil. This increase in oxidation products did not happen when Saaz hops were added during the whirlpool only, showing that boiling is needed for the creation of these spicy oxidation products, likely over 20 minutes.

Although these newly formed oxidation products can remain throughout the brewing process, as the previous studies have shown, they are lost to some degree during the whirlpool and subsequent steps like fermentation, lagering, and filtration. However, there are still enough of these compounds left for a tasting panel to detect hop-derived flavor characteristics during triangle tasting. The panel showed that the early addition of the hops on the onset of boiling, 10 minutes left in the boil, and during the whirlpool, clearly resulted in beers with different flavors.

Overall, the panel seemed to enjoy the test pilsner hopped with Saaz both early and late, as it displayed a more complex and rounded hop profile of spicy/herbal aromas (from the early hopping/oxidation products) as well as floral and citrus notes from late hopping. It might be worth experimenting with multiple hop timings, even with noble hops, if a more complex hop character is desired because the different timing of the additions can alter how they come across on the palate due to reactions with heat.

The beer that was only hopped with Saaz during the whirlpool was rated with less spicy/herbal notes and scored very high in a grassy/green resinous aroma. On the other hand, the beer that was only late-boil hopped was rated as having a woody character. The beer that was only early hopped scored high for the spicy/herbal noble-like hop aroma, which was expected after testing for the sesquiterpene oxidation products created during the boil.[43]

This book is about fruit-forward IPAs, so why does any of this kettle hop research matter? Many brewers I talked to for the book, including myself, still add an early-boil bittering charge of 15-30 IBUs. Not a lot of thought is generally put into what variety is used this early in the boil (usually just what's cheap or on hand) but the kettle hop research shows that hop selection can matter for bittering hops if these spicy earthy flavors are not desired.

So, to apply the kettle flavor research to hazy hoppy beers, here are some hops that you may want to avoid for early bittering because they are relatively high in both α-humulene and β-caryophyllene. If used in the boil, these hops can increase kettle hop flavor through newly-formed oxygenated sesquiterpenes. If these varieties are mildly aged (stored in a fridge for a few months after the bag has been opened for example), they could potentially increase kettle hop flavor even more.

Hops that could contribute to kettle aroma when boiled:

- Hallertau Mittelfruh
- Pacifica
- Vanguard
- Progress
- Northdown
- East Kent Golding
- Nelson Sauvin
- Kohatu
- Perle
- Helga
- Northern Brewer
- Tradition
- Liberty
- Hallertau
- Golding
- Whitbread Golding
- Dr. Rudi
- Fuggle

- Pacific Jade

On the other hand, here are some hops that are high in α-acids but relatively low in α-humulene and β-caryophyllene. Consider these hops safe for early bittering additions when fruit flavors are the focus and spicy earthy flavors are not desired.

High α-acid hops with low kettle hop potential when boiled:

- Waimea
- Loral
- Citra
- Mosaic
- Galaxy
- Bravo
- Galena
- Columbus

Late Hopping

Aroma hot-side hop additions are done very late in the boil to preserve as much of the desired hop compounds as possible. Late hopping is usually done with just a few minutes left in the boil or at flameout (after the heat source has been shut off). There are benefits to late hopping discussed later in the book, but here I cover more research showing why kettle additions may be important for creating a more complex hop character than relying on dry hopping alone.

A study that looked into late hop flavor with liquid carbon dioxide hop extract from Styrian Goldings found the heat of late hopping an important factor in developing hop flavor compounds compared to just dry hopping.[44]

In the tests, a beer made with the hop extract added at 5 minutes left in the boil was compared to a beer that had the extract added as a dry hop. As you might expect, the dry hopped beer (where the extract was added to the conditioning vessel) tested higher in hop-derived volatile components than the late hopped beer. However, the chemical nature of the compounds transferred from the hop extract into the beer was different with the late hopped beer because the compounds that survived from the heat tended to be more polar.

Dry-hopped beers contain more non-polar compounds like monoterpene and sesquiterpene hydrocarbons, which tend to be spicy, herbal, and resinous. These compounds are typically driven off earlier in the processes but can retain in higher concentrations when added post-fermentation.

It makes sense that there is a higher amount of hydrocarbons in dry hopped beers because they are one of the most volatile classes of hop compounds. When introduced during dry hopping (especially after primary fermentation is complete) there is less chance for the compound to escape. Myrcene, for example, can be found in high concentration in dry hopped beers but will be pretty much eliminated from early-boil hop additions. If these green and herbal characteristics are not desired in dry hopped beer, using hops lower in myrcene can help as well as taking steps to strip these volatile compounds, allowing the fruitier ones to remain; for example, dry hopping during active fermentation. A hop like Citra, high in fruity monoterpene alcohols, can come across green or oniony when used in massive amounts in a post-fermentation dry hop because it is also one of the richest in myrcene.

Sensory tests for beers in the study above showed that late-hopped beers scored higher for estery fruity and citrus flavors than beers that were only dry hopped. The reason for this could be because several oxygen-containing terpenes and secondary alcohols were found in the late hopped beers that were not found in the dry hopped-only beers because late hopping allows for the oxygenated hop oils to be biotransformed by the yeast into esters, acetates, and alcohols during fermentation.

Like with studies on boil hopping, these results suggest that via boiling, even a very short time, hop compounds are transformed into a range of oxygenated substances that can alter a hop's oil makeup and impact final hop flavor and aroma.

Oxygen Fraction of Hops

If the oxygen fraction of hops (monoterpene alcohols like geraniol and linalool) is where we are getting some hop flavor in late hop additions (in part because of the polarity), should we be paying closer attention to a hop's total oxygen fraction (where these compounds reside) and setting our dosages accordingly? A study did just this by looking at choosing late hop dosage rates determined by the hop variety's total oxygen fraction as well as total oil amount.

Sensory tests revealed that when a beer is dosed based on the oxygen fraction of a hop variety, it resulted in the lowest difference (more predictable) in perceived hop aroma across all test beers when compared to dosage based on set quantity or based on hop total oil. In other words, the oxygen fraction of a hop variety may be a good indicator of its predicted aroma intensity (low oxygen fraction = less intensity, high oxygen fraction = more intensity).[45] So, if a hop is high in compounds like geraniol and linalool (part of the oxygen fraction), they are more likely to have a greater impact on hop intensity and could potentially be used in lower amounts.

The idea of adding less hops is a financially sound idea (more so for commercial breweries) but also relevant when trying to avoid negative tastes and flavors that can come with over-hopping beers. Covered in more depth in Chapter 7, heavy dry hopping can impart more bittering compounds, polyphenols, and resinous hydrocarbons (like myrcene), which can come across green and harsh on the palate. Strategically formulating hop dosages based on the oxygen fraction of hops using indicators like linalool or geraniol may be an effective way to come up with a good balance of flavor with less harsh characteristics. For example, Citra has a relatively high oxygen fraction and could be used in lower concentrations and still have a big impact on flavor and aroma.

In another paper by Schull, Forster, and Gahr, this concept of oxygen fraction hop dosing was further put to the test.[46] Here, five different hop varieties were tested in trial brews on a 2-hl system. Late hopping was done at the end of wort boiling based on total hop oil content in the whirlpool.

The author's found the solubility (ability of the hop compounds to get into the beer) is a decisive factor for classifying the efficiency of aroma compounds. This doesn't bode well for sesquiterpenes, which are poorly soluble (again, these are generally described as spicy, herbal, resinous, and woody). In fact, when these compounds were dosed in the whirlpool, they didn't approach their sensory threshold values. On the other hand, more soluble compounds within the oxygen fraction of hops are likely to survive the brewing processes and have an impact on the final aroma and flavor. Therefore linalool (a citrus monoterpene alcohol) is often measured to determine overall hop flavor.

To put a further point on this, the paper noted that even though myrcene (nonpolar compound) is 100 times more abundant in hops than linalool, it's threshold value is 15 times higher because of an extremely low overall transfer rate of less than 1%. Linalool was found to have a 33% transfer rate and thus is a more flavor active compound. The transfer rate is how much of the dosed amount is present in the final beer after the boil and fermentation. Keep in mind that dry hopping (especially after fermentation) will impart more of the nonpolar compounds. Again, Myrcene will play a flavor role in late dry hopped beers because there are fewer variables to strip the compound (yeast, CO2, trub, etc.) resulting in concentration well above the threshold with high hopping rates.

This experiment's sensory tests revealed that when the beers were late hoped based on the oxygenated fraction of the hop, the hop intensity of the different beers were comparable. This is interesting because one beer that received just 353 g/hl of pellets in the whirlpool had a similar hop intensity as a beer that was dosed at 1,000 g/hl in the whirlpool (but with a smaller oxygen fraction). The beer dosed at the much higher rate was perceived to have more body, likely because the polyphenol content was so much greater due to additional green hop matter used. So, a hop with a high oxygen fraction may be used in lower amounts compared to a hop with a just a greater total oil figure. However, incorporating total oil and the percentage of oxygenated compounds could be a valuable way to experiment with efficient hop dosages.

An interesting side note in the above paper is that in smaller pilot brewery systems, the late hot-side hopping rates may need to be increased because the evaporation efficiency is higher than with industrial systems (homebrewers may need to boost late hop additions if copying a commercial recipe for example).

I reached out to Yakima Chief Hops (YCH) to see if they could provide a list of hops that tend to have, on average, a high oxygen fraction, which would be helpful to put the information into practice. They mentioned that the oxygenated hop oil compounds are usually at very low levels at the time of harvest and can increase as the hops age. This concept of the oxygenated compounds increasing with age is covered in more detail in Chapter 3.

Using data obtained from YCH on over 50 hop varieties, I came up with a short list of hops that can be used for late, hot-side hopping in lower amounts and still impact flavor. Success is based on a hop's total oil and averages for linalool and geraniol. The reason I look at total oil is because if the hop has more total oil than another variety, even if the oxygen percentage of the oil is less, it could represent a greater amount as a percentage of total hop weight. Again, we use the oxygenated fraction of the hop because it's more soluble and more likely to stick around through the brewing process.

Here are hops with high flavor potential in late hopping due to a high total oil percentage and an above average oxygenated fraction. If the goal is to get as much hot-side fruity hop flavor as possible, these could be good efficient hop choices to experiment with.

- Bravo
- Brewers Gold
- Centennial
- Citra®
- CTZ
- Ekuanot™
- Mosaic™
- Olympic
- Simcoe®

Also helpful is to look at hops on the other end of the spectrum, whose compounds might require more hops used in the late kettle stage when considering total oil amount and the oxygen containing fraction. Here are hops then with likely lower flavor potential in late hopping:

- Ahtanum™
- Cascade
- Cashmere
- Chelan
- Cluster
- Fuggle
- Glacier
- Golding
- Hallertau
- Magnum
- Meridian
- Northern Brewer
- Palisade®
- Perle
- Saaz
- Summit™

- Tettnang
- Vanguard
- Willamette
- Yakima Gold

Extraction Efficiency

A study looking at extraction efficiency examined fifteen single-hopped beers, all with different varieties and tested 59 different hop compounds throughout the brewing process. They, like others, found that oxygenated compounds (specifically monoterpene alcohols), important to hop flavor and aroma. Although these compounds were reduced during various process steps, like fermentation (yeast cell absorption or metabolization), they found both whirlpool additions and dry hopping made significant contributions towards the final beer concentrations.

Of the 15 different hop varieties tested, those that imparted the most monoterpene alcohols were (in order of highest): Nugget, Columbus, Cascade, Centennial, and Sorachi Ace. The hops with the lowest contributions during late hopping were Palisade, Simcoe, and Challenger. What caught my eye in this study, was that each hop seemed to have a different utilization rate of these essential compounds. In other words, despite a hop's initial concentration of the compound, its ability to release the compound into the wort during late hopping varied between the fifteen varieties.

Using linalool as an example, the average transfer rates among the varieties during late hopping was 19%. So, on average, about 19% of the potential linalool in the hop was transferred into the wort during late hopping. Where it gets interesting, however, is that for Columbus the transfer rate of linalool was 49%, over double the average and by far the most efficient hop tested. Simcoe, on the other hand, was one of the lowest, with a 4.5% transfer of linalool during late hopping.[47]

Depending on the desired goal, the literature makes a case that it's not only the hopping process (like hop timing and duration) that is important for overall hop flavor and aroma, but also what variety is used and when. Columbus, for example, appears to be a great hop to utilize in the whirlpool to boost desirable monoterpene alcohols into the fermenting vessel (especially considering its thiol concentrations, discussed later). Nugget is another excellent and affordable, and likely underused whirlpool hop for its ability to impart high levels of linalool into wort. Although there are hundreds of hop compounds discovered to date, linalool is one of the best-known markers for measuring hoppiness potential.

Simcoe made the list for high total oil and above average oxygenated compounds, it tested low for its ability to transfer these oxygenated compounds into wort during late hopping showing how complicated hop science can get! As we will learn in Chapter 11 regarding hop thiols, this is an area where Simcoe shines. Interestingly, as it relates to dry hopping, Simcoe did have a high extraction rate where nearly 83% of its linalool was transferred into the beer. It's becoming evident that benefits can be gained by carefully choosing specific varieties and using them at specific points in the brewing processes.

Although it would be helpful to list the extraction rates of all hops, the data just doesn't exist for that yet. We can only encourage further testing, but it's an area to watch as hop science progresses and brewers try to get the most out of their hop selection and usage rates.

Volatilization of Hop Compounds

Both myrcene (hydrocarbon) and linalool (oxygen containing monoterpene alcohol) have been tested to have an impact on beer flavor and aroma if they are in the final beer above threshold, but the science clearly shows that these compounds drop off significantly during a typical boil. This suggests that if these compounds are desired in the chilled wort, late-stage whirlpool or steeping additions are required to avoid the bulk of the losses. Myrcene levels, for example, have been measured to reduce over 50% in just ten minutes of boiling and were completely removed during a 60-minute boil. Linalool was detected to be removed at about the same rate, even when starting at higher levels than myrcene.[48]

Other commonly tested hop compounds like β-eudesmol, humulene, humulene epoxide I, β-farnesene, caryophyllene, and geraniol, have hotter boiling points and thus a little more staying power in boiling wort. During a 60-minute boil, all these terpenoids decreased gradually, but are still present in varying amounts at the end. Again, the shorter the time the hops are boiled, the more retention of these compounds.

The results above stem from a study where beers were brewed with Saaz, Tettnang, and Hersbrucker, with 67% of the total hops used for each batch added at the beginning of the boil and the remaining 33% added 15 minutes before the end of the boil. The hops were added based on α-acid content, which I presume was to ensure the same IBUs in the beer. Although it doesn't say what the total IBU level was or the amount of hops used, it's interesting that all the terpenoids measured were below threshold values. So, even though some of these desirable compounds were in the beer from the 15-minute addition, their concentrations were below their taste thresholds. This suggests you would need a large kettle dose as late as possible to achieve above threshold concentrations.

Fast extraction of hop compounds with heat is another important factor to consider when trying to maximize oil retention from hops. If losses are as high as 80% for linalool in just five minutes of boiling, then extraction of the linalool appears to be peaking extremely quickly.

Looking closer at how hop compounds react during a whirlpool can help give guidance when determining appropriate whirlpool durations. A 2015 BrewingScience paper tested sesquiterpene hydrocarbons at five-minute intervals during the whirlpool with Saaz hops. For the compounds tested (myrcene, limonene, b-pinene, β-farnesene, α-humulene, b-and caryophyllene) there was an immediate measurable spike after the whirlpool hop charge was introduced to the wort, but the concentrations slowly decreased during the fifteen-minute whirlpool.

Although the BrewingScience paper did not test the more fruit-forward oxygen containing compounds (like linalool and geraniol) to see how they also alter with whirlpool times, it's interesting to see how quickly compounds can decrease with whirlpool length duration. Although I'm not suggesting everyone should do quick whirlpool chilling after adding the hops (as a Rock Bottom Study cited later found longer whirlpool durations resulted in more flavor), perhaps adding hops in stages during the whirlpool could be a way to get a more diverse set of compounds into the fermenter, taking advantage of different extraction rates at varying temperatures and durations.

If quick cooling after adding the whirlpool/steep hops is experimented with, it could also be beneficial because it allows for a larger charge of hops without generating as much bitterness. Massive hop additions might introduce more desirable hop compounds to the beer, but also along with more bitterness. Quick cooling would reduce the chance for the α-acids to isomerize (favoring hop compound retention over hop bitterness). This could also be an argument in-favor of using a hop-back en route to the plate-chiller.

How much isomerization is taking place during the whirlpool? One paper found that iso conversion is still taking place at temperatures as low as 90°F (32°C), but it requires much more contact time. Specifically, it took approximately 207 minutes for 60% iso production. So, when the temperature of the whirlpool is above or near boiling, much more isomerization is happening and quicker. At temperatures below boiling you are still getting isomerization of hop acids, however, if the duration is reduced during the whirlpool paired with an increase in hops and reduced whirlpool temperatures, you could potentially get more hop flavor without a large bitterness increase. I should note that the test above was done in a model solution (not in wort), which means losses of bitter acids to factors like trub and spent hops were not considered.

Hop Timing

A 2017 paper released by the Journal of the American Society of Brewing Chemists on hop timing furthers the science on the importance of late hot-side hopping.[49] Here, beers were made with Simcoe at either 60 minutes left in the boil, 20-minute whirlpool (right after the boil, no cooling was done), or a dry hop addition only (for 48 hours of contact time). In terms of measured concentrations of hop-derived volatiles in the finished beer, there was a clear winner with the whirlpool beer, which was measured higher for linalool (flowery-fruity), α-terpineol (lilac), geraniol (rose), and β-citronellol (lemon, lime).

Interestingly, the dry hopped sample had the lowest levels of β-citronellol, suggesting that adding dry hops to the beer toward the end of fermentation will not likely result in the biotransformation of geraniol to β-citronellol (more on this in Chapter 10). To favor the biotransformation process, whirlpool additions are best as this paper found the final levels of this lemon and lime-like compound was nine times greater than the dry hop-only beer and about 2.5-times higher than the kettle-hopped beer.

So, to summarize the biotransformation aspect of the paper, hops need to be added to the whirlpool to maximize biotransformation of geraniol to β-citronellol, dry hopping late in fermentation was not as effective in the transformation. Further testing of dry hopping as early as brew day would be an interesting follow-up to this paper.

Staying with the same paper, but switching to sensory results, panelists were able to detect a difference between control beers and kettle hopped beers. However, what surprised me was the Simcoe whirlpool beer produced a more aromatic beer than the Simcoe dry hopped beer. In other words, no hops at all on the hot-side resulted in a less aromatic beer than one where whirlpool hops and no dry hopping took place.

In terms of the descriptors used in the study by the tasting panel for the different hop times, they found that the Simcoe kettle hopped only beers were grassy and vegetal. The whirlpool only beer had descriptors of pine, resinous, citrus, stone fruit, and tropical. The dry hopped-only beer scored higher for stone fruit and floral. The results make a strong case for whirlpool hopping to boost hop flavors in IPAs.

I was intrigued by the results of no hot-side hops producing a less aromatic beer, so I decided to try my own experiment testing the concept. I brewed up five gallons of hazy IPA that was dry hopped with a total of ten ounces (283 grams) of hops (Citra and Amarillo) starting with two ounces added to the fermenter prior to adding the wort on brew day. Surprisingly, despite a huge dry hop charge, the aroma of the beer was lackluster, which would align with the results of the study discussed above with Simcoe. In this case, when I didn't add any hops to the kettle (bittering or whirlpool hops) the aromatics of the beer suffered dramatically.

Whirlpool Temperature

Brewers often experiment with reducing the temperature of the wort before adding the whirlpool hop additions hopping to increase the hop oils going into the fermenter from evaporation losses, but does this matter? This was put to the test and the findings were presented during the 2012 World Brewing Congress. Takako Inui, a Specialist in the Beer Development Department at Suntory Beer Ltd., Japan showed that late hopping at 185°F (85°C) retained slightly more measured linalool compared to late hopping warmer at 203°F (95°C) or cooler at 167°F (75°C). The temperature ranges used in the study are like those brewers will often experiment with when trying different whirlpool temperatures.

In terms of sensory differences between the different temperatures, beers late hopped at 203°F (95°C) scored highest for citrusy, spicy, and ester descriptors. The 185°F (85°C) late hop temperature scored higher for floral and herbal descriptors. The 167°F (75°C) scored lowest in nearly every category except for the sylvan (woody) characteristic.[50]

Although some would argue that hops are more complicated than testing just one compound like linalool (I would agree), it does make sense to focus the research on compounds proven to play a large role in hop flavor. One way to put the results into practice is to consider layering whirlpool additions like double dry hopping a beer. Adding hops at flameout and again once the wort has cooled to around 185°F (85°C) could be a good way to create a more complex hot-side hop flavor profile.

On the commercial scale, where cooling can take a long time, there are a couple of methods to cool the wort before whirlpool hop additions. The first is cold water dilution, here you can purposely hold back water from the recipe and add it back cold and filtered directly to the kettle after the boil. For example, in a ten-barrel batch, you can add a barrel of cold filtered water to the kettle to lower the temperature prior to whirlpooling and adding hops. Recirculating through a heat exchanger and back into the kettle after the boil is another way to bring down the kettle temperature prior to the whirlpool hop additions. If this method is used, it's best to avoid adding any whirlpool hops until you get to your desired temperature, so you don't clog your heat exchanger.

Whirlpool Durations

If different whirlpool temperatures can impact oil retention and ultimately flavor and aroma of beer, how might whirlpool lengths have an impact? A study conducted in coordination with 35 different Rock Bottom Breweries (a restaurant chain with locations across the U.S.) looked at whirlpool hop durations and how the variable impacted hop flavor. Every brewery made the same American IPA with the same recipe (yeast strains and water treatments varied however), but with slightly different hopping schedules.

The variations from brewery-to-brewery consisted of three different yeast strains (Wyeast 1272, Wyeast 1056, and Wyeast 1728). Water chemistry of the beers was also different due to varying locations, but proper treatments for mash and wort pH were made for each batch. Every Rock Bottom Brewery was instructed to bitter the IPA with a small boil addition of Amarillo and Nugget, but the final hop treatments varied as follows:

Short: One pound of Amarillo per barrel at the end of the boil for 50 minutes post-boil residence (post-boil residence here means the time from the end of the boil to the end of kettle knockout).

Long: One pound of Amarillo per barrel at the end of the boil for 80 minutes post-boil residence.

Sensory analysis of the beers showed that the longer post-boil residence was statistically significant for increased hop flavor and aroma. Specifically, the increase in 50 minutes to 80 minutes increased the flavor and aroma approximately 9 - 16.5%.[51] According to this study, when using Amarillo, the longer post-boil contact time could result in more hop flavor in the finished beer. It's important to note, however, the study did not measure hop compounds to see if increased post-boil times also led to an increase in actual concentrations. Rather, the results were obtained only from sensory data.

I'm curious if the variations between the different Rock Bottom breweries may have impacted the results in this study, as differences in processes, water profiles, and yeast selection could impact the results. For example, in Chapter 10 we learn that yeast selection alone can impact hop flavor and in Chapter 4 research shows that water profiles were found to also have an impact.

Another aspect to consider with a longer whirlpool time is the amount of evaporation still occurring and the size of the batch. For example, during a typical boil, most homebrewers experience around a 10-12% evaporation rate with an open pot design (over the entire boil). Professional brewers with larger setups have a much lower evaporation rates. For example, one commercial brewer told me they get a rate as low as 2-3%. Considering early research suggested hop extraction times are quick and can decrease almost immediately, a higher evaporation rate, even just during post-boil temperatures, could theoretically result in higher hop compound losses to homebrewers than professional brewers. In other words, more whirlpool hops may be required for a homebrew batch to achieve the same result as a commercial system when considering evaporation rates.

DMS, Hops, and Whirlpool Durations

Another factor to consider when deciding whirlpool durations is the potential for dimethyl sulfide (DMS). DMS is a sulfur compound that is considered an off-flavor in beer when at high concentrations and is introduced from thermal decomposition (wort heating) of S-methylmethionine (SMM) produced in the embryo of barley during germination.[52] The SMM finds its way into wort because it is readily dissolved from malt at all mashing temperatures. During fermentation, yeast can also reduce another precursor called dimethyl sulfoxide (DMSO), that can turn into DMS in the finished beer. This reaction is created by a yeast enzyme called DMSO reductase.[53] The extent of this conversion of DMSO is dependent upon the yeast strain employed.[54] DMS can also arise from wort infected with spoilage organisms, like wild yeast.[55]

Most brewers probably don't think their beer (especially ales) contain detectable levels of DMS, however, a study of thirteen commercially available beers were tested with surprising results. Seven domestic ales, two domestic lagers, two imported lagers, and two non-alcoholic lagers were among the beers tested and found that DMS was at or above flavor thresholds (30-60 μg/L) in all but one of the beers.[56] The authors found that DMS levels in the ales were comparable with the lagers. The flavor threshold for DMS is relatively low at 30 μg/L, so it doesn't take much to contribute to the flavor of a beer.[57] [58]

So why does whirlpool length have anything to do with DMS? During hot stands, any remaining SMM in the wort that wasn't evaporated during the boil will continue to hydrolyze and more DMS will be formed. One study extended a hot wort stand by one hour and found higher DMS concentrations from an average of 49 μg/L to 104 μg/L.[59] This means if a short boil time is combined with an extended hop stand, more DMS could be formed in the final beer. Or, in the commercial realm, if a long whirlpool is conducted in a well-insulated vessel or long transfer times occur at hot temperatures, this could lead to continued breakdown of SMM that survived the boil. Considering evaporation rates are higher for homebrewers than professional brewers, this seems like more of a risk on the commercial level.

DMS can also be introduced into beer via hops. One paper found that after whirlpool hop additions, three sulfides from hops were tested and DMS was among them. Some of this DMS will be reduced during fermentation via CO2, but some could survive and stay in the beer until packaging.[60]

It's thought that highly hopped beers help to mask off flavors like DMS, which is true in part, but with a twist. For example, one study found that moderate levels of linalool from hops increased the flavor threshold of DMS, making it harder to detect. Although, at higher concentrations, the linalool lowered the threshold of DMS making it more detectable. The results suggest that high hopping rates can increase DMS perception due to synergistic effects.[61] Ensuring good practices to keep DMS levels below threshold might be even more important in a heavily hopped hazy IPA.

I can attest that high levels of hopping and high levels of DMS does not result in a good beer! I purposely brewed a hazy IPA with DMS for an article on my blog to test the research. To try and encourage DMS production in the beer. I heated the wort to 212°F (100°C) and immediately cut the heat. I proceeded to scoop out any foam that was created as the wort heated because the evaporation of DMS during boiling was found to be strongly enhanced in the presence of beer foam (the authors speculate that DMS might concentrate in the foam and then be stripped from the wort by the rising vapor of the boil).[62] Because the beer didn't reach a rolling boil, the foam creation was considerably less than normal. Rather than chilling the batch at this point, I opted to do a 60-minute hop stand, which gave the remaining SMM that hadn't boiled out plenty of time to hydrolyze into DMS.

I had this IPA tested at Oregon State University for DMS levels and I succeeded (if you want to call it that). The testing showed a total of 177.2 μg/L of DMS. To put the results into context, ales will generally have less than 30 μg/L and concentrations above 100μg/L DMS flavors are more easily detectable.

How did the beer smell and taste? At first pour it had plenty of what I would cautiously describe as hop aroma, but with a healthy dose of over six ounces (170 grams) of Citra, Galaxy, and Amarillo in two separate dry hop additions (twelve total ounces (340 grams) of dry hops), the aroma was not as expected. The hop aroma was difficult to describe because it was altered so much from the DMS. I've settled on calling it an overripe/rotten fruit smell, which sounds about as good as it tasted. To me, the DMS aroma reminded me of tomato soup and sauerkraut, both great, but not in a hoppy beer! So, if extended whirlpool duration is something you experiment with, upping the boil to 90-minutes might be a good insurance plan to prevent DMS production.

Whirlpool Oxidation and the Green Onion Thiol

Sampling hoppy beers over the years, I can often detect a green onion-like aroma in hazy heavily hopped beers. I've always assumed this flavor resulted in the aging of hop compounds over time, although this may play a small role, it appears the aroma could be coming from oxygen during late hot-side hopping.

Even though a handful of thiols can contribute pleasant fruity aromas and flavors to beer, other thiols can impart negative characteristics (more on hop thiols in Chapter 11). One such thiol is 2-mercapto-3-methyl-1-butanol (2M3MB) which is described as having an onion-like off-flavor. A study examining the thiol found that after fermentation was complete, the off flavor could be eliminated by adding copper sulfate to the beer. Copper can absorb thiols, helping to show that the green onion flavor was likely coming from the 2M3MB thiol.[63]

A 2017 study by Asahi Breweries Ltd., discovered the likely cause of the green onion thiol and why it happens in hoppy beers specifically.[64] The authors searched for compounds that might be responsible for the flavor and then experimented with process variables that might play a role in its production. They determined that 2M3MB was the most likely compound responsible based on threshold limits (3M3MB was also considered). The threshold limit for 2M3MB was found to be very low at just 0.13 µg/L, which is why thiols are so important in flavor development in beer as their sensory impact can be large even in small concentrations.

After determining the likely thiol causing the onion-like flavor, they moved onto testing whether hot aeration of the wort had an impact on 2M3MB concentrations. They aerated wort for five minutes at four different temperatures (68°F (20°C), 122°F (50°C), 158°F (70°C), and 194°F (90°C)) and found the amount of 2M3MB present after fermentation was dependent on the wort aeration and temperature. In other words, the hotter the wort receiving aeration, the more 2M3MB was produced. For example, for the sample receiving aeration at 194°F (90°C), approximately 1.0 ng/L of 2M3MB was created, well over the low 0.13 ng/L threshold. Even more alarming however, 2M3MB was only found in samples of hopped wort. Essentially, the conclusion was the green onion thiol is tied to hot-side aeration, likely from precursors of 2M3MB from hopped wort.

Nobody shoots oxygen into their hot wort, so it shouldn't be an issue, right? Unfortunately, it might not take much oxygen to increase 2M3MB. The paper goes on to say that in commercial settings, hot aeration of wort can happen during cooling when negative pressure generated from pumps can draw air through the valves into the wort lines.

Remember, the hotter the wort is when oxygen is introduced, the more the green onion thiol increased during fermentation. So, avoiding oxygen intake during cooling is important, especially during the early stages. In heavily hopped styles, where hops are entering the boil during the whirlpool stage, it makes sense to assume even more potential for the green onion thiol if there is any hot-side aeration, which would form during fermentation.

This is a good reminder to double check the tightness of tri-clamps on the whirlpool setup before adding the hops to ensure oxygen isn't getting sucked in through the connections. A real paranoid brewer could also purge the whirlpool hoses with CO2 before opening the valves to start the flow in and out of the kettle. At Sapwood Cellars, we start the flow before the boil is complete to both purge the lines of any oxygen as well as to pasteurize the rig before starting the whirlpool and adding hops.

For homebrewers, this might mean the processes of stirring the wort with a giant spoon to speed up the chilling process should be done very carefully as to not introduce oxygen, which might later produce 2M3MB during fermentation. It might be best to avoid stirring the wort until the temperature drops below 100°F (38°C) when cooling with an immersion chiller, especially if you are detecting a green onion aroma in some of your hoppy beers. The study still found levels above threshold at the lower temperatures, but they were directly shooting oxygen into the wort likely magnifying the problem. Because the creation of 2M3MB might also vary with different yeast strains, more studies on the topic are encouraged.

Key Findings

- Kettle aroma (earthy, woody, spicy) mainly comes from the hydrocarbon fraction of hops and can increase when hops (particularly those high in α-humulene and β-caryophyllene derivatives) are added early in the boil, which creates oxidation products leading to more kettle aroma.

- For more rounded and complex hop flavor, hops can be added at multiple stages on the hot-side. Early hop additions for kettle aroma and late staggered whirlpool additions can increase fruity and herbal flavors, depending on the hop variety.
- The bittering hop used can impact the final flavor of beer, so don't overlook this aspect when putting together a recipe.
- Dry-hopped beers contain more non-polar compounds like sesquiterpene hydrocarbons, which tend to be the more spicy, herbal, and resinous compounds.
- Late-hopped beers scored higher for estery-fruity and citrus flavors than beers that were only dry hopped.
- The higher the hops total oil and the higher the oxygen fraction, the more potential for hop flavor and aroma.
- Although there are many hop compounds, linalool and geraniol are often the ones tested to evaluate overall hoppiness.
- Hop compounds are extracted very quickly when added on the hot-side.
- Different whirlpool temperatures can alter the hop compounds and flavor of beer. For example, 203°F (95°C) showed highest marks for citrusy, spicy, and ester descriptors. At 185°F (85°C), beers scored higher for floral and herbal descriptors. Whirlpooling at 167°F (75°C) scored lowest in nearly every category except for the sylvan (woody) characteristic.
- The DMS threshold can be lowered in heavily hopped beers due to synergistic effects, so it's important to follow proper brewing steps to keep levels as low as possible.
- Oxygen introduction during the whirlpool and chilling phase can lead to a green onion thiol (2M3MB).

Chapter 3: Hop Storage

Common knowledge is that hops are best as near to the harvest date as possible. If not used right away, they are generally stored at freezing temperatures in vacuum-sealed or nitrogen-flushed bags. While this is the best way to store hops, the science is interesting when it comes to using slightly aged hops. This chapter takes a closer look at how hop compounds alter with time and might tempt brewers to experiment with hops they have been sitting on for a while!

What Happens to Hops as they Age?

A 1985 study evaluated the hop oil compounds from 20 different hop varieties, all obtained from the same breeding program at Oregon State University. Research focused on comparing fresh hops to hops aged for six months at room temperature. The aged hops saw reductions in α-acids, β-acids, total oil, and myrcene. Because a large percentage of hop oil can consist of myrcene, this can help explain why there is a large drop in total oil during aging. None of this information is surprising, but what the authors also found was that if a hop was dominated by more citrus and floral leaning compounds when fresh, these compounds were more likely to remain at their same, or relative levels when aged.[65]

Looking at more testing of aged hops, a beer was brewed with hops that had been stored at 104°F (40°C) for 30 days and another with hops that had been stored cold at 39°F (4°C) over the same timeframe. The hops were added at the beginning of the boil or after cooling. In sensory tests, the cold-stored pellet hopped beers were characterized as more pellet-like (resinous, green, and floral). The hot-stored pellet beer was described as having citrus and sweet aromas with slightly higher hop aroma intensity.

Further lab testing of the beers with the hot-stored pellets showed an increase of citrus compounds and decreased concentrations of green and resinous components. The drop in resinous components is likely because of the loss in myrcene (which is extremely volatile) in the aged hops. Using Citra as an example, the myrcene content can be as high as 70% of the hop oil, so you can see how a reduction in this green tasting compound could impact the flavor. But this would be less of a factor in boil additions as most of this compound would be removed anyways.

According to model brewery calculations of hop varieties included in the study discussed above, Hersbrucker, Tettnang, Record, Fuggle, Blisk, Eroica, Hallertau Mittelfruh, Willamette, and Styrian might increase in their hoppiness potential with aging. Hops with little change were Nugget, Cluster, Perle, Columbia, and Olympic. Hops with high potential when either fresh or aged were Kirin II, Wye Challenger, Wye, and Target. Of the hops that lost hoppiness potential were Cascade, Galena, and Brewers Gold.

So, although you probably don't think of using hops like Styrian or Fuggle in a tropical and citrus hazy IPA (especially when these hops are slightly aged), it certainly seems worth playing around with these varieties in the whirlpool if you have them laying around. Especially considering you can probably pick up some of these older varieties for cheap!

The study above went a step further and tested the beers for specific compounds. What the authors found was that the beers made with poorly stored hops had increased concentrations for low-threshold citrus components (ethyl 2-methylbutanoate, ethyl 3-methylbutanoate, ethyl 4-methylpentanoate, and 4-(4-hydroxyphenyl)-2-butanone). Geraniol levels were found to be in similar levels in both the warm-stored and cold-stored hops. As you would expect from the sensory results, the cold-stored hopped beers tested for higher concentrations of green and resinous components (myrcene and (Z)-3-hexen-1-ol). The authors assume the change is attributed to the esterification or biosynthesis of short-chain fatty acids derived from oxidation or degradation of hop components, likely humulone or lupulone.[66]

A 2014 paper also found a reduction in hydrocarbons as hops aged. In the study, five U.S. varieties (Columbus, Chinook, Nugget, Cascade, and Mount Hood) in bags were cut open and stored at room temperature or at 32°F (0°C) and analyzed after four and twenty-four weeks for compound concentrations. The authors found a shift in the percentage of terpene hydrocarbon percentages. Specifically, in fresh hops, the terpene hydrocarbons accounted for approximately 85-95% of the hop oils; after twenty-four weeks of storage exposed to air at room temperature the percentage dropped to 30-60%.[67]

Results dating back to 1986 also found some flavor benefits when using aged hops. Here, Cascade and Idaho-grown Hallertauer were carefully aged and brewed (without dry hopping) in a Coors facility. Both hop varieties were split into three groups and stored at 27°F (-

3°C) or 90°F (32°C) for two weeks and at 90°F (32°C) for nine weeks. The authors found that despite the hops increasing in their hop storage index (HSI) and decreasing in β-acids, α-acids, and oil content, the nine-week aged hop beers received the highest flavor ratings. The hop storage index (HSI) was developed to measure the ratio of α-acids and β-acids to oxidized α-acids (humulinones) and oxidized β-acids (hulupones). Both warm-stored hop varieties above had an intense citrus flavor when tasted by a trained panel at Oregon State University during triangular tests. Specifically, the Cascade beer had an increase in grapefruit flavor. Also interesting was only the beer brewed with the cold-stored hops were noted as having a grassy flavor.[68]

As we learned earlier, the drop of total oil in the aged hops is likely due from to the reduction of hydrocarbons, particularly myrcene. This reduction helps to explain when the beer with the cold-stored hops had more of a grassy flavor because more of the resinous-leaning myrcene was present in the hops. Although model brewery calculations mentioned earlier estimated that aged Cascade might lose flavor potential as it ages, when put to the test it was found to increase, particularly the grapefruit flavors. This is a good example of how some calculations may make sense on paper, but don't always pan out in the real-world.

To explain the results with Cascade above, it's helpful to go back to 1981, where six hop varieties (Hallertauer, Perle, Hersbrucker, Tettnanger, Cascade, and Cluster) were stored refrigerated for a year and tested. Not surprisingly, the hops saw a reduction in hydrocarbons, but with Cascade this was especially true as it saw a 98% reduction, and this was at refrigeration temperatures! [69]

If the goal is to boost the fruiter flavors when experimenting with aged hops, it's important to remember that some aged varieties should be avoided for early-boil bittering additions because of the increased chances for kettle hop flavor. Refer to the list of hops that if aged may increase kettle aroma when boiled in Chapter 2.

There doesn't appear to be much data on dry hopping with aged hops, but this could be particularly troubling if tropical flavors are desired, especially with noble-like hops. For example, a 2017 paper tested Hallertau Mittelfruh hop pellets stored under pro-oxidative conditions to dry hop a lager.[70] The hops were stored at either 100°F (37°C) for two weeks and exposed to oxygen a single time or held at 100°F (37°C) and exposed daily to oxygen for two weeks. The lager was then dry hopped with the oxidized pellets at either 1 lbs./bbl or

0.4 lbs./bbl and put before trained and consumer tasting panels at Oregon State University.

The consumer tasting panel largely described the beers with oxidized hops like the control beer, but overall the authors concluded that manipulating hop storage conditions can favor the increase in compounds related to increased "noble-like" descriptors. Consumer acceptance of the dry hopped lagers was not significantly impacted by the oxidized hops. However, eight of ten trained panelists were able to tell the difference between the oxidized hop beers and the control. The trained panel also noted more woody and herbal notes in the oxidized hop samples. In addition, the trained panelists detected an increase in sensory bitterness in the oxidized dry-hopped beers, which agrees with recent literature on dry hopping bitterness via humulinones discussed in detail in Chapter 8.

Another variable when considering brewing with aged hops is the resin quality which can impact head retention. As hops age, the percentage of soft resin falls while that of the hard resin increases, which includes the oxidation products from aging. A study examining beers brewed with an ethanolic solution of hard resin-rich extract found as the content of hard resin increased in a beer (which would mean using a larger number of aged hops) the head retention improved, particularly the cling.[71]

Aged Hops and Cheesy Flavor

A common way of describing the smell of aged hops (think Lambic hops) is that they can be a bit cheesy, sweaty, or rancid. These flavors are thought to come from the reduction of alpha and β-acids in oxidative conditions accompanied by a significant increase in short-chain cheesy smelling acids.

Although these cheesy smelling short chain acids are undesirable, they are key precursors to desirable fruity esters. Specifically, these esters deriving from the cheesy compounds have been described as intensely sweet, estery, fruity, and pineapple-like. This is especially important because the cheesy flavors have much higher thresholds than the esters, meaning that these precursors have the potential to turn into fruity flavors that are much more detectable on the palate.

Specifically, fruity esters that can be biotransformed from aged hops via short chain acids during fermentation have a flavor threshold by a factor of 100 below the short chain cheesy-like acids. So, the more desirable esters can have a big impact on beer flavors, even when in the beer at lower concentrations. Also interesting is that the accumulation of these beneficial esters was shown to proceed late into fermentation after diacetyl was attenuated at elevated temperatures in late hopped beer.[72] In other words, the conversion of the short chain acids from aged hops to fruity esters is taking place during fermentation, so you'd want to get these older hops into the beer before fermentation, likely in the whirlpool and let the temperature rise at the end of fermentation.

One interesting experiment with aged hops may be to use them in a whirlpool, combined with an elevated temperature rest after primary fermentation is nearly complete. This would be a good way to see if these acids noticeably transform into fruiter esters. Perhaps this is one of the reasons Lambic brewers use aged hops, not only for the reduced bittering potential, which may be beneficial to the souring process, but the enhanced unique fruit-like flavors that can be created during fermentation. Let me be clear, I'm not saying the key to making intensely fruity IPAs is to load up the whirlpool with Lambic-style hops, but the science does indicate it's possible to get fruity flavors this way, so why not experiment with it!

Bitterness Quality

There has been debate amongst brewers regarding the bitterness quality you might get from using aged hops. That is, if a hop is severely aged or stored poorly, the bitterness may be harsher or have other undesirable characteristics. This doesn't seem to be the case, however. A study looking at this made two beers, one with long-aged hops stored around 70°F (21°C) for one year in the presence of air and another with slightly aged hops stored at 41°F (5°C) in the presence of air for six months. Sensory tests did not prove statistically significant in the bitterness quality of the two beers. However, the downside was that the long-aged hop beer had to be boiled for a much longer duration to achieve the same bitterness level because of the loss of α-acids from aging.[73]

Hop Polyphenols and Aging

Hop polyphenols are covered in much more detail in Chapter 7, but in general, polyphenols in high quantities in beer can be harsh and astringent. Because the rate of hopping during the late stages of the boil and in the dry hop can be extreme in hazy IPAs, this results in higher polyphenol concentrations. Because of this, I was curious to find research that might show how the polyphenol content in hops changes with age.

One study stored four Czech hop varieties (Saaz, Sládek, Premiant, and Agnus) at 36°F (2°C) or 68°F (20°C) in a sealed vacuum package or exposed to the air. The hops were then tested every two months for total polyphenol content. The authors found that over the course of a year, there was a loss of 30-40% of total polyphenols and storage conditions had very little impact on the losses. Perhaps oxidation at hop packaging was enough to cause long-term polyphenol losses, even when stored cold. During the first two months, there was a loss of about 5-15% and at six months, there was a rapid reduction in polyphenols.[74] It would be interesting to see research like this expanded to other more popular dry hop varieties.

Incorporating Aged Hops in IPAs

When it comes to making hop-forward beers where fruit-like flavors are desired over herbal, spicy, and woody flavors, it might be worth experimenting with slightly aging hops in a pro-oxidative condition and utilizing them in the whirlpool. Pulling some of the research together, it's interesting to consider that using slightly aged hops may reduce harshness from fewer polyphenols, have less green character from shifting away from spicy and woody hydrocarbons, have fewer α-acids (which could mean using a larger amount of hops in the whirlpool), and even potentially taking advantage of the biotransformation of hop-derived short chain acids.

As hard as it might be for some, one easy way to do this is to cut open a bag of hops and store them in the fridge for a few weeks before using them, the colder temperatures will prevent a rapid overall loss in compounds that can happen at warmer temperatures. However, it makes more sense to experiment with slightly aging hops that are already fruit-forward. As we saw with the research, some of the noble hop varieties seemed to get more of an intense woody character as they aged, and this would likely only increase if used in the boil for bittering. Hops that are already higher in oxygenated fruity terpene alcohols might benefit from slight aging, where the shift away from green resinous compounds might allow the fruity oxygenated monoterpene alcohols to shine as they retain their percentages better with age. Considering there is a reduction in both polyphenols and α-acids as hops age, you could likely use a much larger whirlpool charge with them in an attempt to bump fruity compounds without the negative effects of so much hop material like bitterness and astringency.

I've treated hops like a disease that could spread if exposed to the environment for any amount of time. I know I'm not alone, many brewers immediately vacuum seal hops after using them and put them into the freezer. In outreach for this book, I was shocked to learn that some brewers visiting Yakima, WA for annual hop selection in September each year have turned down low HSI hops opting for lots with higher values. In other words, brewers purposely chose the slightly more oxidized hops.

Generally, the higher the HSI, the more oxidized compounds in the hops. Typically, any HSI under 0.3 means the hops are fresh. Between 0.3–0.35, the hops are slightly oxidized but still OK to use and hops with an HSI of 0.35-0.4 and higher are very oxidized. However, different hop lots can have different HSI values, even within the same hop variety.[75]

The study earlier in the Chapter with aged Cascade and the increase in grapefruit flavors tested the HSI as high as 1.04 after storage at 90°F (32°C) for nine weeks. It may just be that if you want to experiment with aging hops to shift the compounds away from floral and spicy hydrocarbons, keeping a bag open at room temperature and periodically smelling them may be a good place to start. It seems difficult to give sound advice on duration and temperature to age when different hop varieties and even hops within the same variety from different fields all can play a role. Don't forget to also consider how they were treated during packaging and shipment.

One potential way to play with this nutty idea of using aged hops could be to save extra hops from brews. Rather than sealing them up, just leave them in their bags in the fridge, freezer, or even at room temperature for a bit. Using these slightly aged hops in the whirlpool stages of your next hop-forward beer seems like a safe way to begin testing out the research. Let your risk-taking threshold be your guide or convince a friend to do it!

Key Findings

- Aged hops will see a large reduction of oils, mainly due to the loss of hydrocarbons (like myrcene), which generally represents a large portion of hop oil percentage when fresh.
- Hops stored at warmer temperatures for short duration (up to a month) and used for late hot-side additions have been found to produce more sweet and citrus aromas compared to more resinous and green flavors from cold-stored hops.
- Aging Cascade hops warm 90°F (32°C) for as long as nine-weeks was found to produce beer with intense citrus (grapefruit) flavors compared to cold-stored Cascade hops.
- Aged hops high in cheesy and sweaty flavors are high in short-chain fatty acids that can act as precursors to lower threshold fruity pineapple-like esters formed during fermentation.
- Using slightly aged hops might allow for greater hop usage in the whirlpool due to reductions in α-acids and polyphenols during aging.
- As hops age, the polyphenol concentration declines likely due to oxygen introduction at packaging (one study found as much as 30-40% reduction over the course of a year).

Chapter 4: Mouthfeel

Along with a great fruit-forward aroma and flavor, a soft mouthfeel is an important aspect to a great hazy IPA. There isn't a silver bullet to generating great mouthfeel in beer, like with flavors, it's a complex matrix with many variables playing a role. The best we can do is try to maximize the variables that have been shown to contribute and this chapter explores those areas.

Sulfate-to-Chloride Ratio

"If the water tastes good, you can brew with it." This was the advice I was given when I first started homebrewing. I thought it was great advice because it meant I didn't have to think much about water as another ingredient, however, experience and research has taught me otherwise. The biggest drawback from this line is that it fails to consider the removal of chlorine or chloramine, which is essential in preventing chlorophenol production (medicinal flavors) during fermentation. So, if water isn't a variable you want to worry about yet, at the very least, you should filter your water with a carbon filter to make sure you are removing the chlorine and chloramine, it's hard to make a good beer otherwise. Only catalytic or surface-modified activated carbon can remove chloramine, standard granular activated carbon and carbon block do not.

I enjoy brewing with 100% reverse osmosis (RO) water when homebrewing, it's not as practical commercially, however. Reverse osmosis setups contain multiple filters and a membrane that will remove particles, chemicals, chlorine, heavy metals, sodium, and more. Most systems are advertised as being able to remove up to 99% of water contaminants. For less than $200, you can purchase an above-counter reverse osmosis system that connects to a sink (laundry, kitchen, bathroom) with an adapter to produce RO water.

One downside of reverse osmosis is the time it takes to gather enough water to brew with. My current filter (five stage system from Reverse Osmosis Revolution) takes approximately three hours to make 5-gallons of RO water (this can change based on water pressure). Another downside of reverse osmosis is the amount of wastewater created. Efficient reverse osmosis systems can have as much as three gallons of wastewater for every gallon of RO water produced.

The nice part about brewing with RO water is that you have a blank slate to work with. With RO you have complete control over the mineral content of the beer (not considering minerals brought from grains), which allows you to create a water profile that's appropriate for what you are brewing. You also get the benefit of a predictable mash pH, because you can calculate the pH impact of the mineral additions combined with the grist. A great resource for calculating mash pH is Bru'n Water (sites.google.com/site/brunwater/).

If you don't go with RO, you can still make great beer! I would recommend obtaining a local water report, learn about seasonal variations in your supply, and get ready to adjust. Variations in water profiles can have a bigger impact than you might think. One example of this is a Brulosophy experiment where they brewed two identical beers (Dry Irish Stout) but altered the water profile of each as follows:

Pale Hoppy Water Profile:

Ca	Mg	Na	SO4	Cl	HCO3	SO4:Cl
90	16	36	167	67	149	2.5

Dark Malty Water Profile:

Ca	Mg	Na	SO4	Cl	HCO3	SO4:Cl
82	11	25	55	123	86	.44

In a triangle test of two samples of the stout made with the pale hoppy water profile and one with the malt water profile, 18 of 29 tasters correctly identified that the beer brewed with the malty water profile was different (it had a lower sulfate-to-chloride ratio). Because of the sample size, this was enough to reach statistical significance, suggesting the water profile alone was enough to alter two otherwise identical beers.[76] What was interesting in this experiment was that even in a beer with intense flavors deriving from the malt (11% roasted barley), the water profile still played a detectable role in the overall taste of the beer.

If you've searched online for water profiles, particularly for hop-forward beer, the sulfate-to-chloride ratio is often the target figure brewers debate. The sulfate-to-chloride ratio is the amount of sulfate (SO4) compared to the amount of chloride (Cl) in the brewing water. While using the ratio as a guide can be a good approach for formulating a recipe, the raw amounts of the minerals themselves are just as important. For example, a chloride to sulfate ratio of 30:10 and 300:100 are both 3:1 but would result in different tasting beers. Generally, I like to stay under 200 ppm of each as to not impart a minerally taste to the beer.

One source cites (with no data explaining why) the "proper" sulfate-to-chloride ratio for dry and bitter pale ales should be 2:1 and full and sweet mild ales should have a ratio of 2:3.[77] The paper emphasized that favoring chloride will create a fuller tasting beer, likely the goal in hazy IPAs.

An article in the *Journal of Automated Methods & Management in Chemistry* examined the impact of the sulfate-chloride ratio can have on beers and agreed with the above paper. The article states that "an excess of sulfate gives a sharp, dry edge to well-hopped beers and the level present should be minimized as much as possible."[78] Unless your goal is a dry and sharp IPA, its best to experiment with low levels of sulfate. My personal experience with heavy sulfate concentrations in hoppy beers is that the hop flavor is reduced while bitterness and dryness tend to be exaggerated.

A paper released in 2010 found that altering the sulfate levels of hop forward beers will have an impact on final flavors. Here, the authors found a "clear negative correlation" with sulfate levels and perceived hop flavors. In other words, when the sulfate level of a beer in the test increased, the perceived hop flavor decreased.[79] This suggests that not only can elevated sulfate levels detract from the softness of mouthfeel, it can also lower the perceived hop flavor.

Chloride impacting softness has been mentioned many times in the research. For example, a 1992 paper titled, "*The Mouthfeel of Beer – A Review*" looked at various factors influencing mouthfeel and included a discussion on calcium chloride. Right away, the review says, "although no sensory evidence exists, it is generally assumed that chloride ions yield beers which are 'rounder' more full and mellower and softer in the palate."[80]

The review goes on to use the work of a previous study in an old *Journal of the Institute of Brewing* that described the taste of chloride ion as "sweet and full." A 1991 *Journal of the American Society of Brewing Chemists* also found a positive correlation with the chloride concentration of 30 commercial beers when describing a beer's fullness.[81] The more chloride the commercial beers were tested for, the higher a taster would rate the mouthfeel of the beer as being full.

Is a fuller mouthfeel necessarily better though? It really depends on what you like, but a 1981 paper found that beers produced with calcium chloride were preferred to beers produced with calcium sulfate.[82] I would tend to agree with this as I like a soft full mouthfeel in hoppy beers, but also across most of the styles, even if it's not technically appropriate.

Looking at another Brulosophy water experiment where different sulfate-to-chloride ratios were tested in a hop-forward beer, they again found a noticeable impact when altered. This time two identical IPAs were brewed with Amarillo, Citra, and Mosaic. The only difference between the two was that one had a sulfate-to-chloride ratio of 150:50 and the other was 50:150. A total of 22 tasters were served two samples of the beer with a ratio of 150:50 and one sample of the beer with a ratio of 50:150. The result was that 14 of the 22 tasters were able to pick out the different beer, which was enough to achieve statistical significance. [83] The author of the experiment perceived the sulfate-rich beer to have more assertive bitterness, which would agree with the research and my experience.

For about two years, I maintained a rather obsessive rating system for my beers where I scored each batch from one to five in a number of areas, one of those being mouthfeel softness. Using the scores from 25 batches of relatively similar hop-forward beers and running correlations, it was clear that calcium chloride had an impact on the mouthfeel of my beers. As the grams/gallon of calcium chloride increased, so did my softness rating. The same is true with the gypsum/calcium chloride ratio, as the ratio of gypsum to calcium chloride decreased (negative relationship), so did my mouthfeel softness score.

I've done several hoppy beers that were brewed with 100% calcium chloride added to RO water and none were the slam dunk I thought they might be. I considered the mouthfeel soft in these beers, but the hop flavor seemed lacking and overall the beer was a bit flabby (no sharpness at all). Interestingly, a number of these beers were high in unmalted grains, which we'll soon find out may contain fewer minerals than their malted counterparts.

Malt's Impact on Minerals

According to Aaron Justus from Ballast Point Brewing Co., sulfates should enhance hop character, dryness, and bitterness in a beer.[84] Surprisingly, some of Ballast Point's IPAs have sulfate concentrations as high as 400 ppm. Ballast Point brewers think of chloride as a way of balancing out the effects of sulfate by mellowing out a beer and adding palate fullness and malt character. Through experimentation with mini-mashes of different malted barley varieties, Justus analyzed the amount of sulfate and chloride each base malt brought to the wort compared to raw barley. He found that on average, base malt was adding around 50-100 ppm of sulfates and approximately 200 ppm of chloride. The malting processes resulted in a higher amount of minerals than the raw grain, potentially from the water the maltsters use.

Taking the information from the malt's impact on sulfate and chlorides, Ballast Point brewed pilot batches to test different sulfate-to-chloride ratios. In a beer dry hopped with Mandarina Bavaria using a 3:1 or 1:3 ratio, favoring either sulfate or chloride, a trained tasting panel preferred the chloride-heavy beers in the 3:1 ratio. The beer brewed favoring sulfate was described as having more hop bitterness and aroma. The beer made with more chloride was described as bready, malty, mellow, and fuller. Perhaps a proper balance between sulfate and chloride is a good way of getting hop aroma without sacrificing body and fullness. Also, of note, when tracking the ions through the stages of brewing, they found that fermentation metabolized sulfate and not chloride. Chloride actually increased (potentially from hops).

Considering Ballast Point's research finding that malted grains will bring additional chloride to beer, when brewing with water-favoring sulfate in a 3:1 ratio would likely result in a beer with an even split of sulfate-to-chloride after the grain minerals are calculated. In other words, the chloride addition from the malted grains is so high that the starting ratio can even out, even when the sulfate was higher to begin with. On the other hand, when brewing water is high in chloride levels, the spread between the chloride and sulfate in the final beer will be significant (favoring chloride).

If your grist is high in unmalted grains like flaked oats or wheat, you'll likely have less pickup of chloride from the grist, which is also something to consider. For example, malted barley can have slightly higher levels of chloride, magnesium, and calcium than flaked barley and flaked oats have a lower concentration of chloride, magnesium, and calcium than malted barley.[85] So, it may be a good idea to experiment with increasing mineral additions as the percentage of flaked grains increases.

From the results above, when making a hazy IPA where fresh hop character is desired as well as a full mouthfeel, a 2:3 sulfate-to-chloride ratio would be a good place to start. You can adjust with subsequent batches and with grist changes.

Knowing a good starting sulfate-to-chloride ratio can be helpful, but how high should you go? High levels of chloride can create side effects like a chalky taste or inhibit yeast flocculation. A study analyzing the anions in beer noted that, "If the level of chloride is >250 ppm, it can enhance the sweetness of the beer but it hinders yeast flocculation."[86] As far as the optimal level of chloride to have in beer, a 1971 journal recommended a level of ~200 ppm to produce a lager with a proper mouthfeel.[87] To experiment with chloride levels, you can try adding small volumes after packaging in the glass to see how a little change can alter a beer and adjust for future batches.

Dextrins

Another factor often cited for contributing to the mouthfeel of beer are dextrins. Fermentables in wort are about 70% maltose, glucose, fructose, sucrose, and maltotriose. The other 30% are mostly maltotetraose (6%) and dextrins (22%). Dextrins are an unfermentable extract that remains in wort from starch that is not broken down to the main fermentable sugars by amylases during the mashing process. In general, dextrins are said to positively contribute to mouthfeel, but will not add any flavor.[88]

How big of a role dextrins play in impacting the mouthfeel of beer is a source of some debate. A 1989 paper looking at the potential of whether dextrins are a significant source of mouthfeel didn't have high hopes prior to the experiment as the opening paragraph stated "whether dextrins contribute significantly to any other beer character than its caloric value is doubtful." This comes despite science at the time of the study which had determined in 1962 that dextrins do increase the viscosity of beer.[89] Also in 1962, dextrins were said to have a thick and pasty effect on mouthfeel[90] In 1977, dextrins were said to be tasteless but still will influence viscosity and add to the mouthfeel of beer.[91]

Back to the 1989 study. A trained panel was given a commercial light beer dosed with dextrins ranging from 20 to 70 g/L. They were then asked which samples were thicker or more viscous. The authors found that for there to be a detectable increase in mouthfeel, there needed to be more than 50 g/L of dextrins added to the beer. How much is 50 g/L in your beer? If we consider that 1 brix/plato is 1 g per 100 ml, we're talking about ~5°P or .020 in gravity points.

The 1989 study disagreed with most of the previous research, saying dextrins likely contribute less to mouthfeel and have more to do with beta-glucans, ethanol, glycerol, glycoproteins, and melanoidins. Beers at this point in time had between 10 and 50 g/L of dextrins. Interestingly, ratings for sweetness from participants were closely matched to viscosity when added at concentrations of 60 g/L or more to beer. Although not surprising, the authors also found that when the samples were uncarbonated, they had a higher rating for viscosity, which they explain is why stouts with less carbonation are perceived as heavier, creamier, and more viscous that ales or lagers that are more heavily carbonated.[92]

A 1991 study measured chemical and physical properties of beer that can contribute to mouthfeel and then correlated these with sensory attributes. Thirty different samples were used in the study, including different beer types and styles, ranging from non-alcoholic lagers to barley wines. The beers were served to a trained tasting panel who were asked to rate the intensity for different descriptors (like density, viscosity, and oily mouthfeel). One of the measurements taken in the study was dextrin concentration (separated out into groups DP4-DP9 and DP10) and they found a low correlation coefficient for the terms "viscosity" and "thickness" and dextrins. Parameters that correlated well to density and viscosity were polyphenols, chloride, and glycerol. Glycerol was correlated higher to viscosity than beta-glucans. The paper concluded that brewing trials need to be conducted to confirm which parameters cause these mouthfeel sensations, however.[93]

A 1993 paper looking at multiple studies on dextrins ultimately concluded they have little or no impact on mouthfeel attributes related to fullness. Citing a study where a series of mashes were done with different dextrin concentrations, researchers found beers with higher dextrin content lacked palate fullness.[94] Also cited was a study where enzymes were added to beer to hydrolyze the dextrins, which did not diminish the fullness of the beer.[95] There was no sensory data to back up these claims, however. The same paper also cited a study suggesting a high wort dextrin level in beer results in low attenuation and gives beer a thick and pasty mouthfeel.[96]

So, although research can sometimes seem like the arguing that goes on in online forums, I have the most confidence in the paper that found 50 g/L (.020 gravity points) of dextrins are needed to achieve a mouthfeel difference because they directly added dextrins to beers until a panel could start to detect a mouthfeel difference. For what it's worth, at Sapwood Cellars, we like to have a final gravity around 1.020 in our hazy IPAs. This seems to give us a nice balance of body and sweetness without tasting like unfermented wort.

50% Carapils Experimental Beer

To test out all the research on dextrins and their impact on mouthfeel, I brewed an experimental hazy IPA with a grist consisting of 50% Briess Carapils and 50% 2-row (not counting acidulated malt added for mash pH adjustment). In the *Oxford Companion to Beer*, Carapils is said to be in some styles such as bocks as much as 40% of the grist for fuller body and mouthfeel. Briess, however, recommends only 1-5% of the grist should contain Carapils. After my experimental beer was finished, I sent a sample to White Labs to get the actual concentration tested.

Briess Carapils is a true glassy caramel/crystal malt, albeit one that isn't roasted enough to develop the color or flavor associated with darker caramel malts. According to John Mallet's book *Malt: A Practical Guide from Field to Brewhouse* specialty glassy malts are made with low temperatures and high moisture to make pale malts with a glassy endosperm. How exactly Briess is making their Carapils is uncertain as it's a proprietary process.

Writing on The Mad Fermenationist blog, Michael Tonsmeire wrote Weyermann Carafoam (Carapils outside the U.S.) is high in protein and under-modified. It's mealy/starchy, so it too is converted into fermentable sugars when mashed but would be unsuitable for steeping. Weyermann suggests it can be used up to 40% of the grist.[97]

I wasn't sure what kind of efficiency I was going to get with 50% Carapils in this experiment, so I overestimated my grain totals assuming I might see a short drop, but I actually got better efficiency than I normally do. In terms of attenuation, I didn't notice a difference from other beers fermented with WLP007. On day ten of fermentation, it already reached its final gravity of 1.014, which is typical for that high of a mash temperature with that yeast strain in my experience. I was expecting to see a much higher final gravity with the huge addition of Carapils, however. I reached out to Briess to see if they had a comment on the normal attenuation with Carapils used at such a high percentage of the grist, because the product is advertised as having the ability to add non-fermentables to wort (below is their response).

"For a multi-step mash with sufficient enzymes we typically see about a 10% reduction in apparent attenuation from the Carapils portion of the wort, i.e. 50/50 brew of pale (80% apparent) and Carapils (72%) would expect to yield an apparent attenuation of 76%. If enzymes are deficient or a β-amylase rest is shortened or omitted you would expect to see much lower attenuation rates from Carapils, maybe down to about 30%."

It's important to note that Briess does not recommend using Carapils at such high rates when formulating recipes. It was surprising how good the attenuation was though with 50% Carapils considering that β-amylase activity is optimal between 140-150°F[98] (60-65°C) and I mashed at 160°F (71°C). I had 76.7% apparent attenuation with WLP007, well above a potential low of 30%.

Looking at the White Lab test results of my beer, it's interesting to see that even with 50% Carapils, I still came under the needed 50 g/liter of dextrins in the finished beer (41.3 g/L actual). Briess seems to slightly disagree with this study, however, responding "as far as dextrin perception is concerned, it seems like 50g/L (~5 Plato, or a .020 increase in specific gravity) is quite high, and the detector is not very sensitive."

Briess also mentioned that the increased body could also be coming from the elevated levels of beta-glucans from Carapils. Although the exact amount of beta-glucans in Carapils is not advertised, it's likely less than other rich sources like oats. For example, a mash consisting of 100% malted barley was tested with a beta-glucan content of only 20 mg/L, adding just 10% unmalted oats increased the beta-glucan content to 393 mg/L. Replacing 40% of the malted barley with unmalted oats increased the beta-glucan content to 1,949 mg/L, which is a 97-fold increase.[99]

Because mouthfeel is likely the result of multiple factors like glycerol, beta-glucans, alcohol, and dextrins, it makes sense to see each as a player in the larger game. In other words, even though the dextrin threshold wasn't reached in my case, it was still very high. If this is combined with high levels of beta-glucans from oats for example, it seems logical there would be an impact on mouthfeel. My opinion on the mouthfeel of the 50% Carapils beer was positive, it had a nice soft mouthfeel, but I wouldn't describe it super thick or chewy. One thing I noticed with this beer was that the head retention was better than I typically see, which was mainly noticeable in the sticky lacing around an empty glass.

Limit Dextrinase

Diastatic power is the term used to know how much starch-converting enzymes a specific malt might have, which break down starches and dextrins into fermentable sugars. These enzymes consist of β-amylase, α-amylase, limit dextrinase, and α-glucosidase. Only limit dextrinase (hence the name) can break down dextrins (by cleaving alpha-1,6-linkages in amylopectin and limit dextrins) into fermentable sugars. Considering that most beers have about 20% small branched dextrins[100], it's important to understand what factors might encourage or discourage limit dextrinase activity. The more active limit dextrinase in the wort, the more fermentable sugars and less total dextrins in the finished beer.[101]

All the starch degrading enzymes are created during the germination phase of malting, so unmalted grains don't have any limit dextrinase activity. When trying to get an idea of the limit dextrinase potential in specific malts, it is helpful to know that limit dextrinase activity has been significantly correlated (in a study of more than 70 different barley varieties) to the grains' extract protein content. The study noted that 80% of the variation is explained by "other factor or factors," suggesting it might be random.[102] So, although protein content might help give us an idea, it still seems like a question mark for the most part.

There is some evidence that certain mashing conditions can have an impact on limit dextrinase. For example, one study showed that with mash temperatures of 135°F (57°C) for fifteen minutes, approximately two-thirds (60-70%) of the total of limit dextrinase activity was inactivated.[103] The more the mash increased above 135°F (57°C), the more inactive the limit dextrinase.

At normal mash temperatures starting around 149°F (65°C), the activity was almost non-existent. However, at 125°F (52°C), most of the starting limit dextrinase remained. The study suggests that if you conduct a protein rest at 113-138°F (45°C-59°C) you would likely have a good temperature range for limit dextrinase activity.

So, a protein rest might do more than just break down large proteins into smaller ones, it can also break down dextrins.

Still focusing on mash temperatures, another study found that limit dextrinase activity was stable at 113-131°F (45°C-55°C) and declined as the temperatures in the mash increased. After 30 minutes (about how long most mashes take to fully convert) at 158°F (70°C), limit dextrinase activity was undetectable.[104] Basically, we can view the limit dextrinase enzyme similarly as we do with β-amylase, which is they are both effective at lower temperatures. So, mashing hazy IPAs without a protein rest and around 158°F (70°C), may encourage higher final dextrin content in beer.

Shifting slightly to research regarding wort production in Scotch, it was found that alcohol yields were higher in unboiled vs boiled worts.[105] In other words, if limit dextrinase survives mashing and goes into the fermenter without being deactivated by boiling or pasteurization temperatures, then the enzyme could continue to break down dextrins during fermentation. In the study, mashing of malted barley was done at 149°F (65°C) for 60 minutes and ran off into a fermenter. Sparging was done in four different batches at different temperatures, with the later runoffs done hotter, bringing the wort to around 185°F (85°C). The first two runoffs were pulled into the fermenter without the hot 185°F (85°C) sparge water and the researchers discovered that most of the limit dextrinase survived at the cooler sparge temperatures.

The authors found that limit dextrinase not only survived the 60-minute mash but remained relatively high during the early stages of fermentation and even increased around the 10-15-hour mark. This means that with limit dextrinase available during the early stages of fermentation can increase wort fermentability (beneficial in Scotch production) and potentially reduce the mouthfeel because of the reduction in dextrins.[106] I should point out that they probably used distillers malt, which is generally much more enzymatic, so it must be seen how true this would also be of a pilsner or pale ale malt base.

What does this Scotch research have to do with hoppy beer? The answer is not much, some things are just interesting! However, for those that occasionally brew no-boil beers, like a no-boil hazy IPA, it's probably best to at least bring the wort up to 185°F (85°C) to stop limit dextrinase activity so the beer doesn't attenuate more than expected as well as lower the final dextrin count which can negatively impact mouthfeel. I've brewed and sampled a few no-boil

NEIPAs, and I personally don't care for them, especially in higher alcohol beers. The massive amount of fresh dough character from not boiling dominates the dry hops and the lack of hot-side hopping leaves the beer with very little hop saturated flavor.

Late Hop Polyphenols and Mouthfeel

A paper that examined how late hopping would impact low alcohol beers (1.2% ABV) tested the polyphenol pickup from whirlpool hops with three different varieties.[107] The results showed transfer rates of approximately 50% (some mid-boil hops were also used). These particular beers were hopped to 15-20 IBUs, which suggests when the majority of the hops are coming from the whirlpool, a substantial number of polyphenols are also being transferred into the wort.

In terms of mouthfeel, the study found that polyphenols from late hopping improved palate fullness. The quality of bitterness did not impart a negative impression of "tannic substance bitterness."[108] This suggests that when making low ABV, hop-forward beers, a good way to improve the mouthfeel is to do heavy dosages of whirlpool hops. One way to do this without picking up too much bitterness is to lower the temperature of the kettle before adding the whirlpool hops. A larger number of lower α-acid hops in the whirlpool can also help increase polyphenols for mouthfeel with less bitterness potential. Hops high in polyphenols can also be used and generally these are also lower α-acid hops (more on this in Chapter 13).

Key Findings

- Two identical hoppy beers brewed with different sulfate-to-chloride ratios produced two distinctly different beers. The higher the sulfate, the more the perceived bitterness.
- A negative correlation has been found with high sulfate levels and perceived hop flavor.
- Chloride helps to increase the roundness and fullness of beer.
- Malted grains will have a large impact on final mineral concentration in beer. For example, base malts can add as much as 50-100 ppm of sulfate and approximately 200 ppm chloride.

- Flaked grains will contribute less minerals than malted.
- A good sulfate-to-chloride ratio in hoppy beers is 2:3 (favoring chloride), you can adjust as you wish in subsequent batches.
- In terms of dextrin concentrations needed for immediate mouthfeel implications, it can take as much as 50 g/L (.020 gravity points). However, amounts close to this threshold combined with other mouthfeel builders like glycerol and beta-glucans all play a role.
- In lower ABV hoppy beers, it can be beneficial to load up the whirlpool with lower α-acid hops at reduced temperatures to increase polyphenol concentration leading to enhanced mouthfeel.

Chapter 5: Flavor Perceptions

"A complex flavor can be mentally analyzed, consciously or unconsciously, we perceive it in the manner in which we hear a symphony."[109]

This quote serves no other purpose than it's what I thought a smart and thoughtful person might use to start a Chapter on flavor perceptions. Moving on.

Each of us has our own threshold for detecting certain flavors. An *American Society Brewing Chemists* study in 1980 found that people showing low thresholds for one compound usually showed high thresholds for one or two other compounds and vice versa. In other words, two people tasting the same beer may report different flavor impressions and both would be right. For each compound in beer, the most sensitive 10% of the group tested showed a threshold approximately 20 times lower than the least sensitive 10%.[110]

Some people may require higher concentrations of one compound to be able to detect it, whereas some can have 20 times less in the beer but still pick it out. Perceived beer flavors can be incredibly complicated. There are many chemical compounds playing a role (especially in hop-forward beers) along with physiological interactions.

A comprehensive fifteen-year study released in 1982 examined approximately 250 compounds that were purified and added to beer to determine different flavor thresholds and how the compounds interact to produce the full flavor of a beer.[111] They found compounds of similar flavors tended to be "additive" where compounds of different flavors acted independently. The study concluded that in general, most beer flavor compounds fit into this additive category, meaning that although one compound may exist below its flavor threshold, combining it with another similar compound may ultimately decrease its flavor threshold.

In theory then, layering hops with similar oil profiles (like Citra and Mosaic) could be a good way to experiment with boosting desired flavors from your favorite varieties. If enough like compounds are added, it could potentially reduce their flavor thresholds. On the other hand, using hops with vastly different compounds (like Citra and Fuggle) might result in more independent and possibly clashing flavors.

Grist Role in Flavor

One area that the grist can impact flavors is the total protein content in beer. Protein has little flavor but can influence perception via binding and/or adsorption of flavor compounds.[112] A 2013 study examined protein and carbohydrate levels in beer and the potential impact on hop compounds.[113] The authors chose five compounds to measure in the test beers: ethanol, myrcene (to represent dry hop flavor), ethyl hexanoate (apple flavor), isoamyl acetate (banana), and benzaldehyde (almond flavor) by testing the headspace of the vessel for compound concentrations at the different protein and carbohydrate levels. Sensory tests were also performed to accompany the measured data.

The test beer was brewed with Nugget hops and fermented with Safale S-04 at 75°F (24°C). After fermentation, one of the beers was diluted with water to obtain a low protein and low carbohydrate beer and the other was not diluted. The authors found that the high protein and carbohydrate beer had significantly more intense dry hop flavor. In sensory tests, the high protein and carbohydrate beer had a 22% increase in hop flavor ratings compared to the low protein and carbohydrate beer.

Using Gas chromatography–mass spectrometry GC/MS testing, the volatile compounds were analyzed at the two different protein and carbohydrate levels. Myrcene was found to be in lower concentrations in the head space (but higher in the beer) in the high protein and carbohydrate beer. This may be because the higher concentration of proteins leads to an increase in binding of compounds, which would lower the concentrations of these compounds in the headspace. In other words, the higher protein content is binding these volatile compounds and keeping them in solution. This might also explain why the higher protein and carbohydrate beer scored lower on the sensory tests for dry hop aroma as it was tested with 55% less myrcene in the headspace (it was actually in the beer).

Carbohydrates were also mentioned as playing a potential role in flavor and aroma differences because of their ability to retain volatile flavors. In the study, as the carbohydrates increased, so did the viscosity. It's this fullness that appears to reduce the ability of volatile compounds to diffuse. Essentially, fewer molecules can reach the surface of the solution where it can be volatilized.

Because carbohydrates may play a role in flavor-binding or by reducing the ability of volatile compounds to diffuse, I thought it would be helpful to take a closer look at the carbohydrate composition of grains, both malted and flaked.

The reported beer carbohydrate values in most beers are 4% dextrins, 0.8% glucose, 0.5% fructose, and 0.2% fructan, 0.4% pentosan and 1% beta-glucan.[114] Of these carbohydrates, those under the polysaccharide group (like pentosans, beta-glucans, and dextrins) are essential for increasing viscosity. If the viscosity increases and fewer volatile compounds (like myrcene) can diffuse out of the beer, we can start to see why more viscous beers could become more astringent if over hopped.

Potentially, if a beer is excessively viscous because of high proteins and beta-glucans, I wonder if the hop character might have more of a resinous and astringent character because more of the hop hydrocarbons are being retained like myrcene, which is otherwise very volatile.

Perhaps one way to add carbohydrates to taste (or to reach certain gravity points) post fermentation is to add maltodextrin. Adding maltodextrin post dry hopping would allow the dry hops to extract in a less viscous solution where more of the greener compounds may volatize leaving their fruiter counterparts behind. You could then build back up the sweetness and viscosity with the maltodextrin, likely to a final gravity around 1.020 in hazy IPAs. At Sapwood Cellars, we always have a sack of maltodextrin on hand, post fermentation doctoring can help OK beers become great beers.

One way these viscous carbohydrates are increased is by using unmalted grains as well as under-modified grains. Beta-glucanase (which breaks down beta-glucans) undergoes a dramatic increase during germination and malting and is non-existent in ungerminated barley. This is why flaked barley has higher beta-glucan concentration than malted barley.[115] Increased levels of beta-glucans (low molecular weight beta-glucans) have also been linked to having a beneficial impact on foam and flavor.[116]

Flaked oats are often used in hazy IPAs to increase beta-glucan content. One study found that a mash consisting of 100% malted barley had a beta-glucan content of only 20 mg/L, but adding just 10% unmalted oats increased the content to almost 400 mg/L.[117] So, if a recipe high in flaked oats is creating too much of a green astringent character, potentially from the beta-glucans retaining the more volatile hop compounds like myrcene, it may make sense to lower the percentage of flaked oats or try malted oats which would have fewer beta-glucans.

Under-modified malts have higher concentrations of carbohydrates than fully-modified malts because during the germinating and malting process protein modification happens first, followed by carbohydrate modification. Specifically, beta-glucanase is produced last. If malting is cut short, like in under-modified malts, and carbohydrate modification isn't complete, the resulting malt would have higher levels of carbohydrates like beta-glucans.[118]

I reached out to BESTMALZ®, who offers an under modified 2-row summer barley malt called chit malt and asked about carbohydrate levels. I was curious most about beta-glucans levels and was told that "the beta-glucan levels in chit malt are higher due to the lower water content and provoked growth at steeping and germination than normal barley malt." They also assume that beta-glucan levels in chit malt are comparable to that of oats, but they haven't tested this yet.

The higher concentration of beta-glucans in chit malt compared to standard 2-row (but still likely less than an unmalted grain) combined with the potential for better head retention and shelf stability (more on this in chapter 14) makes it a good malt choice to experiment with in hazy IPAs. In my experience, replacing about 10% of the grist with chit malt is a good starting point.

Role of Base Malt

The choice of base malt used in beers is often an overlooked decision. More thought is generally put into a 3% crystal malt choice than the 2-row that makes up most of the grist. Research in 2018 into six different base malt varieties has me rethinking this approach.

In the paper, 2-row was tested from Copeland, Expedition, Full Pint, Meredith, Metcalfe, and PolarStar in a malt-forward low bittered (8 IBU) recipe fermented with yeast supplied by New Belgium Brewing.[119] Both sensory analysis and malt chemistry was examined. The beers were stored at room temperature for a month after packaging, then at 39°F (4°C) for another month and evaluated during the first, fourth, and eighth week. The authors found that the six commercial barley sources contained significant metabolite variations, and these did have an impact in sensory test.

The panel found that distinct flavor differences in the beers were detectable after two months of storage. Specifically, the paper noted that "Full Pint and Copeland were associated with fruity, watermelon rind, ethyl acetate, isoamyl acetate, and acetaldehyde/green apple sensory traits. Meredith and Metcalfe were associated with the corn chip, sulfidic (H2S), and Honeycomb cereal sensory traits, and PolarStar and Expedition were associated with umami and cardboard flavors."

The fruitier flavors made with the Full Pint 2-row obviously caught my eye as it relates to making fruity IPAs. Looking closer at why, the authors found that Full Pint had several nitrogenous compounds and terpenes consistent with fruit-like or perfume flavors. Other 2-row varieties also contained compounds consistent with the sensory results. For example, Meredith contained sulfur-containing amines, amino acids, and sugars associated with a corn chip and cereal flavor.

Looking closer at Full Pint, the paper discovered a few additional compounds that may be influencing the fruity flavors, including a volatile metabolite called alpha-ionone, a ketone associated with floral, pear, and watermelon rind flavors, which may be created as a result of α-ionone being synthesized from the beer terpene citral and acetone. The paper went on to cite sources explaining that terpene and lipid degradation pathways may interact to form new fruity terpenes in the beer. [120] The Full Pint beer also had low levels of monoterpenes present, although in low levels, perhaps they could be a nice addition to boost synergy among desirable fruity hop monoterpenes.

Although this paper focused more on flavors after aging, why not try a few beers with the Full Pint 2-row in the same hoppy recipes you've previously brewed to see if you get a fruit boost from the base malt?

Yeast Pitch Rate

Yeast selection will obviously have a large impact on a beer through ester production, mouthfeel, clarity, etc. However, one component that can impact the flavors of a hop-forward beer is not just the yeast selection, but the yeast pitch rate.

A 2017 paper tested various yeast concentrations to imitate primary fermentations with Weihenstephan 68 and 34/70 yeast strains.[121] The results show the higher the yeast pitch rate, the more uptake of certain compounds. For example, β-myrcene decreased, depending on yeast cell counts, and only traces of it remained at the highest counts of 100 million cells/mL. However, linalool concentrations were not noticeably changed by the presence of yeast cells. The authors concluded that the more polar or soluble the compound, the less likely it will be impacted by the yeast. In other words, β-myrcene is not as polar as linalool and thus, more likely to be influenced by yeast cells.

Perhaps we can think of high yeast pitch counts as a potential way to lower the final concentrations of non-polar hop hydrocarbons which tend to be spicy, resinous, herbal, and woody. At the same time, more of the polar oxygen-containing compounds like fruity and citrus monoterpenes alcohols (linalool and geraniol) might remain. So, an early dry hop while yeast is still active has the potential to change the sensory experience based on yeast cell interaction with less polar compounds. However, active CO2 will also push out aromatics (likely more of the volatile hydrocarbons), so early dry hop addition could be less aromatic overall, but also slightly fruitier and less resinous. I speculate that keg conditioning/carbonating a hop-forward beer could also strip more of the resinous compounds from excessive dry hopping.

On the commercial level, I have experimented with early dry hop additions during fermentation and noticed much more overall loss of hop aroma than on the homebrewing level, perhaps due to more aggressive fermentation. However, for some of our more approachable beers where a hint of hop flavor and aroma is desired, we will dry hop on day one of fermentation which seems to provide a subtle base layer of fruity hop flavor with very little to no hop bite or greenness. This could be both from fermentation blowing off the compounds as well as active yeast absorbing some of the more non-polar hop compounds.

So now that we've learned that beers high in flaked oats will have high levels of beta-glucans which might retain more myrcene in the final beer increasing the "green" character. But we also learned that increasing pitching rates may lower myrcene concentrations. So, if the silky viscous mouthfeel of oats is something you are after but are getting beers that are too astringent, consider experimenting with slightly reducing the flaked oat percentage, dry hopping during active fermentation, or increasing the yeast pitch rate.

The science is interesting, but I wanted to see for myself if yeast pitch rates could reduce green, resinous characteristics in beer so I designed my own experiment to test the findings. I brewed a ten-gallons of hazy IPA and split the wort into five-gallon batches to ferment separately. Three days prior to brewing, I prepared a large 3,000 mL starter of RVA 132 Manchester Ale yeast. Swirling the starter as evenly as possible, I poured out 1,000 mL of starter liquid into a separate Erlenmeyer flask and cold-crashed each, so I could discard the starter liquid but keep the yeast. One half of the beer fermented with the 1,000 mL of starter and the other fermented with 2,000 mL of starter double the yeast pitch rate typically required to ferment out five gallons of 1.065 wort.

Each beer was dry hopped early into fermentation with one ounce of Amarillo and two ounces of Citra, then again with the same amounts in the serving keg. The grist was a simple base of 70% 2-row, 15% malted wheat, and 15% chit malt.

I could tell a difference between each sample when served blind. To my palate, the beer with the increased yeast pitch was less harsh with less of a green/vegetal bite and was overall generally smoother than the beer pitched with 1,000 mL of starter. Granted, I was searching for this when tasting knowing the reason for the experiment. I served the two beers blind to approximately ten people, all of whom are brewers themselves, and only one person preferred the beer with the standard yeast pitch. The general comments on why people preferred the increased yeast pitch beer largely resembled my own personal thoughts: it was more pleasing on the palate, offered less astringency and had slightly fruitier hop flavor.

My results would align with the research, which is that increasing the yeast pitch could be a way of reducing the overall green, resinous and astringent characteristics that can come with heavily hopped beers. This could be largely attributed to the increased concentration of yeast present simply pulling out additional non-polar compounds, as well as interacting and removing other potential harsh compounds like hop polyphenols. I will say, as each beer sat in the keg (with hops) for over a month, they became more alike, which suggests to me that some of these harsh green characteristics may settle out over extended cold-conditioning. The increased yeast pitch beer seemed to reach its peak quicker (about a week) compared to the beer with a smaller pitch rate.

I'm not sure I would go as far as to recommend large pitch rates as a solid long-term approach to brewing hazy beer, but it was an interesting experiment that does help to understand hazy hoppy beers a bit more. I would like to see more lab test of actual hop compounds in these types of experiments with hazy beers before making concrete recommendations. I'm hesitant to overpitch commercially, but I do wonder when we rouse dry hops with CO2, if some of the yeast that has settled in the cone is interacting with the hop compounds as we blast it back into solution potentially stripping some of the greener components. Just another area of potential research!

Key Findings

- High protein and carbohydrate beer had more intense dry hop flavor (in the test, myrcene was the measured compound).
- High carbohydrates (like beta-glucans) and protein concentrations in hoppy beer may help retain more of the volatile green, resinous, herbal, and woody hop hydrocarbons.
- Unmalted grains and undermodified grains will have more beta-glucans than malted grains.
- Not all base malts are equal when it comes to flavor implications, one test found a 2-row called Full Pint created more fruity flavors than five other tested base malts.
- Experimenting with different yeast pitching rates may be a way to dial in the desired flavors in a beer. Increased pitch rates can reduce some of the more volatile green and resinous compounds. However, increased pitching rates can have other fermentation impacts like increased esters (when heavily overpitched).

Chapter 6: Esters and Fusel Alcohols

Sometimes referred to as secondary flavor constituents, esters and fusel alcohols can either play a background supporting role in hoppy beers or can completely takeover depending on variables like yeast selection and fermentation conditions. With hundreds of compounds in hop-forward beer fighting a Royal Rumble for your sensory attention, it's worth paying attention to the role of esters and alcohols, particularly if the goal is to let the hops shine.

Both alcohols and esters are important aroma compounds that help shape the characteristics of beer. The most important flavor-active esters are ethyl acetate (fruity, solvent-like), isoamyl acetate (banana), isobutyl acetate (pineapple), ethyl caproate and ethyl caprylate (sour apple), and phenyl ethyl acetate (flowery). The taste thresholds for each ester can vary and are generally very low, ranging from 0.2 ppm for isoamyl acetate to 8-48 ppm for ethyl acetate.[122]

It's not just the individual esters that can shape beer flavor, but the role of multiple esters working together creating a synergistic effect. This means that the esters can impact the flavor below their individual thresholds when present with other esters.[123] In part because of the synergistic effect and low taste thresholds, small changes in the concentrations of esters can impact the flavor and aroma of beer. Generally, ale yeast strains will produce more esters and higher alcohols than lager strains.[124]

The higher alcohols (called fusel alcohols) can also contribute to flavor. The most prevalent fusel alcohols in the research are propanol, isobutanol, active amyl alcohol, and isoamyl alcohol.[125] As we look at the different variables that can impact alcohols and esters, it's important to point out that different ale and lager strains will alter these ratios in fermented beer.[126] It's also important to keep in mind that in each paper detailed below, different yeast strains were used, and the results could vary. However, I think it's fair to use the information to form a general understanding of esters and alcohols to increase the likelihood of brewing beer closer to the desired goal.

Fermentation Temperature

It's generally understood among brewers that higher fermentation temperatures will increase ester production, but amounts can vary across different strains and the individual esters produced. More specifically, one paper found that increasing the fermentation temperature from 64°F (18°C) to 73°F (23°C) resulted in increased acetate ester concentration of 14% and total ethyl ester concentration by 63% (with Safale S-04 yeast strain).

When the above study tested for fusel alcohols, the authors found the alcohols increased "markedly" when the fermentation temperature went from 50°F (10°C) to 59°F (15°C).[127]

One issue I've had as a homebrewer as it relates to wort temperatures is being limited to my ground water temperature when chilling using an immersion chiller. In the summer months, I can usually chill my wort down to about 80°F (27°C), which is much higher than my desired fermentation temperature. I'm always afraid to pitch the yeast to the warm wort in fear of increasing ester and alcohol production. There are a few options; I can pump chilled water through my chiller to get down to pitching temperatures or put the wort in my fermentation fridge for hours waiting for the temperature to drop, both are more work and time consuming.

I wonder if homebrewers can pitch yeast at the warmer summer temperatures right away and allow the beer to cool in the fermentation fridge without any negative ester or fusel alcohol impact detracting from hop aroma and flavor. This question inspired me to research further into the timing of ester and alcohol production.

A study with insight into when ester and fusel alcohol production occur during fermentation was done in 2001 and found a three-phase timetable for production. First alcohol accumulates alone; next both alcohol and ester accumulate; and last ester accumulates alone. Fusel alcohols were produced during sugar and free amino nitrogen (FAN) assimilations during their experiments, which is slightly earlier in the process than ester formation. Ester production rate reached a maximum at approximately 80% of the total fermentation time, depending on temperature. The initial time of ester production was generally around the twenty-hour mark.

Examining the chart included in the study, fusel alcohol production begins in the first ten hours of fermentation and really starts to ramp up around the 24-hour mark, but at a much more drastic rate at warmer temperatures. However, when the beers were pitched warmer in the study, no yeast lag time was experienced, which is likely why alcohols formed slightly faster (60°F (15°C) for a lager yeast strain).[128]

It's important to note that although the study found that the temperature had a significant impact on fusel alcohol production rate through increased sugar and FAN consumption rates, they fermented the beer at the constant hotter temperature. So, pitching hotter in the summer months and allowing the wort to cool in the fermentation fridge could decrease yeast lag time (faster fermentation start), but create a higher concentration of fusel alcohols. However, the fusel alcohol increase would likely be less than the study found because the temperature would be lowering during this fusel production period, not remain at a constant warm temperature as it was in the study.

The time frame at which esters are created during fermentation seems to be less of an issue when pitching hot. In a review on yeast and esters and alcohols in the *Applied Microbiology and Biotechnology Journal*, it's stated that esters are mainly formed during the vigorous phase of primary fermentation by "chemical condensation of organic acids and alcohols."[129] The vigorous stage of fermentation won't be reached during the short time wort is still cooling in a fermentation chamber getting to the desired fermentation temperature from the ground water temperature.

Directly looking at this issue, a 1994 study by the *American Society of Brewing Chemists* analyzed ester formulation during fermentation at different temperatures. Fermentation was carried out at three different temperatures 53°F (12°C), 59°F (15°C), and 64°F (18°C) with a lager strain (NCYC 1324) and ester samples were recorded by headspace analysis. Greater ester concentration was found per degree fermented hotter, which is not surprising. However, as it relates to the time frame, esters (isoamyl acetate) started to ramp up around hour twenty during fermentation, peaking around day three for the hottest ferment and day four for the coolest ferment.[130] So it does seem logical, at least for isoamyl acetate, that pitching hot likely won't have drastic impacts on ester production.

Adjusting the fermentation temperatures during fermentation can also alter the ester and fusel alcohol production, but it's a complex function of the final temperature level, the direction of the change in temperature, and the status of the yeast at the time of the temperature adjustment. A commercial lager yeast strain was tested in oxygenated wort in four separate ferments, one at a constant 52°F

(11°C), one raising the temperature from 52°F-65°F (11°C-18°C) around 60 hours into fermentation (after CO2 evolution rate reaches maximum), one raising from 52°F-65°F (11°C-18°C) around twenty hours into fermentation (after stationary phase), and one at a constant 65°F (18°C).

In the test, the highest esters were found in the beer fermented at the constant 65°F (18°C). The beer that was raised to 65°F (18°C) after the stationary phase (about twenty hours or so into fermentation) finished close to the beer at the constant lower 52°F (11°C). And surprisingly, the beer that was ramped to 65°F (18°C) around 60 hours into fermentation (about 2.5 days) finished with the lowest ester concentration (approximately 8 mg/L less than the constant 52°F (11°C) ferment.[131] It seems plausible, that starting with a higher pitching temperature and gradually cooling it down during the first ten hours or so, could be somewhat offset by ramping the temperatures after the first few days of fermentation.

The above study also looked at the impact on ester production when cooling the fermentation temperature during active fermentation (not a common practice). When the fermentation temperature was decreased from 65°F (18°C) to 52°F (11°C) after 2.5 days resulted in ester levels that were higher than for any other recorded variable. So, lowering the temperature during peak fermentation causes higher ester levels.

As far as fusel alcohol production in the tests described above, they didn't change as much with the temperature adjustments. In general, there was a slight increase with higher fermentation temperatures and when raising the temperature mid-ferment resulted in a lower increase in alcohols versus a consistent hotter ferment. Overall, when making hazy IPAs, it makes sense to allow the fermentation temperature to gradually increase during fermentation to encourage a healthy and complete fermentation, but also to keep esters and alcohols in check.

All the science is fascinating as it relates to the timing of ester and alcohol production, but I wanted to put it to the test to see if homebrewers might be able to pitch their yeast hot in the summer months. So, to test whether pitching hot makes a difference, I brewed a ten-gallon batch of a Glacier and Citra IPA fermented with RVA Manchester Ale yeast and split the wort into two fermenters after chilling to 86°F (30°C). Both carboys went into my fermentation chamber set to 67°F (19°C) (19°C). I pitched the yeast immediately to one of the carboys (which was still at 86°F) and waited approximately fifteen hours until the other fermenter gradually chilled down to 67°F (19°C), at which point I pitched the yeast.

I took a half growler of each beer to a friend's house for a night of bottle sharing (not exactly the most scientific way of doing sensory tests). Overall, the two beers were incredibly similar. Suggesting in this test anyways, that pitching hot doesn't have a big impact on ester or fusel alcohol production. The one difference between the two beers that I was reliably able to detect was the beer pitched hot seemed to have a bigger mouthfeel.

I was curious why the mouthfeel might be different between the two beers, so I dug through some studies and found that glycerol production could be the answer. Glycerol is a sugar alcohol produced as a byproduct of the ethanol fermentation process by Saccharomyces cerevisiae, which can contribute to the body of beer.[132] One study stated that increased fermentation temperature resulted in greater glycerol production and optimum temperature for glycerol production by wine yeast strains of S. cerevisiae are between 71°F-89°F. (21°C-32°C).[133]

Could it be that the short period of just fifteen hours while the beer slowly chilled to the proper pitching temperature enhanced glycerol production? It's possible, as one paper measured the glycerol production timeframe in fermenting liquor and about eight hours into fermentation the glycerol levels started climbing and at eighteen hours glycerol production appeared to reach its maximum level.[134]

Although the mouthfeel impact from glycerol is just speculation from me at this point, I'd love to see more research into glycerol production from common hazy IPA yeast strains. Specifically, what factors might increase or decrease the final levels. It's possible that higher levels could not only impact mouthfeel but may also increase viscosity potentially retaining more of the non-polar green compounds (more speculation).

Trub

A 1982 study looked at the role trub (the mixture of cold and hot break from the boil kettle) played during beer fermentations.[135] Pilot scale fermentations were conducted in two separate tanks with trub and no trub. The study found that esters and fusel alcohols formed during fermentation were influenced by trub levels. Specifically, the levels of esters in the beer fermented with no trub were higher than the beers fermented with the trub added. Further analysis showed that the wort lipids in the beers with trub were significantly higher than the clear no-trub worts.

The same study also found that the beers with trub fermented substantially faster (about two days faster) and had a more vigorous fermentation with a higher suspended yeast count during fermentation. On the other hand, the formation of fusel alcohols slightly increased in beer fermented with high levels of trub.[136]

A follow-up study looking at the potential impact of trub during fermentation was conducted in Japan with BH-84 (commercial lager yeast). Three separate tanks were filled with cooled unfermented wort with varying amounts of trub ranging from 0.13-15.9 mg/ml. The beers were then fermented and tested for esters ethyl acetate and isoamyl acetate. The authors found that when the total trub content in the wort increased, both ethyl acetate and isoamyl acetate were significantly decreased.[137]

So, depending on the flavor goals of the beer you are brewing, allowing some trub into the fermenter from the boil kettle can be a tool to help shape ester formation from the yeast. Based on the studies above, the more trub that's allowed into the fermenter, the lower the ester formation, faster the fermentation, with the potential of slightly higher fusel alcohols.

Yeast Nutrients

A 2014 paper looked at the role of two yeast supplements zinc sulfate (ZnSO4) and the amino acid L-leucine and tested their effects on ester production in beers fermented with the Safale S-04 yeast strain. The authors found that the ester compounds produced during fermentation were greatly increased with the addition of ZnSO4 and L-leucine. Specifically, 0.12 g/L of ZnSO4 resulted in a 27% increase in acetate esters and 123% increase in total ethyl esters compared to unsupplemented sample. The addition of 0.750 g/L of L-leucine resulted in a 41% increase in total acetate ester concentration and an 84% increase in total ethyl ester concentration compared to an unsupplemented sample.[138]

The addition of amino acids of valine, leucine, and isoleucine was found to strongly increase the production of fusel alcohols (isobutanol, isoamyl alcohol, and amyl alcohol). Specifically, 60-70% of the added leucine and isoleucine were transformed into isoamyl alcohol and amyl alcohol, and the all the valine was transformed into isobutanol. A potential downside of no added amino acids (yeast nutrient) to the ferment was a slightly slower timeframe to reach the end of fermentation, in this case, the difference was only about ten hours.[139] However, for most brewers, an additional ten hours of fermentation is probably not a big deal.

So, yeast nutrients are great for healthy fermentation, but could also be altering the yeast-derived flavors. Too much yeast nutrient might create an abundance of fusel alcohols and lead to a hotter alcohol finish. At the same time, yeast nutrients may help boost desirable esters. Experimenting with different nutrient amounts is another tool for brewers to use to try and control fermentation profiles. There's always something to keep tweaking!

Oxygen

Anaerobic (absence of oxygen) and semianerobic (partly oxygenated) fermentation conditions were tested in 1985 by the *American Society of Brewing Chemists* in high gravity worts to find out the effects of esters and fusel alcohol production. The semianerobic fermentations were done with the use of a sterile foam plug (like what many homebrewers use on their starters), which resulted in drastically reduced levels of esters compared to the anaerobic ferment. This was true regardless of the amount of nutritional supplementation given to the beers. The fusel alcohols didn't appear to be significantly influenced by either anaerobic or semianerobic conditions.[140]

Other studies have also pointed to decreased ester production under conditions of increased wort aeration, even across numerous yeast strains and at different pitching rates.[141] Of course, the goal isn't always reduced esters, but if that is a goal, mimicking open fermentations on the homebrew level could be a way to reduce the levels a bit. This can easily be done by covering the opening of a carboy with sanitized aluminum foil during the active phase of fermentation, likely the first day or so.

Beer pH

What about beer pH and its effect on ester production? Although less of a concern when making clean (non-soured) hoppy beers, it's interesting to learn how pH can impact fermentations. The *Journal of Bioscience and Bioengineering* tested three different beers fermented each with a different starting pH (3.0, 5.0, and 7.0). As the starting pH increased, so did the esters formed during fermentation. The beer fermented at a pH of 7.0 resulted in the highest ester concentration with a 13% increase in total acetate esters and 7% increase in total ethyl ester production compared to the control (5.0 pH beer). On the other hand, the beer fermented at a low pH of 3.0 resulted in an 18% decrease in total ester concentration.[142]

Key Findings

Variable	Possible Result
Higher fermentation temperatures	Increased esters and alcohols
Trub present in the fermenter	Reduced esters and increased alcohols
Adding yeast nutrient to fermenter	Increased esters and alcohols
Increased oxygen during fermentation	Reduced esters
Top pressure (dissolved CO2 or capped ferment)	Reduced esters and alcohols
Increased yeast pitching rate	Increased esters (only when heavily overpitched)
Reduced wort pH (3.0)	Decreased esters
Increasing fermentation temperature at climax of fermentation	Decreased esters (lower than keeping constant temperature)
Decreasing fermentation temperature at climax of fermentation	Increased esters
Higher gravity fermentations	Increased esters and alcohols

Chapter 7: Dry Hopping

Dry hopping regimes among homebrewers and commercial breweries can vary drastically and differences (like tank size, recirculation, and duration) can alter extraction rates and ultimately the final flavor and aromas of beer. In this chapter, I analyze research that has been conducted on dry hopping to help brewers maximize the most important aroma addition. Unfortunately, even after reading hundreds of pages of studies on the topic, I can't with any certainty suggest the best way to approach dry hopping. However, the research can help guide brewers into experimentation with different methods, recipe designs, and equipment to boost results.

Introduction of Oxygen

Oxygen is the number one enemy of dry hopped beers. It can quickly transform a fresh and fruity hoppy beer to a sweeter cherry cardboard darker version of itself. In my experience, this can happen even faster in the hazy hoppy style. For example, I've had a hazy IPA oxidize in primary after just two weeks because of a leaky lid! I would avoid using buckets on the homebrew scale for hazy hoppy beers for this very reason, they seem to be notorious for leaking, which is particularly concerning post-fermentation.

Dry hopping is often overlooked as a potential source of oxygen introduction, but a thesis by Peter Harold Wolfe, titled, "A Study of Factors Affecting the Extraction of Flavor When Dry Hopping Beer," notes that the introduction of dissolved oxygen is "inevitably introduced" when dry hops are added to beer, "resulting from the multitude of crevices inherent to their anatomy."

Because of this inevitable oxygen introduction, Wolfe suggests that dry hopping early in fermentation while the yeast is still active allows oxygen to be metabolized by yeast before it can oxidize the beer.[143] We know that active fermentation dry hopping may reduce oxygen introduction, but may also impact final hop compound levels from CO_2 production and removal and absorption from yeast cells.

Considering most ale fermentations, when adequately pitched and oxygenated, are typically done fermenting around five days or so, it would seem then that dry hopping to ensure as little oxygen introduction as possible should be done around day 3-5 of fermentation. What if you want the post-fermentation dry hop profile? A few brewers I spoke to who like to dry hop after fermentation will add a small amount of sugar with the dry hops to encourage quick refermentation in hopes of scrubbing some oxygen introduced with the dry hops.

Another way to avoid oxygen pickup during dry hopping is to add dry hop additions to an empty keg (or brite tank) and purge the entire keg and the dry hops with CO2 (filling to 15-20 psi multiple times). You can then transfer the beer into the keg through the liquid keg post but be sure to release pressure from the keg to keep the flow of beer going.

If you are fermenting in a keg or another vessel hooked to CO2, you can use a spunding valve when making the transfer to the serving keg. The spunding valve helps maintain a nice slow transfer by slowly releasing pressure from the receiving vessel helping to prevent foaming. Ideally, you want the receiving keg's PSI to be slightly under the PSI of the source keg. If the receiving keg's pressure is too high, there won't be flow into the keg. On the other hand, if the pressure from the pushing keg or vessel is much higher than that the receiving keg it will cause the beer to transfer too quickly.

Commercial brewers can do a version of this as well, just expect to use a lot more CO2! In my discussions with commercial brewers, most are doing CO2 transfers of beer from tank-to-tank (for example, fermentation tank to brite tank) but also first purging the receiving tank with CO2 (like purging a keg for homebrewers). Some brewers have reported lower dissolved oxygen readings when using CO2 to transfer beer between vessels compared to using a pump and a balancing line. I outline how Sapwood Cellars does this with hoppy beers in the last chapter.

Another option to keep oxygen levels low is to fill a receiving vessel with water or sanitizer and push it out with CO2 and then transfer in the beer. When the vessel is filled with the liquid and pushed out with CO2, it requires less CO2 than continuous purging and can remove even more of the oxygen. This can be done with kegs on a homebrew scale, but I wouldn't recommend doing this if you cut your dip tubes because sanitizer or water will be left in the bottom of the receiving keg and will mix with the beer.

Another method to reduce oxygen exposure during dry hopping is by continually flushing the headspace with CO2 while adding the hops. For homebrewers, if fermenting in a keg, simply hook up the CO2 to the gas side of the keg and flush the headspace while opening the lid and adding the hops (5-10 psi). If fermenting in a carboy, you can place a hose hooked to your CO2 above the beer to fill the headspace while dropping in the hops. Commercial brewers might have CO2 go through the spray ball while pouring in dry hops. This method of flushing the headspace with 15-20 PSI of CO2 has been tested and shown to reduce variability in the aroma intensity of dry hopped beers caused by oxygen.[144]

Homebrewers are unfortunately at a disadvantage when it comes to oxygen exposure potential during dry hopping. The smaller the batch size, the more the total quantity of beer is exposed to oxygen introduced during dry hopping. With larger commercial brewing systems, the massive amount of beer being produced acts to dilute the oxygen to a much greater extent. It's similar to why a five-gallon barrel has the potential for faster oxygen intake compared to a standard sized barrel. In smaller barrels (like with smaller fermenters), there is greater surface area to volume ratio, which means more of the beer will be in contact with oxygen.

Because smaller batches can be impacted more by oxygen exposure during dry hopping, I would consider the purging of CO2 for homebrewers during dry hopping an important step. I'm not even sure making extremely small batches of hazy hoppy beer is worth the effort as the study mentioned above found that dry hopping should be done at volumes at least equal to 20 L (5.3 gallons), suggesting oxygen issues with small batches is especially at risk to oxidation.

Commercial brewers can dry hop using a hop doser, which is a device that attaches to the dry hop port on the top of the tank via a tri-clamp fitting and a butterfly valve. The hop doser allows you to open the butterfly valve that is connected to the dry hop port on the tank and drop in the hops without exposing the beer to oxygen. An added benefit of the dry hop doser is the ability to purge the hops with CO2 prior to dropping them into the tank. The hop doser is generally big enough for an eleven-pound bag of hops and is especially great for dry hopping after primary fermentation has completed. When dry hopping late, brewers will often put a few pounds of pressure on the tank (since fermentation is complete) to help trap in volatiles and the dry hop doser allows you add the dry hops without releasing the pressure on the tank.

Dry Hop Contact Time

How long to dry hop is a common discussion among brewers. Some prefer hops on beer for weeks, while others prefer 24 hours or less. Sometimes contact time is just a matter of practicality. But luckily, there has been research that may influence how you approach dry hop durations going forward.

A study authored by Peter Wolfe, Michael Qian, and Thomas H. Shellhammer focused on how extraction of hop compounds during dry hopping can be impacted by the duration of the dry hop. Here, three separate lots of pelletized Cascade hops were dry hopped for a week in a beer-like solution at 1/3 lbs./bbl in a flushed and sealed stainless keg with no agitation. Samples were taken and analyzed on day one, four, and seven.

The results of the week-long dry hopping showed that for both linalool and myrcene, day seven concentrations weren't higher than day one concentrations. In fact, most of the results showed a decrease at day seven than the first day of dry hopping, which suggests that for these two compounds, 24 hours might be enough to get full extraction. In fact, terpenes like linalool and myrcene may reach their solubility threshold in a matter of hours. Even more surprising, due to the hydrophobicity of some hop aroma compounds, extended dry hopping can cause removal out of the beer and back into the spent hops.[145] Keep in mind, this experiment was tested in a keg without agitation or special procedures to try to speed up or increase extraction.

The size of a dry hopping vessel might also play a role in the extraction rates. For example, Peter Wolfe suggested in an online Q&A session that as the tank size increases, dry hop extraction efficiency decreases. Potentially, you would need more hops when brewing on a larger scale to get the same results as you would on the homebrew scale.

Wolfe also suggests that extraction times will be faster on the homebrew scale compared to commercial size tanks. For example, it might take three to five days in a 500-barrel tank to get full extraction without recirculation or agitation. Homebrewers would get faster extraction because of the smaller volume, even quicker if you swirl the carboy or keg a few times during the dry hop.[146]

Wolfe explained to me that dry hopping is entirely dependent on local diffusion speeds, not reaction rates (in contrast to say, hop acid isomerization in the kettle). Thus, anything that speeds up diffusion (stirring, temperature, etc.) will speed up extraction rates, and all of those things are generally slower as you scale up tank size - there will be less liquid in direct contact with hop material and it's harder to move that liquid around.

Looking closer at short dry hop durations, one paper tested dry hopping at 1/3 lbs./bbl at 68°F (20°C) in both a beer-like solution as well as fermented beer (1.044 original gravity fermented with an ale yeast strain and hopped to 12 ppm iso-α-acid). The biggest difference in this test was that the beer was agitated with a shaker table during dry hopping to maximize extraction. Again, quick extraction was shown with the hydrocarbon compounds, which were extracted in just four hours (greener compounds). The fruiter monoterpene alcohols also fully extracted in about four hours, peaking and then gradually reducing, especially linalool.[147] Again, the tests were done while the beer was agitated via the shaker table, so it seems safe to assume typical idle dry hopping would experience slower extraction times.

Wolfe's results indicate that dry hop extraction times are much quicker than most of us originally thought. Even at colder temperatures of 34-39°F (1°C-4°C), Wolfe suggests that extraction could still occur in less than three days. Looking closer at temperatures during dry hopping, a paper tested dry hopping at 39°F (4°C) and 68°F (20°C) and measured linalool solubility over the course of two weeks. The authors found the lower temperature resulted in slightly faster extraction, which peaked around day three, but was near maximum extraction on day two. The warmer temperature followed a similar extraction pattern but was just under the lower temperature linalool concentrations. After the full fourteen days, they were both at same levels.[148]

Homebrewers could use this data to experiment with dry hopping and carbonating at the same time. If colder temperatures still achieves extraction, adding hops to a keg at the same time it goes into the fridge for carbonating could help speed up your grain-to-glass time without having a negative impact on extraction rates. You could even accelerate extraction by gently swirling the keg.

In a follow-up study, Wolfe again looked at dry hop extraction, but this time adjusted the test to better replicate brewing conditions and brewed a pale ale bittered with 21 ppm iso-α-acid via an extract. The beer was fermented with Wyeast 1056 and filtered prior to dry hopping. Dry hopping was done in three-barrel stainless steel tanks with bagged Cascade pellets dosed at 1 lbs./bbl. The tank was either stirred (by pumping the beer in and out of the tank at a constant rate of 1,000 rpm) or held passive.

The findings of the experiment showed that stirring the beer during dry hopping significantly yielded more extraction, which resulted in more aroma intensity, but at the expense of increased in astringency and bitterness. The increased astringency from recirculating dry hops was also something that came up during my interviews with commercial brewers for this book as a complaint of recirculating dry hops, almost as if the hops are getting over extracted.

The increase in bitterness and astringency found in the experiment above correlated to the total polyphenol content in the beers. As the extraction rate increased with the dry hop duration (six hours to twelve days) so too did the polyphenol content and perceived bitterness. Pellet hops had an overall greater extraction of compounds than leaf hops and with that, a much greater total polyphenol content.

Bitterness levels also increased with extended extraction time, despite reduced levels of iso-α-acids, which agrees with findings in more recent work showing that leaf material in hops absorbs and reduces iso-α-acids.[149]

In terms of extraction time, the pellet hops were nearly fully extracted in just 24 hours and the leaf hops took a bit longer but stirring helped more with leaf hop extraction than with pellet hops. Looking at sensory results rather than just measured hop compounds, the non-stirred pellet hops at just six hours had essentially the same aroma intensity scores compared to day four, suggesting a short contact time with dry hopping may be enough to get extraction.

Overall, pellet hops have been found to extract at higher rates. For example, Hopsteiner found that pellet dry hopped beer had linalool concentrations nearly 50% greater after two days of dry hopping compared to whole leaf.[150] So, you may need to increase the quantity of leaf hops used to get the same intensity you'd get with pellets. As a starting point, I'd suggest increasing the whole leaf additions by about 25% compared to what you would dry hop with in pellets.

At the commercial level, one way to experiment with recirculating while also attempting to keep astringency down is to do short recirculation periods with lower dry hop amounts. For example, one experiment showed that after just two hours of recirculating (via a pump) immediately after adding the dry hops and then allowing the hops to sit idle in the tank, resulted in increased aroma compounds compared to a non-recirculated beer. Specifically, in the test above, linalool averaged an increase of about 58% when recirculated for the two hours.[151] I would like to see this experiment repeated at even shorter recirculation periods.

Dry Hopping and Polyphenols

To expand on polyphenols and dry hopping, a study looked at how polyphenolic bitterness of hops could influence the harshness of beer when combined with iso-α-acids.[152] The authors found that when polyphenols increased along with iso-α-acids, bitterness was described as harsh, medicinal, and metallic. Interestingly, not only did this character increase with more polyphenols and iso-α-acids, but so did the duration of the sensation on the palate. This suggests that beers with high levels of polyphenols that you might get from heavy dry hopping (especially when combined with a heavy protein grist) might induce a lingering harshness. The authors didn't rule out the possibility that humulinones could contribute to this along with polyphenols. As we'll learn in the next chapter, is likely.

One of my biggest complaints with heavily-hopped, hazy IPAs is an aggressive vegetal bitterness, sometimes referred to as "hop bite." Part of this could be explained by a large portion of polyphenols making their way into beer via dry hopping. In a study examining the transfer rates of hop substances during dry hopping, researchers found the rate of total polyphenols pickup is about 50–60%.[153] In terms of a hop's potential for polyphenols (although they vary by hop variety) hops generally have a total polyphenol content of around two to six percent. Obviously, as the dry hopping rates increase, so would the overall polyphenol concentration.

A 2018 study by Hopsteiner found that a unique polyphenol found only in hops (xanthohumol) is in significantly higher rates in hazy beers than other styles. Compared to a West Coast IPA which had 0.7 ppm of this polyphenol, the highest commercial hazy IPA was tested at 3.5 ppm and the average of all the hazy IPAs tested in the study was 2 ppm of xanthohumol (more than double the West Coast IPA).[154]

The same body of research also tested other non-polar compounds (like myrcene) in commercial hazy IPAs and found they are also much higher than in the West Coast IPA tested. The West Coast IPA had <0.3 ppm of myrcene and the hazy beers averaged 1.4 ppm (the highest was 2.5 ppm). So, although myrcene is non-polar, the more viscous protein-rich base is encouraging these compounds to stay in solution, potentially with more hop bite.

This same Hopsteiner study looked at how putting a hazy beer through a centrifuge might impact some of these compounds and found that centrifuging removed half of the myrcene and half of the measured polyphenol (xanthohumol) content. Although incredibly expensive devices, centrifuging hazy IPAs may be a way to decrease the conditioning time required to reduce hop bite by removing some of the harsh tasting polyphenols by as much as half their levels almost immediately.

There is even more evidence suggesting that dry hopping can impact the perceived bitterness in beers. Here, a paper considered the total polyphenol content of 34 commercial lager beers brewed in different countries, combined with sensory testing of the same beers. The authors found that beers that were dry hopped had the highest phenolic, polyphenol, and humulinone concentration. These same beers were also perceived as having a harsh and progressive bitterness.

In the same study, researchers found that beers bittered with a blend of tetra and pre-isomerized iso-α-acids products were rated as having a smooth and diminishing bitterness compared to more traditionally hot-side hopped beers.[155] This could potentially be an option for the bittering addition for a beer that will be heavily dry hopped. If you know that lots of dry hopping may contribute to some polyphenol and humulinone bitterness, then replacing the hot-side bitterness with a pre-isomerized iso-α-acid product could be something to consider. Especially if your system is limited to a maximum amount of whirlpool hopping.

One method to try and minimize polyphenol bitterness from dry hopping (other than running the beer through a centrifuge) is to dry hop while the yeast is active. Polyphenols can interact with yeast and drop out of solution as yeast flocculates, which will reduce the overall polyphenol content.[156] For some varieties that have higher polyphenol content (generally lower α-acid hops), early dry hopping could be worth an experiment. Leave the lower polyphenol varieties for late hopping when fermentation is done or nearly done.

I would like to see experiments done testing the various hop compounds and polyphenol content when fining agents like Biofine® Clear are used. Advertised to formulate the rapid sedimentation of yeast and other hazy forming particles, I wonder if it would help drop out some of the harsher astringent qualities of a hazy beer, like centrifuging, but at a much lower price point. But won't that make the beer clear? It hasn't in my experience on the commercial level.

Looking closer at polyphenol concentrations with different hop varieties, I obtained hop data sheets for different German hops including their tested polyphenol content.[157] The chart on the next page shows different hops listed in order of the highest polyphenol content with the measured α-acid content. As you can see, as the α-acid content increases, the polyphenol content tends to decrease. Running the data through Excel, it shows the correlation is -.647, which means that ~65% of the difference in polyphenols is attributable to the α-acid change. That's pretty big!

Hop Variety	Polyphenols (%w/w)	α-acids
Hallertau Blanc	5.4	8.5
Spalter	5.3	4.1
Saazer	5.3	3.2
Tettnanger	5.2	4
Spalter Select	4.9	5.1
Hallertauer Mfr.	4.6	4.1
Saphir	4.5	4.1
Smaragd	4.5	5.9
Hersbrucker Spat	4.4	3.1
Cascade	4.3	6
Hallertauer Maerkur	4.2	13.3
Perle	4.1	7.4
Hallertauer Tradition	4.1	6.2
Mandarina Bavaria	4	7.9
Polaris	4	18.6
Huell Melon	3.9	5.8
Northern Brewer	3.9	9.2
Herkules	3.8	16.7
Opal	3.7	7.9
Nugget	3.4	11.3
Hallertauer Taurus	3.1	15.9
Hallertauer Magnum	2.6	13.9

Another study looked at two varieties and tested them for α-acids and polyphenols. The authors found that a 17% α-acid variety imparted fewer polyphenols into a tested beer during dry hopping compared to a much lower 3% α-acid variety.[158] So, although this is a relatively small sample size of hops tested for polyphenols, from the information I could gather, it seems that brewers can likely assume higher polyphenol concentrations in lower α-acid hops and higher concentrations of polyphenols in lower α-acid varieties.

In conversations with the researcher who authored the study above, it was mentioned that the highest polyphenol content hops (averaged 5%) and were the classic aroma varieties with greener aroma and flavors. The medium polyphenol content hops (averaged 4.4%) and were the aroma varieties. The lowest polyphenol hops (averaged 3.6%) and are the classic bittering varieties.

Moving to other variables that can impact the total polyphenol content of dry hopped beers, the same paper looking at dry hop temperature, dry hop duration, and the impact on polyphenol extraction had some interesting results. The authors found that the temperature of the dry hop significantly increased polyphenol extraction. When dry hopping at 66°F (19°C) compared to 39°F (4°C), there was an increase in polyphenol concentrations of nearly two-fold for the low-α-acid hop and nearly 2.5-fold for the high α-acid hop.

How quickly do polyphenols get into beer during the dry hop? One study suggests that peak concentrations are around three days of dry hopping, which is about where the research suggest most hop compound extraction peaks in large commercial batches. The peak concentration of polyphenols remains consistent when tested up to a fourteen-days of dry hop duration.[159] In this case, the beer was dry hopped in 30 L (approximately eight-gallons) of wort. With what we know about extraction times and tank size, it's possible that polyphenol extraction time on the commercial level could be slightly longer than three days. Small batch homebrewing may see full polyphenol extraction even sooner.

Combining temperature and dry hop contact time research, if we want to try and reduce the total polyphenol content in our dry hopped beers to reduce astringency, it's best to dry hop at temperatures below typical ale fermentations and for a short durations. Experimenting with dry hopping while crashing is one way to try this. Another is to dry hop during the cold carbonation period, especially since certain hop compounds like linalool were tested to still extract at colder temperatures. At Sapwood Cellars, we typically start our post-fermentation dry hopping around 58°F (14°C) and have had success as low as 40°F (4°C).

Although I don't have any direct experience with polyvinylpolypyrrolidone (PVPP), it's another method to try and reduce polyphenol content of beer and reduce astringency. As it has been tested, beers with reduced polyphenol content scored lower on harsh characteristics.[160] It's possible, however, that removing polyphenols might also reduce the mouthfeel and fullness of beer.[161] Trevor Fisher, a good friend and accomplished homebrewer, did a hop experiment with PVPP as I was doing this research and we concluded in relaxed sensory tastings that the beer made with PVPP had reduced hop flavors along with reduced astringency. Neither of us were particularly impressed overall with the PVPP beer, but this is just one example.

Pellet Disintegration and Sedimentation

When dropped into beer, pellets simultaneously begin to swell and disintegrate into primary particles. During this time, the particles break off and will drop or stay suspended. Eventually, all the hop particles will settle to the bottom of the vessel, but the velocity of the settlement depends on the size and density. In other words, the larger the particle size that breaks away from the pellet during swelling, the faster it will drop out of the beer and extraction will stop or slow. On the other hand, the smaller the particle size, the longer the particle will stay in suspension and contribute to the extraction of hop compounds.

Since sedimentation of the hop particles, especially large flocs, can happen rather quickly, it's essential to keep hops in suspension to continue the extraction process. This is likely why some studies found better or faster extraction when using stirring or pumping techniques to keep the hops in contact with the beer.

In addition to suspension times and particle size, swelling process can influence hop compound extraction because the surface area depends on the particle size and fluid uptake of the primary particles. Small particles have a large specific surface, but fluid uptake (swelling) increases the surface area. So, it's ideal to have fast and efficient swelling of the hops and small particle size distribution. One way to encourage speedier swelling is by increased temperatures. Swelling velocities increase with the dry hopping temperature.

Interestingly, the higher the α-acid of a hop, the less swelling because α-acids don't isomerize at dry hopping temperatures: they stay hydrophobic (repel or fail to mix with liquid) and don't uptake the surrounding beer. This means you might get better extraction when dry hopping with low α-acid hops because they will have a higher swelling volume, leading to a larger surface area for extraction of the hop compounds.[162]

The above information on how pellets behave during dry hopping helps explain the results of a Hopsteiner study on the extraction of linalool when dry hopping with loose pellets vs. hops contained in a sack. Here, the beer dry hopped loosely had nearly 50% more extraction than the beer dry hopped with the use of a hop sack. Getting reduced extraction when using a hop sack makes sense because keeping the hops contained reduces the surface area of the hops, leading to less extraction. Dry hopping loose could then increase extraction, reduce hop usage (which might also reduce harsh polyphenols), and speed up dry hopping time required.

I wouldn't think that containing hops (like in a hop-spider) on the hot-side of brewing would have as much of a negative impact as was tested with cold side dry hopping. This is because elevated temperatures and constant agitation from the boil should increase extraction.

As a homebrewer, I know that dry hopping in kegs and dealing with clogged poppets can be a problem. Because of this, I worked with a company (Utah Biodiesel Supply) to create a stainless 300-micron filter designed to go around the keg's dip tube. You can then insert a #6 or #6.5 pre-drilled silicone stopper into the open end of the filter and slide the dip tube through the stopper and into the filter, which seals up the filter from rogue hops. The 300-micron filters are intended to be used with hop pellets and the 400-micron filters with whole leaf hops. I would recommend going with the 300-micron filters to use for both. You can also use a filter setup like this if you choose to ferment in kegs, which allows for pressurized hop-free transfers out of the primary fermenting keg.

Other homebrewers have also had success dry hopping loose in kegs with a Clear Beer Draught System, which forces the keg to pull beer from the top rather than the bottom. At colder serving temperatures, most of the hops in the keg will sink allowing for clear hoppy beer to be pulled from the top via the floating device.

Dry Hop Amounts

With so many factors that can impact variables like extraction rates, using a standard dry hop amount figure might do more harm than good. However, there is research into how different dry hop volumes might impact final flavor and aroma.

A 2017 study looking at dry hop amounts tested Cascade hops from the same 2015 hop crop on a pale ale dry hopped at a range of 200-1,600 g/HL (0.5-4.1 lbs./bbl). The beer was then analyzed for oil concentration and sensory testing was also performed. Tested with 40L of beer (10.5 gallons), dry hopping was done for 24 hours of contact time at 68°F (20°C).

Not surprisingly, the higher the concentration of Cascade hops, the higher sensory scores for hop intensity. However, the gap between 8 g/L (2 lbs./bbl) and 16 g/L (4 lbs./bbl) was relatively small. Hop intensity may not always be the goal, however, as results also found that as the rate of dry hops increased, so did scores for herbal and tea characteristics. Cascade hops scored the highest for citrus marks when used at 4 g/L (2 lbs./bbl), but at higher rates, herbal and tea descriptors were cited more often. The conclusion (for Cascade hops, anyways) is that dry hopping at a rate of 4-6 g/L may be the best way to maintain the citrus qualities of the hop.

Another key takeaway from this study is a look at the extraction percentage of terpene alcohols at the different dry hopping rates. In other words, how much of the possible fruity monoterpene alcohols, like linalool, geraniol, and nerol, were extracted at the different dry hop amounts? They found that as the dry hopping percentage increased, the efficiency of the extraction decreased. So, these monoterpene alcohols were extracted more efficiently when dry hopped in smaller doses. Specifically, when the beers were dry hopped at just 2 g/L, they had higher extraction percentage increases compared to dry hopping at 4 g/L (about 8% increase in linalool, 2% for geraniol and approximately 4% for nerol).

Looking at even bigger dry hop volumes, the authors found that dry hopping at 2 g/L compared to 16 g/L showed an increase in efficiency of 17% for linalool, 4% for geraniol, and 4% for nerol with the smaller dry hop charge.[163] Although not massive differences, this suggests that dry hopping in smaller stages with fewer hops (double or triple dry hopping) may be better for getting more flavor compared to one big dry hop charge. It's unclear if the limiting factor here is the extraction itself or on the saturation of the components.

Another study examining extraction of hop compounds confirmed that as the amount of dry hops increases, the extraction percentage decreases. Here, the authors dry hopped a 5% IPA using a recirculating filter and T90 Citra pellets at either 250 g/hl, 500 g/hl, 1,000 g/hl, and 2,000 g/hl. Measurements of linalool showed a roughly 20% decrease in extraction from the 250 g/hl to the highest dry hop charge of 2,000 g/hl. For homebrewers, this would mean a drop of about 20% extraction when dry hopping around five-gallons of beer at a rate of 400 grams vs. 50 grams. Considering the highest total extraction achieved for linalool was only around 38% of it's potential, reductions from large dry hop additions could be significant.

The data makes a case for experimenting with low dry hop dosages (maybe 1.5-3 ounces at a time (42-85 grams) for homebrewers), but two to three different times throughout or post-fermentation to increase extraction rates. Increasing dry hop charges with fewer hops could potentially mean less extraction of harsh polyphenols and bitter humulinones that could come with higher hopping rates.

For homebrewers, in regard to the Cascade study, it would mean that for a 5.5-gallon batch (leaving room for a half gallon of losses), it might be best to use a modest dry hop charge of just 124 grams (about 4.5 ounces) of Cascade to keep the citrus profile of the hop. It might be even better to split up the 124 grams into 41-gram increments to try and boost extraction potential, being sure to purge the headspace with CO2 with each dry hop addition to prevent oxygen exposure post-fermentation. Commercial brewers can experiment with breaking up dry hop charges into eleven-pound increments (depending on the batch size) as this is the typical size hops are purchased in.

Another factor to consider with dry hopping is how batch size can play a role in extraction. One paper tested the same dry hopping rate of (100g/100L) in three different batches ranging from large industrial-scale, semi-industrial, and laboratory scale (done in five-gallon kegs). The authors found that at the same dry hopping rate, the smaller five-gallon keg had substantially higher concentrations of hop compounds than the two larger batches. Sensory testing also revealed that the reduced batch size resulted in higher intensities in smell and taste.

However, the smaller batch size had hop characteristics that were defined as less fruity than the larger batches with more of a raw hop

and herbal character.[164] The sensory information would appear to agree with previous research in that greater extraction in smaller batches means less is probably more in terms of how much dry hops to use.

Ultimately, the authors concluded that the composition of hop compounds from dry hopping depends on scale because the mass transfer rates of hop aromatics are not comparable for different batch sizes. This means that trying to scale up a homebrew recipe to a large commercial batch may come up short regarding desired hop aromatics. On the other hand, trying to emulate the same dry hopping rates from commercial breweries on the homebrew scale would also not likely get the same results.

One of the biggest downsides to extreme dry hopping rates are beer losses. This may not be as big of a deal to the homebrewer who can brew slightly over five gallons to accommodate for the hop-derived losses. However, professional breweries need to make money, so losses from excessive dry hopping can add up. The study above looking at batch sizes and dry hopping rates looked directly at beer losses at different dry hopping rates and found that absorption of beer from hops ranged from less than 2% at 250 g/hl to almost 14% with 2,000 g/hl. Somewhere in the middle at 1,000 g/hl (around 7 ounces for a five-gallon batch) had losses just shy of 6%.

The authors suggest that to avoid losses and keep a strong aromatic profile in the beer, brewers can supplement dry hopping with hop extracts and oils. Oil products produced from cold CO2 extracts can take the oils of single hop varieties, which still enables flavor control, but at the same time can be used at 100% transfer efficiency with zero beer loss. In other words, dry hopping Citra at 250 g/hl (0.65 lbs./bbl) resulted in about 69 ppm of geraniol (41% extraction efficiency), where just 2 g/hl of hop oil resulted in 84.2 g/hl at (100% efficiency). But an important disclosure: this study was produced by Totally Natural Solutions, who sells the hop oil.[165]

Total Oil

I always assumed that if a particular hop variety was high in total oil content, then it had a better chance of producing a beer with more flavor and aroma. But is this the case? In 2016, researchers at Oregon State University put this concept to the test by evaluating beers dry hopped with Cascade hops from 29 different lots. Total oil content from each lot ranged from 0.60 ml/100g to 2.10 ml/100g. A trained panel evaluated the beers five times, each in a randomized fashion.

The authors concluded that Cascade dry hopped beers containing higher amounts of total oil did not necessarily result in a beer with higher overall hop aroma intensity. In fact, the Cascade hop with the lowest oil content had one of the highest aroma intensity ratings and one of the higher total oil hops had the lowest evaluated aroma intensity.

The authors suggested that one possible reason could be the quality of the oil, which can be impacted by a number of different variables like geographic location, climate, irrigation, disease pressure, harvest date, post-harvest processing, storage, transport, and evaporation. It's also possible that relationship exists within the tested hop compounds (synergy) that certain compounds may work together in a way when in greater amounts to produce hop aroma.[166]

Research conducted in 2018 at Oregon State University also found that a hop's total oil content is a poor indicator for predicting hop aroma potential from dry hopping.[167] In the study, 84 hop samples were tested spanning three different harvest years (2014, 2015, and 2016) within two different hop varieties (Cascade and Centennial). Sensory and hop oil analysis was performed on the dry hopped samples from unhopped beer produced commercially. Dry hopping was done for 24 hours at 59°F (15°C) in half barrel kegs at a rate of 386 grams of hops per HL of beer (1 lbs./bbl).

Using multiple linear regression analysis found that for Cascade one particular compound (geraniol), not total oil, was the most effective at predicting aroma quality and intensity. It should be noted that the dry hopping was done after fermentation was complete and in the absence of yeast, as active fermentation can biotransform geraniol to citronellol (more on this in Chapter 10). As it relates to Centennial, the authors again determined the total oil figure not the best indicator for determining aroma quality and intensity, rather, the compound β-pinene was the better indicator.

Using the results from the study above, it's interesting to note that Centennial has one of the highest β-pinene concentrations averaging 0.8-1% of the total oil. Other hop varieties with high levels of beta-pinene are Bravo, Tahoma, and Comet.

Why is total oil likely a bad figure to use to determine hop potential? Most of a hop's total oil is made up of hydrocarbons, which can be less important to hop aroma compared to terpene alcohols and esters when dry hopping. Using Centennial as an example, myrcene (a hydrocarbon) can be as much as 60% of the total oil, but doesn't appear to be as important as β-pinene which is only about 1% of Centennial's total oil.

In a previous section in the book titled, "Oxygen Fraction of Hops," it was assumed that total oil may be an important factor in determining hop intensity paired with the total oxygen fraction of a variety to estimate hop intensity. I still like this logic because when the total oil figure is combined with the percentage of a hop's oxygenated compound makeup, there's likely more of the desired fruity monoterpene alcohols to impart flavors and aroma into the beer.

Impact of Filtering on Hop Compounds

If you filter a beer, is it at the expense of losing the volatile hop compounds? The answer appears to be both yes and no. A study using GC-MS to determine the hop-derived volatile compounds in beer looked at both a filtered pilsner and an unfiltered pale ale. Both beers were made with similar hopping schedules and dry hopped with the same amount of Lemon

Drop post-fermentation. The biggest difference, other than yeast strains, was that the pilsner beer was filtered.

The results of the study revealed that filtering the pilsner had very little to no differences in the more polar fruit forward monoterpene alcohols (linalool, geraniol, and α-terpineol). However, there was a significant difference with the hydrocarbons (myrcene, β-caryophyllene, α-humulene, β-farnesene, and β-limonene). The pilsner, which was filtered, had lost most of these hydrocarbons compared to the unfiltered pale ale. For example, the pale ale had nearly 250 ug/L of myrcene, and the filtered pilsner had slightly over 50 ug/L. Although the point of the paper was not to determine the impact of filtering solely, the authors still suggest that

the filtration probably contributed to the loss of the more volatile hydrocarbons in the pilsner.[168]

Based on this study, it appears filtering has the biggest impact on removing the woody, spicy, and resinous/green flavors and doesn't have as much of an impact on the more polar monoterpene alcohols. The results suggest that filtering could potentially give a brewer more control over the final flavor, however, the synergy between various compounds would also be impacted. Although I don't have any direct experience with filtering, it could be a way to speed up the conditioning time some hazy IPAs require by removing some of the greener characteristics, but likely at the expense of some of the haze. The filtering processes appears to be like centrifuging in terms of what compounds are removed.

Dry Hopping and Head Retention

Not surprisingly, the role of hops and head retention is a complicated matter. Although good head retention has a lot to do with the makeup of the grist, research does show hops also play a role. However, depending on hop selection and timing, outcomes can be either negative or positive for foam.

It's generally understood that beer foam is the result of a combination of multiple factors, including foam-positive proteins from malts, α-acids, iso-α-acids from hot-side hops, metal cations, alcohol concentration, and the reduction of lipids. In addition to iso-α-acids, one study found a hop acid called dihydroisohumulone can also substantially improve foam stability and lacing.[169]

A study focused on beer foam tested factors that could potentially influence foam quality: protein, iso-α-acids, and ethanol. They found a significant increase in beer foam from IBUs of 0-15. However, there was relatively no change when the IBUs increased from 15 to 30, with a foam increase occurring again around 35 IBUs.[170] The paper also found that the higher the pH of the beer, the more it had a negative impact on head retention, which is interesting when considering dry hopping will increase beer pH.

A presentation looking at how different acids in hops impact foam found that α-acids improved beer foam and lacing better than iso-α-acids. Further, α-acids had an even greater impact on improving foam stability on beer at colder temperatures when tested from 57°F to 69°F (14°C-21°C). The presentation concluded that because α-acids are low in bitterness, they could be isolated and added post-fermentation at just 3-4 ppm to enhance both beer foam and lacing.[171] Dry hopping at cooler temperatures may be a way to introduce foam positive α-acids to your beer.

Looking closer at the research, pellets of Cascade were used for dry hopping at dosage rates of 0.5, 1, 1.5, 2, 2.5 lbs./bbl and measured for foam stability. As the dosage of Cascade increased, foam stability decreased. This would agree with the finding above that as pH increases, foam quality decreases, since dry hopping will increase the pH by approximately 0.14 units per pounds of hops used per barrel. In addition, the longer Cascade hops sat in the beer during dry hopping, the more the foam stability was reduced. This decrease in stability was slight after two days of dry hopping, then accelerated on day three, and continued to slowly decrease until day eight. Ultimately, long term dry hopping can have a negative impact on head retention.

Perhaps the loss of iso-α-acids during dry hopping is causing some of the foam reduction. For example, in the study above a beer with 48 ppm of iso-α-acids had better foam stability compared to a beer dry hopped at a rate of 1 lbs./bbl, which reduced the iso-α-acid to 30 ppm. The dry hopped beer also had an increase in humulinones (oxidized α-acids) and α-acids. So, is it the humulinones decreasing the foam stability?

When a beer with 30 ppm of iso-α-acid was dosed with just 17 ppm of humulinones, the foam stability increased slightly. This suggests that humulinones on their own can help foam, however you can't isolate humulinones extraction only when dry hopping. When the beer with 30 ppm of iso-α-acid was dosed with only α-acids, the foam retention increased significantly, even higher than the original beer with only 48 ppm of iso-α-acids. This would agree with the study mentioned earlier that isolated α-acids are a great way to increase foam. Isolated hop acids can be added via hop extracts post-fermentation.

One such hop extract product, called Tetra (a reduced iso-α-acid), has been tested with a concentration of just 6 ppm and was found to increase the foam stability of beer from approximately 270 seconds to almost 340 seconds. When using an iso-extract post fermentation for foam retention, it's important to take into consideration the increase in bitterness the extract will bring. For Tetra, you can count on 1-1.7 times the perceived bitterness compared to the same IBU level from traditional hopping. So, although there is a measurable increase in bitterness at low concentrations for foam retention, this increase is marginal. I should note that Tetra is a product of Hopsteiner, who also conducted the analysis.

Hop Variety and Foam Retention

Just to throw brewers a curveball, the same body of research above also found that hop variety can play a role in foam quality. The research tested five different varieties: Apollo, Bravo, Cascade, Centennial, and Eureka. At dosage rates of 1 lbs./bbl there was a reduction of foam stability in Bravo, Centennial, and Cascade, but an increase in foam with Eureka and Apollo. Again, long term dry hopping, even with the foam positive hops, had a negative impact on foam (the foam positive hops began to have a negative impact after three days of contact time). One possible reason for the increase in foam from Eureka and Apollo is that of the tested hops, they had the lowest amount of fatty acids, which is foam negative.[172]

Fatty acids are important for yeast growth[173] and help ensure a healthy fermentation.[174] However, hop fatty acids that survive the brewing process are foam-negative, in part by adsorbing into the protein layer of beer and breaking interactions between proteins.[175] Specifically, longer-chain fatty acids (C12-C18) are more effective at destabilizing foam than short chain fatty acids (C6-C10)[176] because longer-chained fatty acids are more surface active, which can destabilize adsorbed protein film.[177]

I speculate that adding foam negative hops to the fermenter as early as brew day may be a way to ensure these fatty acids are used by the yeast and not have an impact on fermentation. Although, the longer contact time may also not bode well for foam retention. I wouldn't worry too much about specific hops and their impact on foam when you can add extracts post-fermentation to boost the foam. You can plan for the slight increase in bitterness by using slightly less hot-side bittering hops.

Malts and Head Retention

Although not specific to dry hopping, it's important to understand the important role malts play in head retention. In general, the better the protein content of a beer's grist, the higher the head retention potential. However, the processes of malting and the impact it has on proteins is important to understanding head retention. For example, studies show that foam enhancing proteins primarily form during the germination of barley, which suggests unmalted grains won't be as foam-positive as malted ones. It's not just the germinating that matters either, but how long it's germinated, as beers brewed with under-modified malts (less time germinating) can retain as much as 30% more foaming enhancing proteins than beer brewed from typical modified malts.[178]

One way to know how long the grain has been modified is by looking at the Kolbach index percentage, which is a measure of protein modification. In the study mentioned above, the lower modified malt (Kolbach index of 39.9%) produced more foam enhancing proteins than the control beer malt (Kolbach index of 43.7%). There are certain malts created with the exact purpose of being under-modified to help with head retention and chit malt is a good example of this. Even though the protein percentage of chit malt is like 2-row (because it *is* 2-row barley) it's the reduction in the modification of these proteins during malting, not the total percentage of protein, that ultimately helps with head retention. As a bonus, chit is high in starter enzymes and can also increase conversion of starch.

Looking closer at chit malt, a study was done where five different beers were brewed substituting either 10%, 20%, 30%, and 40% of the pilsner grist with chit malt. The authors found that all the beers made with chit malt had higher foam stability (NIBEM values) than the control of 100% barley malt. The best foam stability was tested in beers made with 10% and 30% chit malt beers.

The authors of the above study suggest that chit malt can increase foam-active polypeptides at the same time it reduces the number of negative polypeptides, which are haze-active compounds.[179] In other words, chit malt can enhance head retention while also slightly increasing clarity. This is the opposite of other protein-rich options like malted wheat, where modified proteins from malting can increase haze when paired with hop polyphenols. Again, I find myself praising chit malt, but it's an interesting option for hazy IPAs that get too murky or have too much polyphenol vegetative bite. Reducing some of the haze to a "sheen" with chit malt while also lowering protein/polyphenol astringency and boosting head retention are all good reason to experiment with chit malt. In my experience, using chit malt at around 10% of the grist helps produce dense foam that looks whip crème-like.

Key Findings

- Oxygen will inevitably be introduced to beer when dry hopping. To keep oxygen levels low, try adding hops during first 3-5 days of fermentation or continually purging the headspace with CO_2 while adding dry hops, especially post-fermentation.
- Dry hopping for just 24 hours has been tested for nearly complete extraction, however the size of the batch plays a role. Homebrewers will get faster extraction than commercial breweries.
- With agitation or recirculation, extraction can peak as quickly as four hours, but may also enhance the astringency, especially when hop usage rates are high.
- Dry hopping at colder temperatures will still see extraction, likely peaking in three days.
- Hop pellets have higher extraction rates than whole leaf hops.
- As dry hop rates increase, so will the amount of more non-polar compounds like myrcene (green) and aggressive tasting polyphenols. This is particularly true with high-protein and beta-glucan grists.
- In general, hops low in α-acids will have more polyphenols than hops high in α-acids.
- Polyphenols peak after three days of dry hopping and will have higher extraction rates at warmer dry hop temperatures.
- Increased yeast pitching rates may help to remove more non-polar hop compounds and polyphenols.
- Dry hopping too much of a particular variety can alter that hop's profile, likely going from fruity flavors to more herbal and raw flavors.
- Dry hopping in stages will result in greater extraction than one large dry hop addition.

- Both α-acids and humulinones (oxidized α-acids) will increase beer foam, but higher beer pH from dry hopping can negatively impact beer foam as well as hop varieties high in fatty acids.
- Chit malt can help increase foam stability as well as slightly increase beer clarity.

Chapter 8: Dry Hopping and Bitterness

It took thirteen years after scientists discovered hop α-acids isomerize into iso-α-acids to agree upon a standard test to measure these bitter acids. The agreement resulted in the international bitterness unit and the IBU test. The IBU test uses a spectrophotometer to measure the iso-α-acids in beer.[180] For the most part, the test has been used successfully by brewers to help create recipes and maintain bitterness consistency. The biggest downside is that it cannot differentiate between different hop acids. This inability to single out hop acids is important because not all bittering acids are equally as bitter on the tongue, among these are humulinones, which is the focus of this chapter.

What Are Humulinones

The three α-acids in hops that contribute to beer bitterness are cohumulone, humulone, and adhumulone. When boiled, they isomerize into the major contributors of beer's bitter taste. Specifically, these three acids isomerize into six iso-α-acids, which are trans-isocohumulone, trans-isohumulone, trans-isoadhumulone, cis-isocohumulone, cis-isohumulone, and cis-isoadhumulone.[181] However, hops also contain small amounts of oxidized α-acids (humulinones) and oxidized β-acids (hulupones), which form via spontaneous peroxidation of the α-acids and β-acids.[182] In fact, humulinones are one of the most abundant oxidized hop acids in aged hops.[183]

Humulinones are similar in molecular structure to iso-α-acids, but they have an extra hydroxyl group that makes them more polar.[184] Because humulinones are more polar they are easily extracted into beer. Dating all the way back to 1955 humulinones were described as being bitter,[185] which is why their solubility is so important. A follow-up study in 1965 described humulinones as a substance in hops which are not α-acids but have bittering power and when present in beer in small amounts will have a “marginal effect on flavor.” When introduced to beer (through hops), the study continues, it gives a “harsh lingering bitterness.”[186]

For brewing purposes, the first study to put an actual figure to the bittering potential of humulinones came in 1964, when it was found that humulinones are 35% as bitter as iso-α-acids.[187] This figure has since been updated with further testing and it's now understood that humulinones are closer to 66% as bitter as iso-α-acids.[188] So, 1 ppm of humulinones would equal .66 IBUs. The bitterness from humulinones are suggested to be "smoother" because they are more polar than iso-α-acids and should not stick or linger on the tongue as long as iso-α-acids.

Humulinone Concentration in Hops

Baled hops contain fewer humulinones then pelletized hops, about 0.3% for baled to approximately 0.5% or more with pellets. Because only about 10-20% of the lupulin glands are broken when baling hops (in stark contrast to pelletized hops where 100% of the lupulin gland is broken) this process may enhance the oxidation of the α-acids into humulinones. Dry hopping is where humulinones play the biggest role in impacting bitterness, hot-side additions of humulinones have very little impact. I'm not entirely sure why this is the case, however, and I hope this gets studied further. It's possible the humulinones are being lost to trub, yeast, or hot-break, but I couldn't find data confirming this.

Because of the high solubility of humulinones, they will dissolve into the beer at relatively high rates during dry hopping. Specifically, beers that are dry hopped at .5 to over 2 lbs./bbl (equivalent to 35-142 grams on the homebrew scale) will see high concentrations of humulinones. On the other hand, beers that are solely kettle hopped contain few humulinones (less than 2 ppm). To get a sense of typical humulinone levels in dry hopped beers, 29 commercial IPAs were tested and ranged from to 2-24 ppm.

Looking closer at how efficiently humulinones can find their way into beer, an experiment was performed with low (8.6 IBU) and high (48 IBU) beers and dry hopped with Centennial pellets for five days at rates of 0, 0.5, 1, and 2 lbs./bbl. The findings showed the lower the dosage rate, the higher the extraction of humulinones. The 0.5 lbs./bbl beer had nearly 98% of available humulinones dissolve into the beer. However, higher rates of dry hopping also had incredibly high extraction rates (80%).

Just like how hops can pull out iso-α-acids in the boil kettle during wort cooling,[189] they will also pull out iso-α-acids during dry hopping. Specifically, the higher the dry hopping rate, the more iso-α-acids will be absorbed by the spent hop material. For example, one test found a 38% reduction in iso-α-acids with a dry hopping rate of 2 lbs./bbl.

I reached out to John Maye, who authored much of the work on humulinones described above and it's Maye's opinion that the "sweet spot" to determine the bitterness impact of humulinones through dry hopping and iso-α-acid removal is around 25 IBUs. Beers with starting IBUs under 20 can become more bitter by dry hopping and beers with starting IBUs above 30 can become less bitter from dry hops.

A 2014 paper also found that of iso-α-acids were being removed during dry hopping in addition to measurable increases in humulinones. In the experiment, after fermentation with Wyeast 1056 was complete, a Pale Ale was dry hopped at 64°F (18°C) with Chinook pellets. Samples of the beer were taken and hop acids tested at 6, 24, and 72 hours. The results showed that no β-acids were found in the beer after dry hopping, which was not surprising, considering they are insoluble in beer.[190] Oxidized β-acids called hulupones were also not found in the beer, however they are more soluble than β-acids. β-acids can oxidize into hulupones during the boiling process but their overall concentrations into beer are small because of the low solubility. They likely contribute very little to the overall bittering of beer.[191]

During the dry hop in the same experiment, polyphenols, α-acids, and humulinones all significantly increased with dosage and dry hop duration. A sensory test revealed a highly correlated increase in bitterness intensity after dry hopping. This increase in bitterness was strongest with the increase in humulinone concentration from dry hopping. The author estimated that humulinones had up to ten times greater influence than polyphenols on dry hop sensory bitterness. In other words, the increase in polyphenols likely increased the IBUs 2.2 points and humulinones increased IBUs by 15 points.

Importance of HPLC Testing for Bitterness

The biggest flaw in the international bitterness unit test adopted nearly 50 years ago is that it cannot differentiate between iso-α-acids and humulinones when determining beer bitterness. This is important because humulinones are 66% as bitter as iso-α-acids and α-acids are about 10% as bitter as iso-α-acids. The differences in bitterness levels in the different hop compounds means the IBU test isn't accurately measuring the true sensory bitterness of a beer. In addition, about 12% of the IBU test results comes from other hop compounds which can further confuse the results.

A potential way to increase the sensory accuracy of bitterness testing is via high-performance liquid chromatography (HPLC) testing because HPLC testing allows for the separation and accurate measuring of the various hop acids. For example, through HPLC testing, John Maye was able to show that by dry hopping, a considerable amount of iso-α-acids were removed and replaced by less bitter humulinones and α-acids.

By using HPLC to calculate bitterness of dry hopped beer, you can add bitterness intensities of the different hop acids relative to iso-α-acids. An example laid out in the Maye study is a beer that contained 51 ppm of iso-α-acids and was dry hopped at a rate of 1 lbs./bbl with Cascade hops at 60°F (16°C) over three days. The beer was then tested with HPLC and determined to contain 32 ppm of iso-α-acids (reduction of 19 ppm), 13 ppm of α-acids, and 13 ppm of humulinones. So, looking just at what an IBU test shows, the beer after dry hopping would jump to 58 IBUs, but would decrease in sensory bitterness when taking into consideration the bitterness potential of each individual acid.

To put a calculated sensory bitterness figure to the above example, you can calculate the 32 ppm iso-α-acids + (13 ppm humulinones x 0.66) which would equal a sensory bitterness figure of 40.5 ppm. You could improve this sensory bitterness figure even more if you also add the α-acids added to the beer via the dry hop, since they are also soluble. Since α-acids are estimated to be about 10% as bitter as iso-α-acids according to Maye, the updated formula would look like this:

Calculated Sensory Bitterness = ppm iso-α-acids + (0.66 × ppm humulinones) + (0.10 x ppm α-acids).

It seems that current brewing methods and more advanced hop research methods has outpaced the old IBU test for determining beer bitterness levels (particularly in dry hopped beers). It makes sense to start moving toward a figure tied closer to sensory bitterness that separates different hop acids and adjusts for bittering intensities of each. Unfortunately, not every brewery has access or can afford constantly getting beers tested by HPLC. Advertised IBU figures (especially in heavily dry hopped hazy IPAs) can be misleading to consumers because after dry hopping, the sensory bitterness figure would be drastically different than a tested IBU figure.

Determining Humulinone Content in Hops

There is a relationship between the humulinone concentration of hops and the hop storage index (HSI) figure. The hop storage index is a used to estimate the losses of α-acids and β-acids during aging. Specifically, the HSI is determined from the ultraviolet absorbance measured in the spectrophotometric analysis of hops.[192] Essentially, HSI is the measurement of the deterioration of hop bitter acids. The higher the HSI a hop variety has, the more humulinones that hop also has.[193] This makes sense because as the HSI increases in hops (less stable varieties) there is an increase in oxidized α-acids, which are humulinones.

It may not take much time for humulinones to form on fresh hops. For example, the Maye study found that in just fourteen days, fresh Galena hops stored under a vacuum and cold already had a concentration of 0.47% w/w humulinones. So how quickly do α-acids oxidize into humulinones? If the hops are stored in a freezer or even at refrigeration temperatures, the oxidation process will happen at a much slower rate and warmer temperatures will speed up the oxidation process.

One paper evaluated the oxidation changes of α-acids and humulinone concentration of hop pellets stored at 68°F (20°C) and 104°F (40°C) for 40 weeks, and 140°F (60°C) for eight weeks. When stored at 68°F (20°C), the decline in α-acids and increase in humulinones was rather slow. The α-acids began a sharp decline after ten weeks, where the humulinones slowly increased throughout the entire 40-week period. [194]

Looking closer at the above study, at 104°F (40°C), α-acids decreased quickly to less than 5% of their initial amounts after five weeks. Humulinones increased rapidly at just three weeks, but then started to decline rapidly. At 140°F (60°C), the changes in α-acids and humulinones were about ten times faster than at 104°F (40°C).

It seems that properly stored and relatively fresh hops will not see significant swings in α-acids and humulinones. On the other hand, if you are dry hopping with hops stored at room temperature for a few months, you could experience a greater amount of bitterness from the increased humulinone concentrations. However, poorly stored hops at warm temperature, especially for long periods, will lose almost all the humulinones created after ten weeks or after just two weeks if stored 140°F (60°C). Realistically, after smelling these poorly stored hops, you wouldn't want to dry hop with them at that point, anyway.

Another factor that can influence the concentration of humulinones in hops is the α-acid concentration of the hop variety. For example, when dry hopping with the high α-acid Zeus compared to low alpha Hersbruker, a 2017 study found that Zeus imparted significantly more humulinones to the beer. Peaking at just 24 hours (shows how soluble humulinones are) the Zeus-hopped beer already had a humulinone content of approximately 60 mg/L, compared to 7 mg/L with the Hersbruker beer. [195] This makes sense: the higher α-acid hop imparts more humulinones because it has more α-acids available to oxidize into humulinones. Humulinone solubility was not found to be significantly impacted by the temperature of the dry hop when tested at 66°F (19°C) compared to 39°F (4°C).

Dry Hopping and pH

Along with humulinones from dry hopping, the pH of beer can also impact the bitterness perception. In tests performed by John Maye in the papers discussed above, after dry hopping, it was determined that the pH of beer increases with dry hopping amounts. Specifically, a pH increase of 0.14 units per pound of hop pellets used can be expected. In homebrew terms, if you dry hop with 142 grams you might see an increase in pH of 0.28. This is important because beers tested with the same iso-α-acid content tasted more bitter when the pH was increased.[196]

An earlier paper submitted to the University of Wisconsin-Stout Graduate School also found that dry hopping leads to an increase in pH. In the study, four different commercial beers and six hop varieties were examined. The author found a mean pH increase between 0.040 and 0.056 when dry hopped at 0.5 lbs./bbl. When the amount of dry hop volume increased to 3 lbs./bbl, the mean pH increase was 0.233 and 0.332, which is slightly under the increase Maye found. Of the six hop varieties tested at a dry hop rate of 3 lbs./bbl, Styrian Aurora and Centennial raised the pH the most, followed by Willamette, Columbus, Polish Lublin and Northern

Brewer. No significant correlation between the hop attributes and the increase in beer pH was found. [197]

The temperature at which the dry hop is performed will have an impact on the pH adjustment, but just barely. The colder the beer is during the dry hop, the more the pH will increase. Specifically, one test found that when starting at a pH of 3.84 and dry hopped at 66°F (19°C) at a rate of 4 g/L, the pH went up to almost 4.0 after six days compared to a pH of 4.05 at 39°F (4°C) with the same hop variety and duration.[198]

Hop Aroma and Perceived Bitterness

A 2016 study in *Food Research International* studied the impact of hop aroma compounds on the perceived bitterness intensity in beer by having trained tasters sample beers at three different bitterness levels (13, 25, and 42 IBUs) and spiked with three different levels of hop aroma extract (0, 245, and 490 mg/L). The tasters sampled the beers both with and without wearing nose clips and noted bitterness levels.

The authors found that the addition of hop aroma extract resulted in an increase in bitterness perception across the IBU levels. Specifically, when the nose clips were off, and the hop aroma was apparent, the tasters scored the beers as being more bitter (despite ranking the same beer at a lower bitterness level with the clips on). This was also the case for the medium and high IBU beers, which had higher bitterness scores without the nose clips at both the medium and high hop aroma dosage. Only the higher dose of hop aroma caused an increase in bitterness perception in the lower 13 IBU beer.[199]

So, in a modern heavily dry hopped IPA, the strong fruity hop aroma will on its own likely increase the bitterness perception of the beer (unless you are drinking with a nose clip because you're weird). This is something to keep in mind when formulating recipes, if the goal is a smoother less aggressive IPA with heavy dry hops, you could start on the low end of the targeted IBU figure assuming the perceived bitterness boost from the aromatics of the dry hops. In a beer with a starting gravity of 1.050, I like to aim for about 15-30 IBUs as a good starting point for hot-side IBUs coming from boil additions as a base bitterness prior to whirlpool hopping.

Dry Hop Bitterness Experiment

To test out research in dry hopping and bitterness, I brewed a hop forward session beer with a very small number of hot-side hops and followed this up with a heavy dry hop. I then shipped a sample of the beer to Oregon BrewLab to get the IBUs tested. Keep in mind that the IBU test used here cannot distinguish between different hop acids.

Specifically, the experimental beer was a 5.5-gallon batch that only received 16 grams of Citra hops during a 90-minute steep that was added right at flameout (no prior cooling). Brewing software estimated around 10 IBUs would form from the small, but long steep addition. I then added 56 grams of Mandarina Bavaria and 28 grams of Cluster hops on day two of fermentation. I followed this dry hop addition with 56 additional grams of Cluster and 28 grams Mandarina Bavaria as a keg hop addition.

The lab results showed drastic increase from the estimated 10 IBUs, coming back with 33 tested IBUs. The higher than expected IBU increase likely came from humulinones from the dry hops. My tasting notes for the beer described the bitterness as a "smooth subtle bitterness that is apparent at first but quickly dissipates."

Now, while these results were interesting, I also wanted to test actual humulinones levels in a heavily dry hopped beer. For the next experiment, I brewed a beer with no hops in the boil or whirlpool, but heavily dry hopped. I brewed a Citra/Amarillo hazy IPA and sent samples of the beer to John Maye to get tested for bittering acids via HPLC. I also sent a small sample of the hops used, which were tested for humulinones, α-acid, and β-acid content.

Experiment Details:

Batch Size: 5.5 Gallons
Water Profile: 100% reverse osmosis water treated at 1.5 grams/gallon calcium chloride
Mash pH: 5.51
Final Beer PH: 4.64

Grist:
50% 2-Row
25% Organic Flaked Oats
25% Malted Wheat
Acidulated malt as needed

Yeast:
RVA Manchester Ale @ 66-68°F (19°-20°C)

Dry Hop Schedule: 28 grams each Citra and Amarillo added to fermenter (prefermentation hops)

56 grams Citra and 56 grams Amarillo added at day four of fermentation (capped fermentation at this time)

56 grams Citra and 56 grams Amarillo added to the serving keg (left at room temperature overnight and into the fridge the following day)

Lab Test Results:

24.3 ppm humulinones
2.7 ppm iso-α-acids
71.5 ppm α-acids
10.7 ppm β-acids
6.6 ul/l myrcene
3.7 ppm Xanthohumol (polyphenol)

Calculated Sensory Bitterness = 2.7 ppm + 16 + 7.1 ppm = 25.8 ppm

The traditional IBU test came back with a bitterness level of 76.9 for this beer, remember it had zero hops on the hot-side, including in the whirlpool. So, you can see how misleading the IBU figure can be when considering that 57 out of the 76 IBUs are coming from the α-acids and humulinones and only 2 IBUs are coming from iso-α-acids, the rest most likely from polyphenols.

You might be thinking, wait a minute, how can you possibly get 2.7 ppm of iso-α-acids in beer without ever adding hops to the boil or whirlpool to isomerize? I had the same question and asked John Maye. His guess was that the amount of iso-acids in this beer was incredibly low for the volume of hops used, meaning the isomerization efficiency was tiny. Maye suggested two potential avenues for the cold-side isomerization.

First, Maye has seen minerals like magnesium (which you can get from malts, even if you don't add it to your brewing water) can cause α-acids to isomerize. The second possibility is a very small amount might isomerize slowly over time while the beer was at room temperature and during fermentation. In this case, I added 56 grams of dry hops prior to the start of fermentation and another 112 grams mid-fermentation. As far as hops in the keg and in the fridge, Maye said this long-term storage wouldn't result in α-acids isomerizing because of the cold temperatures.

I found a paper that showed a small amount of iso-α-acids getting into beer through dry hopping. In the study, a wheat beer, Pale Ale, and a lager were dry hopped with different varieties for one, two, and three weeks (Hallertauer Mittelfrüh, Saphir, Polaris, and Mandarina Bavaria). Although the dry hopping durations are likely much longer than most brewers would consider, it's interesting that with longer dry hop times more iso-α-acids were measured in the beer. For example, with Polaris, the iso-α-acid content started at 8.3 mg/L prior to dry hopping and increased to 8.5 mg/L at week one, 9.4 mg/L at week two, and 11.7 mg/L at week three.[200] Although only an increase of 3.4 of total iso-α-acids during the dry hop duration, it goes against the common knowledge that iso-α-acids only get into your beer on the hot-side of brewing.

Back to the results of my no hot-side hop experimental beer, it's interesting to see such a high α-acid content in the finished beer, which was higher than the lab had ever tested before. The reason the α-acid content tested so much higher than humulinones is that despite humulinones being more soluble than α-acids at dry hopping temperatures, there are so many more α-acids than humulinones in the hops to begin with, so more find their way into the beer.

Again, α-acids aren't contributing much to bitterness, being only 10% as bitter as iso-α-acids, but the powerful antibacterial nature of hop acids means it's unlikely to get a lactobacillus infection! Even more so if you are adding hops to the boil, considering that Maye suggested to me that only 8 ppm of iso-α-acids are needed to inhibit bacteria.[201]

Although humulinones are said to have a smoother bitterness and are calculated around 66% as bitter as iso-α-acids, I had mixed reactions to the overall bitterness quality of the experimental beer. It's smoother in the sense that it doesn't linger in your mouth like a highly-bittered West Coast IPA. On the other hand, the initial blast of bitterness came across harsher and more vegetal than I would prefer, likely from over dry hopping.

The aroma of this beer was surprisingly weak considering the high amount of dry hopping involved. I asked Maye if he had any ideas as to why the overall hop character was so low despite the large dry hop additions, essentially being triple dry hopped. Maye thought it could be possible that the leaf material introduced to the beer was so great that it removed/absorbed much of the hop oil, which could effectively reduce the aroma. I also speculate that the high levels of myrcene in this beer might be masking fruitier compounds. Overall, the beer lacked the hop saturated flavor I'm after, suggesting that late hot-side hops are an important part of hazy IPA flavor.

It's interesting to look at how my beer with zero hot-side hops but dry hopped with ten ounces of hops in a five-gallon batch stacks up against twelve commercial NEIPAs tested for similar compounds. In terms of bitterness from humulinones (which can contribute as much as 50% of the bitterness in a NEIPA)[202] my beer was near the commercial average of 26 ppm (at 24.3 ppm). My beer had almost double the amount myrcene content (green and resinous flavors) than the commercial beers. My beer also tested the highest for the polyphenol Xanthohumol (3.7 ppm to the average of 2.0 ppm in the commercial beers).

Again, my complaint with many hazy IPAs is they come across too vegetal and aggressive, masking the hop flavor from the late hot-side additions. This beer is a great example of this, it wasn't very good. The lab results show that this vegetal taste is likely coming from high levels of myrcene and polyphenols. We learned earlier that the more viscous the solution, the more we are retaining these volatile compounds from hops. This experimental beer had 25% malted wheat and 25% flaked oats, which is likely the reason it held on to so much myrcene. I'd suggest dialing back the protein levels (particularly malted proteins) and dry hop amounts if your hazy IPAs are too green and aggressive like this. For example, I'd reduce the flaked oats to 10% and the malted wheat to 10% to help reduce the vegetal flavors from dry hopping in this experimental beer if I were to rebrew it.

Key Findings

- Humulinones are oxidized α-acids that are 66% as bitter as iso-α-acids and are highly soluble and make their way into beer via dry hopping.
- Dry hopping will reduce the amount of iso-α-acids added from the hot-side.
- The IBU test can be misleading, especially for dry hopped beer because it doesn't differentiate between the different hop acids and their sensory bittering potential.
- Higher α-acid hops will impart more humulinones during dry hopping because it has more α-acids available to oxidize into humulinones.
- Dry hopping will increase the pH of beer by about 0.14 pH units per pound of hop pellets.
- Perceived bitterness increases when the pH of a beer increases.
- Intense dry hopping rates combined with a heavy protein and beta-glucan grist can produce beers with high myrcene and polyphenol levels, potentially masking otherwise fruity flavors from hops.

Chapter 9: Hop Creep

Although the idea that hops contain enzymes that can break down dextrins into fermentable sugars is new to most brewers, it's not within the academic brewing literature. In 1893, Dr. Horace Brown discovered the diastatic power of hops when researching why "after-fermentation" was happening in casks that had been dry hopped. After-fermentation (or refermentation as we would call it today) was a result of the dry hops freeing up fermentables, the very subject of this chapter. As a side note, not only were they dry hopping in 1893, but dry hopping at a rate of 3/4 lbs./bbl, not a lot, but still higher than I would have thought![203]

Follow-up research regarding the diastatic power of hops can be found in a 1941 paper by J. Janicki, which concluded that "dry hopping does produce significant quantities of sugar in beers containing appreciable amounts of dextrins."[204] Amazingly, research into this area screeched to a halt until 2017.

How could a topic as relevant as dry hopping producing additional fermentable sugars go so long without being studied? The answer is likely in part due to the transition among brewers and consumers slowly going from brewing and drinking primarily lagers to modern-day hoppy beers where substantial post-fermentation dry hopping is taking place. However, it is still surprising how long hops have been liberating sugars in the shadows.

Interest in the enzymatic potential of dry hopping is primarily due to the work of Allagash Brewing Company, a brewery not necessarily known for their dry hopping. Allagash began noticing over-carbonation in their Hoppy Table Beer after dry hopping. Targeting 2.6 volumes of CO2 during bottle conditioning, following a two-to-three-day dry hop with Comet and Azacca, brewers noticed the CO2 reached 3.35 volumes after one week, 3.94 after two weeks, and all the way up to 4.30 volumes after three weeks! Clearly, something was going on.

After dumping 60 barrels of over-carbonated Hoppy Table Beer (imagine trying to get all that beer foam down the drain), Allagash started an investigation. They first eliminated yeast strain selection, wild yeast, grist choice, and bottling extract dosages. Focusing then on the most significant difference between this beer and others was the fact it was dry hopped before bottling. Because of this, Allagash set up an experiment to test over-attenuation with a base beer split three ways bottled by 1) dosing sugar and conditioning yeast 2) dry hop and dosing sugar/yeast and 3) dry hopping only (no sugar). What they found was that bottling by dosing just sugar and yeast (no dry hopping) revealed expected carbonation levels and extract decrease in the bottle. The second beer, which was dry hopped and dosed with sugar (just like Hoppy Table Beer), became over carbonated with the extract level of the beer decreasing much more than anticipated.

Interestingly, the extract level continued to decrease over about twenty days. Finally, the third beer, which only received dry hopping, was also over-carbonated. The extract level continued to decrease with time in the bottle at nearly the same level as the beer that was dry hopped and received a sugar addition!

Further testing (with various yeast strains) again showed that dry hopping (with Cascade) caused over attenuation with higher levels of extract loss during bottling than control beers that were not dry hopped. This refermentation of dry hopped beer with yeast present is now referred to as "hop creep." To Allagash, it seemed obvious that something was going on with the dry hopping that was causing over attenuation during bottle conditioning, so they reached out to Thomas Shellhammer, Professor of Food Science and Technology at Oregon State University for guidance.

Not only did the Brewing Science Lab at Oregon State validate Allagash's tests by duplicating their experiments, but they also tried leaving the beer for a 40-day conditioning period and saw the extract level continue to decrease. Specifically, with a starting real extract around 3.5°P (1.014), the beer with yeast and dry hops dropped to 2°P (1.008), with no sugar added. Their test also revealed that when hops were added to the beer with no yeast present, researchers did not see a drop in the extract levels. It's almost like extended dry hop periods was mimicking long-term attenuation you might see with Brettanomyces.

What is causing such high levels of extract loss during bottling conditioning dry hopped beers? Oregon State discovered that in the Cascade hops tested, four different enzymes were found (Amyloglucosidase, α-amylase, β-amylase, and limit dextrinase). These enzymes may sound familiar because during the mash, they are responsible for producing fermentable sugars. Although these enzymes were found in hops at much lower levels than malt, they are still present and likely playing a role in over attenuation.

Essentially, enzymes from dry hopping are creating additional fermentables, like glucose and maltose, from dextrins. Yeast in the bottle or tank then consume them during conditioning. The enzymes most responsible for refermentation are hypothesized to mainly come from amyloglucosidase, combined with low levels of α-amylase and β-amylase activity.[205]

Ultimately, further testing revealed that the production of fermentables from the enzymes varies depending on different brewing variables like temperature, duration, and dry hopping rates. Oregon State research concluded that shorter (one or two day) dry hopping at a lower temperature of 50°F (10°C) compared to 68°F (20°C), shorter durations (reduced contact time), and lower dry hopping rate created fewer fermentables.

As it relates to making hazy IPAs, what interests me about these findings is how early-fermentation dry hopping may impact the final gravity of the beer. For example, if dry hops are added as early as brew day while lots of yeast are present, it seems plausible that enzymes would release additional fermentables that the active yeast would then consume. Also, the extended time those early additions are in contact with the beer may further increase available sugars during fermentation, which would increase the final ABV readings by lowering the final gravity.

I asked Oregon State's Kaylyn Kirkpatrick, who researched hop enzyme activity, about early dry hopping and potential lower final gravities. Kirkpatrick said they have heard reports of lower final gravities from early dry hopping, and the style of beer has a lot to do with the extent of hop creep. Kirkpatrick explained this follows Michaelis-Menten kinetics, which states that if the substrate (dextrin) concentration increases, so does the rate of enzyme activity until a saturation point. So, if beer dextrins are substrates (some hazy IPAs have higher than average dextrins), then it is possible to modulate the enzyme activity by altering the mash for example, although it would be complicated for the average brewer to do so.

If you are a homebrewer or professional brewery that keeps beer cold after dry hopping and packaging, this hop enzyme activity doesn't seem like it would have much of an impact as the cold temperatures would prevent yeast refermentation. However, for other dry hopped beers that do well with time in bottles, like mix-fermented beers, or if you are dry hopping after primary fermentation warm, this may cause issues. Colder and shorter dry hop durations of one-to-two days is likely best if problems start to arise from over carbonation. It also seems best to try and drop out as much yeast as possible before packaging. Shellhammer suggested that even if you reduce the yeast level in a beer before packaging, you may just delay the issue because additional fermentables created by enzymes from the dry hops may be consumed eventually.

Diacetyl and Dry Hopping

A presentation at the 2017 American Society of Brewing Chemists Annual Meeting by Melvin Brewing's Andrea Baillo, sheds some light on the potential of vicinal diketones (diacetyl, which taste and smells like buttered popcorn, buttermilk, butterscotch, and movie/theater popcorn) stemming from hop enzymatic activity during dry hopping. Baillo set up an experiment to test VDK and dry hopping with two separate beers, dry hopped for seven to ten days with fermentation temperatures of 68°F (20°C) to 70°F (21°C) or after dropping the tank temperature to 60°F (16°C).

Both beers in the experiment were dry hopped after primary fermentation and after yeast was harvested. Baillo found that with their Melvin IPA, when dry hopped at 70°F (21°C), a secondary fermentation started from the enzyme activity of the dry hops, which also led to an increase in VDK. The VDK was able to get back to low levels but not till after six or seven days post dry hop. When the IPA was dry hopped colder at 60°F (15.5°C), the secondary fermentation, as well as gravity drop, and VDK spike was subdued.

Another variable that appears to increase VDK production during dry hopping is the act of rousing the tank with Co2, which is done during dry hopping to keep the hops in suspension and encourage hop extraction. It appears that when the yeast at the bottom of a tank is agitated from the Co2, the yeast is encouraged to start working on the new fermentables freed from the dry hop enzyme activity. With little yeast left in the tank and nutrients from the primary fermentation depleted, this is likely the cause for the spike in VDK.[206]

What the test shows is that you can reduce the spike of VDK that might occur from dry hopping if you lower the dry hop temperature. If the temperature is left at or near fermentation temperature, you might see a higher spike in VDK, but the yeast seems to be able to remove most of it if given enough time (like a diacetyl rest with lagers). For example, Great Notion Brewing in Portland Oregon was able to address their issues with VDK and dry hopping by simply lowering their dry hop temperatures, which is discussed in greater detail in Chapter 15. At Sapwood Cellars, we like to agitate our dry hops with bursts of CO2 through the cone, because this can encourage refermentation by waking up the yeast, we tend to dry hop at 58°F (14°C) and below and after dropping most of the yeast from the cone to prevent diacetyl production.

Key Findings

- Dry hopping can produce significant quantities of fermentables in beer, especially if there are an abundance of dextrins. This refermentation is now commonly referred to as hop creep.
- Dry hopping can cause over carbonation in bottles via refermentation from enzymes (specifically, amyloglucosidase).
- Shorter dry hop durations of one or two days will reduce the amount enzymes created that could eventually free up fermentable sugars.
- The colder the dry hop temperature (below fermentation temperatures is best) the fewer enzymes will be active.
- Lower dry hop rates will also reduce the number of enzymes that could lead to over carbonation.
- Dry hopping early in fermentation with high dextrin hazy IPAs could result in a lower final gravity due to hop enzymatic activity and extended hop contact time during active fermentation.
- Enzymatic activity from dry hopping in the absence of enough yeast and nutrients can lead to unhealthy refermentation causing VDK (diacetyl) issues, especially at warm dry hop temperatures paired with extended dry hop contact time and burping the tank with CO_2 to encourage dry hops to get back in suspension.

Chapter 10: Biotransformation

Bioflavoring is a way to enhance or alter the aroma and taste characteristics of beer without the introduction of synthetic chemicals. These flavors are created through the production and conversion of flavor compounds and flavor precursors by biological methods. Extraction from plant material like hops, flowers, and fruits yields possible avenues to achieve the bioproduction of flavors.[207] Perhaps one of the most commonly used and misunderstood terms among brewers of hazy hoppy beers is biotransformation, this chapter should help define this activity and show how different process steps and ingredients can promote the enhancement of compounds (primarily hop compounds) through biological conversions.

Glycosides

Goldstein and Ting discovered and presented in 1999 at the European Brewery Convention the presence of hop flavor precursors in the soluble fraction of hop solids (which make up 20-25% of the solids) and showed these precursors can end up in beer in some form. Goldstein determine the hop solids contained 82.6% carbohydrates, with 92.4% of these made up of glucose, which contains glucose-conjugated compounds called glycosides. Glycosides are odorless nonvolatile compounds that can be hydrolyzed to produce sugars and freed aglycones (alcohols) with acid or enzyme catalysis. The compounds produced from beta-glycosidase can be put into three categories: 1) simple alcohols, 2) terpene alcohols, and 3) carbonyl compounds.[208] Most important to brewing are those that include terpene alcohols because of their connection to hop flavors.

This chapter focuses on enhancing beer flavors and aromatics through the enzymatic hydrolysis of flavor precursors in glycosidically-bound flavor compounds in fruits and hops. The enzymatic hydrolysis of glycosides first requires the cleavage of the inter-sugar bond in di- or triglycerides, yielding β-d-glucosides. The most appropriate enzyme for hydrolysis of these β-d-glucosides is 1,4-β-glucosidase.[209] In order to get the β-glucosidase enzyme into beer so that the glycosidic aroma precursors in fruit and hops can be released, brewers must use yeast strains with proven β-glucosidase activity, which can be released during fermentation or with commercial enzymes isolated from plants, bacteria, molds, and yeasts.[210]

Put another way, plants like hops and fruits contain many volatile flavors detectable in their original state. However, they also contain many non-volatile aromas called aglycones that can also contribute to the aroma and flavor, but first must be released through enzymatic hydrolysis (requiring the β-glucosidase enzyme). In fact, plants contain as much as five times as many non-volatile aroma molecules compared to the volatile ones.[211] Several studies have shown that in hops, glycosidically bound aroma precursors in the vegetative hop material may be released and contribute to the hoppy aroma of beer.[212]

Ways to Achieve β-glucosidase Activity

One way to encourage β-glucosidase activity is by purchasing commercially available enzymes with proven β-glycosidase activity, like AR2000 and Rapidase Revelation Aroma, which are both commonly used in the wine industry to enhance the aromatic profile of white wines. These commercial enzymes have glycosidase side activities that can be dissolved at 35-70 grams/1000 gallons in white wine for example toward the end of fermentation (if this same dosage rate is used in beer it's about 0.5 g/10 gallons of beer). The advertised conditions for commercial enzymes typically say they work best at a pH range between 2.8 and 5.0 (although further testing of AR2000 in indicates a pH of 4.5-5.75 is likely best) and to keep sulfate levels low (usually done in hazy IPAs anyways).

Commercial enzymes will remain active and are stopped in the wine industry with bentonite. The β-glucosidase enzyme is a protein which could cause haze if not stopped, which some may not care about. The haze formation from enzyme activity is of more concern if the beer is warmed up to >100°F (38°C), which hopefully isn't happening to your beer anyway! If a beer is stored cold immediately and kept cold, the haze formation may not occur and use of bentonite might not be necessary.

As for dosage suggestion when using commercial enzyme powders, it's tricky for beer because to date, they are designed and tested for wine. I would encourage you to conduct trials, but in talks with suppliers, a good dosage to start experimenting with is 0.5-1 grams per 5-10 gallons.

Some studies have found that commercial enzymes may not be as effective at releasing trapped glycosides in fruit and hops as yeast or bacteria can be. A study focusing on wine partially explains yeast ability to outperform commercial enzymes for bioflavoring because indigenous yeast has already adapted to the ecological environment and have become part of the wine ecosystem. These may serve as better options to embody the regional characters of wines.[213]

An example of this is Metschnikowia reukaufii, an isolate by The Yeast Bay. This isolate was taken from freshly opened flowers of a bramble bush in the Berkeley Hills of California. Quoted below is how The Yeast Bay describes Metschnikowia reukaufii, a fun option to experiment with when attempting to achieve bioflavoring in hop-forward beers as a small blend of the yeast (using a typical hazy IPA strain for the bulk of the percentage).

> M. reukaufii poorly utilizes maltose and longer chain maltose derivatives like maltotriose, though the genus in general is thought to have fairly strong expression of glucosidases, or enzymes that can transform and modulate the character of the beer by altering glycoside substrates.
>
> While only attenuating to 20-25% on its own in brewer's wort, in co-fermentations it has been shown to drop gravity and pH of the fermentation faster, accentuate and modulate the aroma profile and soften the perceived bitterness of the finished product.
>
> This accentuation of the aroma profile is likely due to not only the complex though rather subdued fruit cocktail ester profile of M. reukaufii, but also likely owing to the production of glucosidases that utilize hop glycosides as substrate to free flavor active molecules from the sugars to which they are bound. [214]

An alternative approach to encourage biotransformation is to introduce β-glucosidase activity to beer is by using specific yeast strains that have been tested and proven to have β-glucosidase activity. In the example of M. reukaufii above, test brews resulted in accentuated aroma when co-fermented with Saccharomyces. Multiple studies have examined the β-glucosidase activity of hundreds of different yeast strains. Most of this research has been focused on species indigenous to winemaking and the highest activity of β-glucosidase has been continually found to reside in non-Saccharomyces yeast strains.[215]

A study in the *Journal of Applied Microbiology* looked for β-glucosidase activity in 58 brewing yeasts (both Saccharomyces and Brettanomyces) and, after an initial screening for glycoside hydrolase activity, narrowed the strains down to six for further testing. They found that S. cerevisiae U228, Br. intermedius CMBS LD85, Br. custersii CMBS LD72, Br. anomalus CMBS LD84 and D. anomala CMBS LD88 all clearly showed the presence of a β-glucosidase activity. A commercial wine strain S. cerevisiae U228 was the only Saccharomyces strain to show β-glucosidase activity. Of most interest was that Br. custersii (isolated from fermenting Lambic) showed the highest activity.[216]

A 2016 study on the subject of bioflavoring screened 428 different yeast strains for β-glucosidase activity and found two Brettanomyces strains with "pronounced" β-glucosidase activity (B. anomalus YV396 and B. bruxellenis YV397) with B. anomalus showing the highest enzymatic activity (aka claussenii).[217] Further testing of the B. anomalus strain in mixed seven-day fermentations with a non-producing β-glucosidase Saccharomyces strain, Yannick found significant differences in cherry beers with B. anomalus. Sensory panels described these beers as "fruitier" and "more cherry and honey like." Panelists preferred them over a beer treated with the commercial enzyme AR2000 and a beer not treated at all. Yannick also found aroma differences in fermentations with hop extract and B. anomalus, although not as drastic as the cherry fruit beer.

A 2004 study in the *Journal of Applied Microbiology* screened for β-glucosidase activity in 180 indigenous yeast isolates from grape surfaces.[218] Of these, eleven were selected for further study, as they showed the highest β-glucosidase production. The authors found the best β-glucosidase producers belonged to non-Saccharomyces yeast called C. guilliermondii, C. pulcherrima, and K. apiculata.

Hops also contain enzymes, including β-glucosidase. A paper screening just two hop varieties (Progress and Hallertauer Tradition) found that both showed some β-glucosidase activity. However, they were both below 125 U/g.[219] To help make sense of this figure, consider that the wine strain 71B-1122, which is known to be a high producer of β-glucosidase, produces over 100,000 U/g.[220] Brewers should then be looking toward enzyme production from yeast or a commercial enzyme for bioflavoring and not from the hops themselves to get more β-glucosidase activity.

Certain hop varieties will result in remarkably different beers based on the elaborate makeup of compounds within each hop. We also know that different yeast strains may interact differently with these compounds, creating distinct aromas and flavors. For example, one study brewed 36 different beers using four French hop varieties and three yeast strains to examine how hop compounds varied between each beer. The authors found that of 39 compounds measured, 28 were influenced by the hop variety and yeast strain. Specifically, fifteen of the compounds were hop-derived, and thirteen were yeast derived. These complex interactions show how both yeast selection and hop combinations can play an important role in determining flavors.

In the paper above, a beer made with Aramis hops and fermented with the lager strain CLIB279 resulted in a beer with approximately 45% less geraniol than when fermented with CLIB267, another lager strain. Remember, this is despite using the same hop in equal amounts.[221] The result has more to do with CLIB279's inability to convert geraniol into citronellol.

A study that examined post-fermentation hop aroma profiles and metabolized hop aroma compounds between two yeast strains also found yeast selection important for bioflavoring potential. When using the same wort for fermentation, the authors found significant differences in hop aroma compounds. For example, one strain showed nearly twice as many fruity compounds after fermentation, whereas the other strain had a higher concentration of compounds that are more floral, herbal, and citrusy.[222]

Although the science shows that yeast selection can play a role in the amount of biotransformation of hop compounds, sensory data to date does not show that these compounds formed via the hydrolyzing of nonvolatile glycosides is easily detectable. For example, the paper mentioned above focusing on B. anomalus and a cherry fruited beer had a higher sensory impact than when fermented with hops. In other words, even though many of the same compounds which exist in both fruit and hops that can be biotransformed, the results showed that fruit biotransformation was more easily detected by a tasting panel.

In 2016, glycoside biotransformation activity was studied again with an ale, wine, and lager strain. The wine strain had the highest tested β-glucosidase activity of the group, producing a beer with clove, medicinal, and phenolic aromas so intense it would likely mask any small biotransformation differences coming from hop compounds. The American Ale 1056 strain tested was capable of β-glucosidase activity, but to a lesser extent then the wine strain

(OSU2).[223] This finding is interesting as it's one of the first mentions of an ale strain capable of β-glucosidase activity, hopefully more ale strains will continue to be tested.

Conditions Favoring β-glucosidase Activity

A study in the *Annals of Microbiology* looked at the β-glucosidase activity of a proven strain MDD24 (Pichia anomala isolated from table grapes in Thailand) against a commercially available enzyme for use in enhancing wine aroma. In this test, researchers found that glucose in the medium reduced β-glucosidase activity by 80%. Both fructose and sucrose also decreased β-glucosidase activity in the commercial enzyme with MDD24, but to a lesser extent than sucrose. Specifically, activity decreased as much as 20% in the presence of 20% fructose (commercial enzyme activity decreased by 75%) and about 55% of activity remained in the presence of 20% sucrose (80% remained with the commercial enzyme).[224] So, the presence of sugar reduces the potential for bioflavoring from β-glucosidase.

Maltose is the most dominant sugar in wort (60-65%), followed by maltotriose (20-25%) and glucose accounts for only 10-15%, while sucrose and fructose content is relatively low in total fermentables.[225] Given this, it seems that to maximize the bioflavoring potential, it's best to add enzymes (either commercially or by yeast) at the end of fermentation when sugar levels have been reduced.

A 2013 *Food Chemistry Journal* study examined the β-glucosidase activity of three non-Saccharomyces yeast (Trichosporon asahii) on Cabernet Gernischt and found that pH was a big factor in maximizing activity. The authors found that the optimal pH for the tested enzymes was 5.0 and higher. The lowest levels of activity were when the pH was reduced to 3.0, however, not all of the enzymes were as sensitive to lower pH values.[226] The study also found, and confirmed, that although there were different resistances to glucose among the two strains, it also played a significant role in diminishing β-glucosidase activity.

In tests of the commercial β-glucosidase product AR2000 also found pH as an important factor in enzymatic activity. The authors found that AR2000 worked best at a pH of 4.5 than at lower values. Also tested was B. anomalus which had the best β-glucosidase activity at a pH of 5.75.[227] The paper above looking at the presence of sugar impacting β-glucosidase activity also confirmed that lower pH values (below 4.0) had a negative impact on enzyme activity.

Temperature is another factor tested to have an impact on β-glucosidase activity. Generally, higher temperatures improved enzyme activity and lower temperatures slowed it. However, optimal temperatures in the studies above are often way above fermentation temperature (above 100°F or 38°C) which isn't practical for healthy ale fermentations. When measured against a commercial enzyme in wine, the yeast strain (MDD24) was more effective at typical ale fermentations than a commercial enzyme tested,[228] suggesting yeast strains may be better choices for lower temperatures than commercial products, but this was a small sample size.

Because the studies suggest a higher pH is ideal for maximum β-glucosidase activity (although this may be strain dependent), for an aged sour beer for example, it might be worth experimenting with double hop or fruit additions. You could add hops or fruit at the beginning of aging to take advantage of the higher pH and the lower sugar content of the beer (post primary fermentation). You could again add a fresh charge of fruit or hops to the beer prior to packaging for renewed fresh fruit volatiles, similar to double dry hopping a hazy IPA post-fermentation.

Walt Dickinson of Wicked Weed has successfully used this method with Red Angel, a popular American Wild Ale, adding raspberries to the beer when it goes on oak (beginning of aging/souring but after primary Brettanomyces fermentation). Dickinson has said doing this lends a "jaminess" to the fruit addition which is a different fruit aroma than what he has said he experiences with a post-souring fruit addition.[229] Knowing that most Brettanomyces strains are good bioflavoring options, adding fruit after primary (low simple sugar environment), with plenty of Brettanomyces still active, and at a reasonable beer pH, it's a good bet that bioflavoring is behind this enhanced jaminess flavor.

Exo-β-Glucanase and β-Glucosidase Activity

Yeast production of exo-β-glucanase also releases glycoside-related volatile compounds in fruit and hops like β-glucosidase. The main difference is that exo-β-glucanase can be produced at different levels in some Saccharomyces strains, where the research discussed above suggests that β-glucosidase activity is stronger in non-

Saccharomyces strains. This can be important because exo-β-glucanase is also capable of liberating aroma compounds directly from glycosylated precursor, but to a lesser degree than β-glucosidase.

A study in the *International Journal of Food Microbiology* tested the ability of an "over-producing" exo-β-glucanase Saccharomyces wine yeast strain (Lalvin T73) ability to release flavor compounds from grape must fermentations and found that the exo-β-glucanase enzyme did in fact release additional flavors. Interestingly, they found that exo-β-glucanase might be a more versatile enzyme as it wasn't as impacted by ethanol, SO2, or glucose/fructose, and because it reaches peak activity quickly (around two days).[230]

Combining the best of both enzymes offers exciting opportunities for brewers. For example, if a Saccharomyces ale strain is tested and shows the ability to overproduce exo-β-glucanase, it seems possible that in the presence of hops during the normal ferment (from prefermentation dry hops or from late kettle hops) you could potentially release additional aromas because of its ability to operate under normal fermentation conditions. Hopefully, levels of exo-β-glucanase activity from normal ale strains is something that will be tested in the future.

The concept of combining the two enzymes was tested in the study above. In it, authors found that a Saccharomyces strain (CMBS LD40 a Belgium yeast strain) showed a higher release of certain aglycones from hop glycosides during fermentation, likely from exo-β-glucanase. They suggest utilizing a mixed fermentation of both the Belgium strain and Br. custersii to get the highest release of volatiles from hop glycosides.

Because previous studies found a much greater impact of bioflavoring from fruit over hops, combining the two could also be an interesting way to experiment with new and different flavors in fruited IPAs. For example, it may be worth combining fruit and hops at the same time as a β-glucosidase producing strain (or commercial enzyme) prior to kegging and after primary fermentation. You would need to wait for complete refermentation from the additional fruit fermentables prior to packaging. The refermentation from the fruit sugars would also likely strip dry hop volatiles, so another round of dry hopping before packaging could be employed.

While there is data to suggest that exo-β-glucanase activity can reach its peak in just a few days, I couldn't find any studies specifically testing the duration for β-glucosidase activity. However, one paper suggested that β-glucosidase activity might reach its peak in a similar time frame. If this is the case, it could allow for the opportunity to spike a clean, hoppy beer with a β-glucosidase-producing Brettanomyces strain or commercial enzyme post-fermentation with hops, fruit, spices, or even flowers, for two-to-five days. Doing so could take advantage of bioflavoring without getting typical Brett aromas if kept at serving temperatures after packaging. Be careful packaging a beer with Brett added as refermentation and bottle explosions could happen (you would need to keep the beer cold after packaging) a commercial enzyme is probably a safer bet for this type of experimentation.

Ultimately, it seems that bioflavoring can be achieved from exo-β-glucanase activity produced by Saccharomyces yeast, but it's likely not as effective and it's difficult to know the exo-β-glucanase activity present in traditional brewing strains until they are tested. However, if a strain is known to produce exo-β-glucanase, you might get above average bioflavoring results with hops or fruit by doing a mix fermentation with a β-glucosidase producer as part of an ale blend.

As a helpful reference, there is a chart on the next page summarizing the strains tested in the research and their specific bioflavoring activity.

Strain	Species	Activity Shown	Notes
AR2000	Commercial enzyme	β-glucosidase	Best at end of fermentation with pH of 2.8-5.0 (although testing showed a pH of 4.5-5.75 depending on temperatures), sensitive to high levels of S04
Rapidase Revelation Aroma	Commercial enzyme	β-glucosidase	Best at end of fermentation Hindered by high sugar concentrations, activity increases above 122°F (50°C), sensitive to high levels of S04
Rapidase Expression Aroma	Commercial enzyme	Likely β-lyase	Advertised extraction of precursors of thiols.
U228	S. cerevisiae	β-glucosidase	Restrained by glucose
CMBS LD85	Brettanomyces intermedius	β-glucosidase	
CMBS LD72	Brettanomyces custersii	High β-glucosidase	

CMBS LD84	Brettanomyces anomalus	B-glucosidase	
CMBS LD88	Dekkera anomala	β-glucosidase	
CMBS LD40	S. cerevisiae	Exo-β-glucanase	
MDD24	Pichia anomala	β-glucosidase	Optimum pH of 4.5 at normal ale fermentation temperatures
	Trichosporon asahii	β-glucosidase	Optimum pH of 5.0 and sensitive to glucose
QA23	Saccharomyces cerevisiae bayanus	β-glucosidase	Wine strain excels at focusing the fruit either alone or as part of a blend
58W3	S. cerevisiae	β-glucosidase	Wine strain
T73	Saccharomyces cerevisiae bayanus	Exo-β-glucanase	Wine strain with an optimal pH 4-5, not as sensitive to glucose or fructose, So2 and ethanol.

PSY-001	B. anomalus	β-glucosidase	
YV397	B. bruxellenis	β-glucosidase	
YV396	B. anomalus	High β-glucosidase	Performs best at a pH of 5.75 at 98°F (36°C)
	C. guilliermondii	β-glucosidase	
	C. pulcherrima	β-glucosidase	
	K. apiculata	β-glucosidase	

Biotransformation of Terpenoid Alcohols

So far it seems that bioflavoring potential of typical ale strains is minimal as it relates to β-glucosidase activity releasing bound compounds, but there is another route that has been tested in Saccharomyces strains: the biotransformation of fruity terpenoid alcohols during primary fermentation from free compounds extracted into beer from hops.

A 2003 study looked at the ability of lager and ale strains to transform terpenoids during fermentation. Specifically, they looked at geraniol, linalool, myrcene, caryophyllene, and humulene. The study found that yeast can in fact transform terpenoids. Specifically, geraniol was converted into citronellol (sweet, rose-like) and linalool was converted into terpineol (lilac-like). They found that "most of the terpene alcohols were lost from the fermentations within the first few days and after that, the decreases occurred at much lower and steadier rates."[231]

A more recent study also looked at the hydrolysis of hop glycosides by testing the terpenoid alcohol concentrations with both an ale (Lallemand West Coast) and lager (Saflager-55) yeast, as well as directly adding β-glucosidase enzymes and acid (pH 2.7) to samples prepared with spent hops. Spent hops are the leftover material after supercritical CO2 extraction of hop pellets, which they found still have low levels of aroma compounds. In terms of biotransformation, the enzymes and the acid treatment had the highest levels of linalool (flowery-fruity) and the ale and lager yeast had much less. Specifically, the ale and lager strains had linalool levels lower than the control (especially the lager yeast), whereas one enzyme treatment increased almost three-fold from the control.

Regarding the acidic 2.7 pH treatment in the study, the low pH increased 15-fold the α-terpineol (lilac), which was way higher than all the other samples, both enzyme and yeast. It's an interesting thought that if an acidic beer is paired with hop compounds, you could get acidic-induced biotransformation.

In the same test, β-citronellol (lemon-lime) concentration increased during fermentation with both the ale and lager yeast strains from the control and was even at higher levels than the enzyme treated samples. The concentration of geraniol (rose) decreased in the ale and lager beers, which would align with previous research into this bioconversion route (geraniol to β-citronellol). Interestingly, the enzyme samples saw an increase in geraniol (bound geraniol was freed). So, in the presence of β-glucosidase, even more geraniol might be available from the hops which could then be converted to β-citronellol. Overall, the ale yeast strain showed a higher bioflavoring ability than the lager strain.[232]

It should be noted that the hopping rates used in this study were much higher than typical amounts (50 g/L), so the authors note that the actual sensory effect of the findings may be low. This rate of hopping is similar to about 1,000 grams of hops in a five-gallon batch! However, they did use spent hops, which would have fewer total oils than fresh hop pellets.

The brewing process can also impact the concentration of monoterpene alcohols. A study that selected four hop varieties (Citra, Cascade, Millennium, and Nugget) and tested hop oils after simulating late-hopping for five minutes. The authors found that linalool was found in high concentrations in all the hops before and after the simulated late-hopping, showing it's one of the most likely compounds to survive the brewing process.

Because Citra had the highest level of geraniol amongst the varieties tested above, it was chosen for further evaluation. In brewing trials, the amount of β-citronellol was found to increase throughout fermentation in the Citra beers and the geraniol concentration drastically decreased, particularly during the first three days of fermentation.[233] This is another example of the geraniol to β-citronellol biotransformation.

For brewers, it's clear from this study that you can increase the number of geraniol-rich hops during the whirlpool phase of brewing to encourage more β-citronellol production. Hops high in geraniol that could be experimented with are Centennial, Brewers Gold, Simcoe, Chinook, Bravo, Olympic, Cluster, Mosaic, Galena, Warrior, Ahtanum, and Crystal.[234] Using cheaper and more accessible hop varieties high in geraniol during the flavoring stages of the boil seems worthy of experimentation as a way to economically boost hop flavor, especially when paired with a commercial enzyme during fermentation.

In a paper that studied the different timing additions of hops, it was found that the yeast growth phase (first couple days of fermentation) was when most of the geraniol decreased, which agrees with previous research. Even when geraniol was added after fermentation at two different timings, they didn't see a decrease as much as those first couple days. In other words, the later the hops are added during dry hopping, the less chance of biotransformation of free geraniol to β-citronellol. On the other hand, if you want geraniol transformed into the lime-like β-citronellol, add geraniol-

rich hops during the whirlpool and possibly even at the start of fermentation to ensure you have as much extracted as possible before yeast growth. As a side note, some of this initial loss in geraniol during active fermentation could also be partly explained by cell absorption by yeast cell metabolisms.[235]

A 2017 paper looked at 42 hop varieties and compared the monoterpene alcohols of linalool, geraniol, and β-citronellol throughout fermentation and after one week of storage. Again, it was confirmed that bioflavoring with these monoterpene alcohols is primarily happening during the early stage of fermentation (days two-to-four). For some of the hop varieties in the study (Comet, Hallertau Blanc, Polaris, Amarillo, HBC366, Summit, and Vic Secret) the geraniol levels didn't decrease during the first three days of fermentation, but still increased after fermentation was complete. These results suggest that some hop varieties (like those mentioned above) may have more geraniol precursors than free geraniol.

Of the 42 hop varieties tested, those that had the highest concentrations of free geraniol were 0612B, Motueka, Bravo, Cascade, Chinook, Citra, Mosaic, and Sorachi Ace. These varieties would see most of their geraniol bioflavoring to β-citronellal early into fermentation and will have more bioflavoring potential. This is because of the easily accessible free geraniol compared to geraniol-precursors (bound geraniol) available during the primary stage of fermentation.

This same study investigated glycosidically-bound flavor potential in the different beers made with the 42 hop varieties. Using a commercial β-glucosidase enzyme to release the monoterpene alcohols, researchers found that Amarillo showed the most glycosidically-bound geraniol potential. The results suggest that if a commercial enzyme is used, or a known β-glucosidase producing yeast, then Amarillo would be a fun hop choice to try and boost flavoring potential.

Combining Amarillo with β-glucosidase could potentially shift the aroma and flavor of Amarillo more toward lime/citrus and away from floral characteristics. Of the geraniol dominant hops tested, Bravo, Chinook, and Mosaic showed the most glycosidically-bound geraniol potential, which also makes them excellent choices when a known amount of β-glucosidase is present during fermentation.[236] Again, as β-glucosidase activity frees bound geraniol from the hops, then more geraniol is then present during fermentation to be converted to the lime-like β-citronellol.

This same paper also detected an increase in some monoterpene alcohols during what they described as the "storage period," the time after fermentation is complete. For example, in a beer made with geraniol-rich Bravo, after fermentation was complete and during a one-week storage period, there was a slight increase in linalool, geraniol, and β-citronellol. It's likely during this period the increase can be attributed to the occurrence of hop-derived glycosidically-bound precursors and yeast-derived β-glucosidase hydrolase activity. This would align with what we've learned regarding conditions that favor glycosidically-bound release of flavors, which is an environment low in fermentable sugars (after fermentation) and at slightly increased temperatures. It's interesting to consider pitching a high β-glucosidase producing strain (or commercial enzyme), around the tail end of fermentation to try and increase the bioflavoring during a short resting/conditioning period for one last fruity push (perhaps with .003-.005 gravity points to go).

If glycosidically-bound precursors can be enhanced in a one-week storage period after fermentation is complete, can they also be released with additional storage time in a bottle? This doesn't seem to be the case as it relates to linalool, geraniol, and β-citronellol, which were found to decrease in a dry hopped Pale Ale fermented with an English ale strain. During testing at 3, 6, and 12 months, the concentrations slowly declined.

However, this was not the case for α-terpineol (lilac-like aroma). After 12 months in a bottle, measurements of α-terpineol measured over 200% of the initial concentration, which likely increased via the biotransformation process. Not surprisingly, this increase accelerated when the storage temperature was 68°F (20°C) compared to 41°F (5°C). However, even when the beer was stored at 41°F (5°C), the amount of α-terpineol still increased each time the beer was measured at 3, 6, and 12 months.[237] This particular research is interesting as it relates to α-terpineol, but not necessarily practical as aging fresh hoppy beers isn't recommended.

You may not even have to rely on hops to get some bioflavoring, as some spices are rich in the same compounds as hops. A paper looked at using a non-hop geraniol source, coriander seeds (which is also high in linalool). Using the coriander seeds like late hop additions, they were added at five minutes before the end of the boil at a rate of 0.5 g/L. Again, during the first three days of fermentation, the high amounts of geraniol in the beer from the coriander seeds decreased and the β-citronellol concentration increased. This again verifies this biotransformation, but also is eye opening to the use of non-hop products (potentially cheaper) to purposely drive hop-like flavors in the beer. The sensory impressions from the coriander beer revealed floral and slight citrus notes.[238]

Michael Tonsmeire wrote a blog post on February 6, 2017 titled, "Gose: NEIPA Principles for Coriander" which tested the bioflavoring potential of coriander. Michael chose to add coriander seeds directly to the fermenter at the same time the yeast was pitched. The tasting results align with the research, as the beer didn't resemble the typical coriander aroma, likely due to biotransformation of the compounds. The beer had a bright and zesty citrus aroma and I can confirm these tasting notes, as I was lucky enough to have a sample of the beer![239]

Key Findings

- Glycosides are odorless nonvolatile compounds that can be hydrolyzed to produce sugars and freed aglycones (alcohols) with acid or enzyme catalysis.
- Commercial β-glucosidase enzymes may enhance the biotransformation of hop compounds but work best at higher pH (generally above 4.5), warmer temperatures (ale fermentation temperatures and above), and low simple sugar environments.
- In terms of yeast producing the bioflavoring enzyme β-glucosidase, non-Saccharomyces strains typically have higher activity (like Brettanomyces strains), but certain wine yeasts have also been tested as high producers.
- Exo-β-glucanase (found in some Saccharomyces strains), is also capable of liberating aroma compounds directly from glycosylated precursor, but to a lesser degree than β-glucosidase. It is also less sensitive to fermentation conditions.
- Typical ale strains can biotransform free hop terpenoids like geraniol into citronellol. This biotransformation can happen without the presence of β-glucosidase but may be enhanced in the presence of the enzyme as more geraniol would likely be available from the hops. This conversion (geraniol to citronellol) is happening quickly during

fermentation, so late dry hop additions likely wouldn't see much of the conversion.

- Hops contain both bound and free compounds. Hops high in bound compounds (precursors) would benefit from enzyme treatment to release these additional trapped flavors. For example, Amarillo showed the most glycosidically-bound geraniol potential and could be enhanced with β-glucosidase proven yeast or a commercial enzyme.

Chapter 11: Thiols

It's said that a green sauvignon blanc wine is created in the vineyard and a tropical sauvignon blanc is created by fermenting with the right yeast strain. Volatile thiols are one of the reasons for this, because of their ability to create flavors of gooseberry, pineapple, grapefruit, passion fruit, and citrus flavors.[240] These fruity thiols are actually sulfur compounds, to most brewers, this probably conjures up negative thoughts of DMS but hop and fruit-derived thiols are fruity flavor enhancers!

What are Thiols

The sulfur compounds of a hop's total oil are extremely low at less than 1%, but low flavor threshold values make them an interesting flavoring variable. These sulfur compounds can be broken into four groups: 1) Alkylsulphides and polysulphides; 2) thioester; 3) sulfur-containing terpenoids; and 4) polyfunctional thiols.

Alkylsulphides and polysulphides are produced by the degradation of proteins and smell sulfurous like cabbage, onion, and boiled vegetables, perhaps better suited aromas for a hot dog than a beer. Thioesters are formed by the biosynthesis pathway of the α-acids and likely result from the fatty acid metabolism. They're also considered a negative in beer.[241]

Polyfunctional thiols are the portion of a hop's sulfur compounds that can be desirable in beer because of the potential for intense fruity flavors. Polyfunctional thiols possess a sulfhydryl group together with another chemical function like aldehyde, ketone, acids, or esters. As it relates to beer, most of these volatile thiols originate from hops, both in a free state and a bound form. The difference is in a free state, the thiol aromatics can be released immediately when introduced to the beer via late hopping and dry hopping. The bound form of a thiol must be released to have an impact on flavor and aroma. This is very similar to free and bound terpenes discussed previously.

The liberation of bound thiols is done via an enzyme called β-lyase, which is produced by yeast where the carbon bond of the S-cysteine conjugate is cleaved to release the free thiol.[242] Of the polyfunctional thiol of hops, about 10 to 20% are bound to cysteine and need this enzyme to be released during fermentation[243] (#freethethiols). Because of their low concentration in hops and low thresholds, you can see how yeast strains producing this enzyme would be beneficial in enhancing an already fruity hop by releasing bound thiols.

Some of the more researched fruity thiols are 4MMP (also known as 4MSP) which has descriptors of box tree, ribes, and blackcurrants. The second is 3MHA and has descriptors of passion fruit and guava and is converted from the third thiol often studied in the literature id called 3MH (grapefruit, gooseberry, guava characteristics). The 3MH thiol has a perception threshold measured as low at 0.06 ppb.[244] The blackcurrant-leaning 4MMP has one of the lowest of the fruity beneficial thiol thresholds measured at just 0.00055 ppb.[245] Compare 4MMP to something like linalool, which has a threshold of 2.2 ppb,[246] and you can see that just a little of the 4MMP thiol can play a big role in flavoring a beer. Kind of like a little wasabi on sushi can go a long way.

4MMP in Hops

In terms of where 4MMP resides on the hop, it has been determined that at least 82% of the thiol is found in the lupulin gland and the remaining 18% on leaf material that might come from the leaf's contact with the lupulin gland. This suggests that new hop products like cryo hops (LupulN2®), which removes most of the leafy material, would still likely contain some aromatic thiols, but less than pellets or whole leaf hops.

In one test, it was found that drying fresh hops via kilning (of Cascade and Mandarina Bavaria) lead to an increase in 4MMP, which the authors suggested might stem from the liberation of thiol precursors during kilning. Another variable that can have an impact on 4MMP is storage. As you would suspect, the colder the hop is stored, the more the hop will retain the thiol.[247]

One study examined the concentrations of 4MMP in different hop samples and found that American, Australian, and New Zealand varieties had higher amounts of the potent thiol. This could be explained by the use of copper sulfate as a fungicide in Europe, as copper can absorb thiols. One sample of Citra, for example, had way over the threshold value at 114 ppb. This was followed by Eureka (59.1 ppb), Simcoe (51.2 ppb), Apollo (28.6 ppb), Cluster (9.84 ppb), and Zeus (8.48 ppb).

Other tested hops that fell into the medium range of 4MMP concentration were Amarillo, Cascade, Chinook, Denali, and Nugget. The lower tier of concentration was found in Bravo, Calypso, Galena, Lemondrop, Super Galena, and Willamette. Other studies have also found high concentrations of 4MMP in Simcoe (112 ppb), Summit (88 ppb), and Apollo (61 ppb), and Australian Topaz (48 ppb).[248]

Combined research suggests the following for baseline 4mmp levels in certain hop varieties.[249]

High 4MMP levels: Citra, Simcoe, Eureka!, Summit, Apollo, Topaz, Mosaic, Ekuanot, Galaxy, Nelson Sauvin.

Significant 4MMP levels: Zeus, Cluster, Chinook, Cascade, Centennial, Amarillo. German Northern Brewer, Hallertau Blanc, German Cascade, Mandarina Bavaria, Polaris.

Measurable but low 4MMP: Bravo, Calypso, Denali, Galena, Lemondrop, Sorachi Ace, Super Galena, Willamette, Halltertau Tradition, Herkules, Perle, Taurus, Tettnanger, Styrian Golding, New Zealand Pacific Gem. Perhaps Saaz (found in one study, not another).

None: Hallertau Mittelfrüh, Hersbrucker, Hull Melon, Magnum, Saphir, Spalter Select, Bramling Cross, East Kent Golding, First Gold, Fuggle, Pilgrim, Progress, Wye Challenger, and Wye Target.

How quickly is the transfer rate from 4MMP-rich hops into beer during dry hopping? An experiment with Eureka hops into a Pilsner style beer found quick extraction. When testing for 4MMP on different days of the dry hop, the authors determined that the majority of the 4MMP extracted into the beer the first two days of dry hopping and very little was extracted between days two-eight. Sensory evaluations of the beer agreed with the paper results.[250] Much like with other hop compounds, extraction of thiols during dry hopping happens relatively quickly.

Thiol Potency Indicator

A 2017 paper investigated the thiol concentration of 17 hop varieties, both in bound and free form. The authors then came up with a mathematical equation for determining "Thiol Potency Indicator," which incorporates chemical data, sensory perceptions, and statistical operations to help brewers make smart choices when choosing hop varieties and usage timing of those hops.

The paper suggests that hops high in bound thiol precursors should be added during the late hopping phase (whirlpool/steep) to help cleave these precursors during fermentation. On the other hand, hops that are rich in free thiols can be added to the dry hop, where enzyme activity from yeast isn't required to release the aromatic thiols. The thiol 3MH for example, is best suited for the late hopping because more than 99% of 3MH is present as a thiol precursor in hops.

The specific findings of the 17 hop varieties tested were interesting. Citra was determined to be one of the most versatile hops, meaning it works great as a late hop and a dry hop because it contains similar amounts of both free and bound thiols. Three other varieties that have a good percentage of both free and bound concentrations of 4MMP are Apollo, Eureka, and Simcoe. On the other hand, Cascade, Hallertau, Hallertau Perle, Saaz, Citra, and Calypso are great choices for late hot-side hopping because of bound 3MH levels.[251] Again, 3MH (grapefruit-like) can be converted to 3MHA (passionfruit-like) during fermentation, especially in the presence of β-lyase. Although not specifically studied in the paper, I'm interested if dry hopping with these 3MH-rich hops early in fermentation might also be a way to cleave the precursors.

The concept of targeting certain hops and their addition timing based on free and bound fruity thiols is interesting. For example, Calypso was tested with 99% bound 4MMP and 100% bound 3MH. Calypso has loads of potential but is likely underperforming if used as a late dry hop, because fermentation is needed to liberate the precursors.

The 3MH precursor (G3MH) measured during the study showed the highest concentration in Saaz. For comparison, the amount of this precursor in Citra was 5,209 ppb and Saaz measured at 20,678 ppb. Other hops tested with high G3MH which can be converted to 3MH were Calypso, Cascade, Hallertau Tradition, and Hallertau Perle—all with potential and could be experimented with late in the boil because the precursor needs to be introduced to the wort prior to fermentation.

Remember that the liberation of bound thiols is done via an enzyme called β-lyase produced by yeast. Most yeast that have tested positive for β-lyase are not typical ale strains, but wine strains, which isn't to say that typical ale strains don't produce the enzyme, but they just haven't been tested yet. Another option to try and liberate some of these bound thiols from hops like Calypso is by adding an enzyme directly to the beer at the start of fermentation. One such product is called Rapidase Revelation Aroma, which is designed for extraction of aroma precursors, typically thiols for white grapes, but theoretically could extract the same thiols in hops.

Thiols, Beer Aging, and Bottle Conditioning

A study that examined how thiols evolve during the aging of a Belgian beer found that after a year of storage, the originally detected, aroma-active thiols (4MMP and 3MH) were completely gone. Interestingly, the study also found that during the early stages of storage, the concentration of these aromatic thiols increased with a spike during the second and third months. This suggests the S-cysteine conjugates can be chemically degraded in beer to release these thiols in the bottle, but they won't stick around with too much aging.[252]

Taking a closer look at the role of bottle aging, this time focused specifically on bottle refermentation (carbonation stage), a study examined the polyfunctional thiol concentrations of lagers bottled with sugar and the yeast strain MUCL 34627 and tested the beer each week. A reference beer was also used, which didn't get yeast or sugar, as well as a beer that only received the yeast strain and no sugar. After three weeks of refermentation in the bottles, the authors identified 19 thiols that were absent or present at lower levels compared to the reference beer. The biggest spike occurred during the second and third weeks of bottle refermentation, likely after most of the fermentation was over from the added sugar. The authors speculate this increase during later stages might be due to yeast autolysis facilitating thiol synthesis.

Of the thiols that increased during refermentation were 3S4MPA (sweet), 3SHol (exotic/rhubarb-like), 3SPA (flowery), 4SNol (fruity), and 4S4M2Pone (box tree). The authors found that the addition of sugar wasn't necessarily required to enhance thiol concentrations above threshold values. However, they were generally in lower concentrations than the bottles with the added sugars. A trained judge could identify differences in a triangle test between the control and the three-week bottle-reconditioned beer where only 30% of other tasters could tell a difference between the beer with no sugar added (just yeast), compared to the beer with both added.[253] It's interesting that the addition of the strain MUCL 34627 at bottling impacted the levels of thiols over time in the bottle, with or without sugar.

It's worth considering experimentation with adding these same wine strains during a post-fermentation dry hop where it may enhance these fruity thiols (likely the free thiols at this stage) from the hops. This might avoid the potential negative aspects of fermenting with wine strains as part of a blend, where phenolic characteristics can dominate.

One potential reason bottle conditioning may enhance thiol conversion may come from a wine study that looked at how different fermentation temperatures might impact final levels of fruity thiols. In the study, the authors found that when the fermentation temperature increased from 55°F (13°C) to 68°F (20°C), the final levels of 4MMP and 3MH were higher.[254] This information may be important as it relates to bottle conditioning beer, which is done at room temperature and warmer than a normal fermentation temperature.

Again, leaning on research from the winemaking world, another possible explanation for enhanced thiol conversion during bottle conditioning could be in part because of the different fermentation environment after primary fermentation is complete. This particular wine study looked at how nitrogen might play a role in the release of thiols and found that the addition of DAP (yeast nutrient high in nitrogen) resulted in a decrease in thiol production.[255] During bottle conditioning, most of the nutrients, including nitrogen, have already been consumed, potentially increasing the liberation of thiols in the bottle. In addition to nitrogen content, oxygen is also very low during bottling (or should be), oxygen can reduce the intensity of thiol-odors.[256] This shows that thiols appear to be both sensitive to oxygen and nitrogen, which are both low during the refermentation and bottling stage.

Hop Thiol Potential

A study looking at the potential of four different hop cultivars took hop extracts and incubated them with a commercial enzyme exhibiting β-lyase activity to test the release of any volatiles from S-cysteine conjugates that might be present in the extract.

The test looked at Saaz, Cascade, Tomahawk, and Nelson Sauvin, all from the 2011 hop crop. The authors found that Cascade had the highest potential with 14 to 22 times the amount of 3SHol (grapefruit) that has previously been found in the variety when not in the presence of the enzyme. In other words, when Cascade was in the presence of the enzyme, it released 22 times the amount of the free thiol. This suggests that Cascade is likely a great whirlpool hop choice if a grapefruit-like taste is desired (especially if using an enzyme during fermentation). Tomahawk, Nelson Sauvin and Saaz released less than Cascade in terms of total 3SHol, but still 29, 23 and 126-fold higher than previously reported in the hops.[257]

Saaz saw a 126-fold increase of 3SHol when it was in the presence of the β-lyase enzyme! This makes sense, as a previous research also showed that Saaz has a high number of bound thiols. With the right yeast strain (or commercial enzyme), you can see how carefully selecting hops, even varieties not typically valued for their aromatics, can enhance the aroma of a beer through biotransformation.

The same paper also looked at 4S4MPone (catty, black-currant) and found that Nelson Sauvin increased 79-fold to a very high 598 ug/kg when incubated with the commercial enzyme. Tomahawk saw a larger increase of 87-fold, but the overall concentration was lower than Nelson Sauvin.

What is interesting is that the above study shows a large potential of bound aromatic thiols in hops released when in the presence of β-lyase, compared to wine where only a very small number of precursors found in grapes are converted to free thiols during fermentation. For example, 3SHol from grapes has been tested to be released at a conversion rate of 3-4.4%.[258][259] Another paper suggests that in wine no more than 5% of the cysteinylated precursors contained in the must are biotransformed into thiols.[260]

The exciting prospect with hops is that unlike wine grapes where only about 5% of the precursors are converted, hops can have much higher conversation rates. For example, with 3SHol, one of the highest increases were 41% (Tomahawk), 8% (Cascade), 5% (Saaz), and 13% (Nelson Sauvin).[261] Remember, the thresholds for these thiols are rather low, so even a small increase could bump you over required values.

Applying the research to the modern IPA, we can start to experiment with the β-lyase enzyme during fermentation to get a little more flavor and aroma from certain hop varieties either by using a commercial enzyme or blending in yeast strains that can produce the enzyme. For example, using a cheaper hop like Cascade which has lots of bound grapefruit potential in the whirlpool, and adding a small dose of β-lyase (like Rapidase Expression) in the fermenter. The enzyme may also help create a more overall complex hop character by altering the hop compound concentrations in the beer.

Lessons from Winemakers

In the case of wine, fruity thiols are present in the form of precursors on the grape itself, residing on the outer layer of the fruit (exocarp). For wine strains, this bioflavoring ability is linked to the metabolic activity of yeasts, which is necessary to cleave cysteine-conjugated precursors on the grapes.[262] The release of these volatile thiols varies with different strains, which means that some wine yeast have shown to have a better ability to release flavors than others.[263]

The thiol bioflavoring process is similar to how β-glucosidase activity can release glycosidically-bound flavor compounds in grapes and hops. The difference with thiols, it's not glycosidically-bound flavors, but thiol precursors (two separate pathways to biotransformation). Although research in this area is still relatively new, it's charting a promising path to understanding and potentially unlocking bound flavors and aromas in fermented wine and hop-forward beer.

Studies have shown that the higher amount of the cysteine conjugate thiol precursors in the must, the higher the thiol concentrations in the final wine, but it may be as little as only 3.2% of the precursor that is released during fermentation.[264] This may make the research around thiols seem trivial, but remember that these thiols have low taste thresholds, thus are extremely potent, so it doesn't take much to have an impact.

The three main thiols in wine are 4-mercapto-4-methyl-pentan-2-one (4MMP), 3-mercaptohexan-1-ol (3MH), and 3-mercaptohexyl acetate (3MHA). These thiols are also found in hops and potent, which is shown by their low perception thresholds in wine: 0.0008 ppb (4MMP), 0.06 ppb (3MH), and 0.004 ppb (3MHA).[265] The thiol 4MMP has the lowest threshold, but at high of concentrations can come across like catty.[266]

A study that tested different yeast strains and their ability to release volatile thiols was studied with commercially available strains VL1 and VL3. In the study, VL3 (Sauvignon Blanc strain), released more thiols than VL1, which is also considered a high β-glucosidase enzyme producer.[267]

Another study examined seven wine strains for their ability to release volatile thiols, including strains L2056, NTII6, VIN7, VIN13, VL3, X5, and QA23. The results showed that VIN13 released the most 3MH, VIN7 had the second most, and VIN7 released far more 4MMP and 3MH than the other strains. VIN7 had the highest concentration of 3MHA, which is converted from 3MH.[268]

The results from these different wine strains showing their ability to release fruity thiols is of interest to hoppy brewers because these same thiols tested in wine fermentations are also found in hops. There could then be some potential incorporating a wine strain like VIN7 into a beer fermentation as part of the yeast pitch if you are trying to boost the passionfruit flavors converted from the 3MH thiol from a hop like Cascade for example.

Sensory analysis of the wines tested above also make a case for experimenting with VIN7 as it was significantly preferred to the other wines by tasters, likely because of the stronger passionfruit aromas. The Vin7 results seem to confirm the commercial description for the VIN7 strain: "VIN 7 releases passion fruit, grapefruit, gooseberry and guava aromas and flavors from their non-aromatic precursors in the must."[269] Granted, wine fermentations are completely different than beer fermentations.

It makes sense to see these results and be curious about blending different wine strains for ultimate results. For example, if you know that a certain strain is great at releasing 3MH and another is great at converting 3MH to 3MHA, then why not blend the two to get the best of both worlds? The Australian Wine Research Institute (AWRI) has done just this. They offer a blend of strains called Alchemy II, that is a scientifically formulated blend of wine yeast strain designed to encourage the synergistic action of the specific yeast strains that release and convert the volatile thiols.[270] Not surprisingly, Vin7 is one of the strains advertised in the blend.

The concept of producing complex aromas and flavors through thiol enhancement by combining more than one strain (coinoculating) has been tested to be a good idea. A study looked at three wine strains fermented separately and again when fermented together (the strains were Vin7, QA23, and Vin13). In terms of measured thiols, the coinoculated wine treatments contained higher amounts of 3MH than the single-strain fermentations. The Vin7/QA23 coinoculated wines were higher in 3MHA (Sauvignon, and passionfruit) concentrations than the single-strain.[271]

Another strain of wine yeast called Pichia kluyveri deserves attention for its bioflavoring ability. The strain was harvested naturally from New Zealand grape juice. Pichia kluyveri is a non-Saccharomyces yeast that has been tested to boost fruit-forward flavors by enhancing thiol precursors in grape skins during fermentation, specifically tropical, passionfruit, and blackcurrant flavors. It's advertised as being the most potent thiol producing non-Saccharomyces yeast on the market. If you get a hold of Pichia kluyveri, keep in mind it cannot ferment more than 4 to 5% alcohol, a second strain of yeast should be pitched with it to ensure complete fermentation.[272]

Pichia kluyveri has been put to the test with beer fermentation with some success. Specifically, initial ferments with P. kluyveri produced high amounts of isoamyl acetate (fruity, banana), but also an ethyl acetate off-flavor ester. The authors described P. kluyveri as having a "unique potential for enhancing fruitiness in beer." The longer P. kluyveri can ferment as the solo strain, the higher this solvent-like, ethyl acetate off-flavor will develop. A follow-up pitch with a S. cerevisiae strain after a day or two could help "arrest" this excessive solvent flavor production. [273]

Because Pichia kluyveri can work to enhance some desirable fruity polyfunctional thiols from hops but also can produce intense isoamyl acetate, it's probably best to use it as a small percentage of a yeast blend. I would start as low as just 5% and start working up with subsequent batches.

My Experiments with Wine Yeast in Hoppy Beer

It's great digging into all of the research on the potential of wine strains enhancing thiols and glycosidically bound compounds in hops, but it's more fun to brew some beers with the studied strains and enzymes! I've had mixed results playing with the strains as part of blends and solo ferments in hoppy beers.

The wine strain 58W3, which can be purchased easily from homebrew and wine shops in 8-gram packets (some of the wine strains require commercial size pitches) is a fun strain to play with as it's been tested to free bound terpenes in grapes because of β-glucosidase activity. The strain is also advertised to create a full rich mouthfeel in wine, a hazy IPA characteristic. I experimented by fermenting a hazy hoppy beer with 100% 58W3 with a base of 65% 2-row, 20% chit malt, and 15% malted wheat. The hot-side late hopping was done with Mosaic and Columbus and dry hopped with Medusa, Simcoe, and Citra.

Of the wine strains I've used in beer ferments, this one tends to leave the highest finishing gravity 1.022 (starting with a 1.060 gravity reading). Despite high hopes for the beer, the strain created a strong smoky and plastic phenolic character that masked any bioflavoring taking place. There was still a nice pineapple and lime tropical fruit flavor, but the phenolic flavors were just too dominant. Mouthfeel wise, the higher finishing gravity and likely higher glycerol levels that typical ale strains achieve worked together to create a full and creamy mouthfeel.

58W3 could be used as a small percentage of a yeast pitch, potentially blending with S-04 (it's easy to blend dry yeast by weight). Using as little as 5-10% of a strain in a blend can have a big impact still on final flavors in beer, the hope here is that it's enough to get the bioflavoring enzymes from 58W3 to get to work on the hops without the phenolic characteristics.

One method to try and tamper a phenolic character from taking over a hop-forward beer with a strain like 58W3 is to experiment with removing wheat from the grist. Analysis of wheat has shown that phenolic acid content levels are overall higher than barley, particularity, ferulic acid. Organically grown malted wheat may have even higher levels of ferulic acid than conventional wheat.[274] This is important because the phenolic character in Weissbier is created in part by the metabolism of ferulic acid extracted from wheat by a POF+ yeast strain, creating 4-vinylguaiacol (spicy clove aroma).

Assuming the wine strain is POF+, using less wheat malt in the grist will leave less ferulic acid to be converted during fermentation, ultimately lowering the phenolic 4-vinylguaicol flavors allowing the hops character to potentially come forward.

Another hoppy wine strain experiment I tried was to split a batch three ways, changing the wine yeast strain used to ferment each beer. All three of the strains used (QA23, 71B-1122, and 58W3) have been tested as positive β-glucosidase producers. The base was 60% 2-row, 20% flaked oats, and 20% malted wheat with Columbus as the whirlpool hop and dry hopped during active fermentation with Nelson Sauvin. 71B-1122 was the most aggressive of the three strains in terms of fermentation, getting down to a final gravity of 1.010 (it was also the quickest to finish fermentation). QA23 finished at 1.016 and 58W3 finished at 1.017.

QA23 was the least aromatic of the three beers and despite the 1.016 final gravity still tasted dry and had a bit of alcohol warmth. The 58W3 beer was the most tropical of the beers and had the best mouthfeel (it was also the haziest of the three), but like in other beers I fermented with it, there was a phenolic character that competed with the fruity aromas. The beer fermented with 71B-1122 had the most overall aroma intensity that was very grapefruit-like, but with a spicy characteristic that I wouldn't typically want in an IPA.

Using wine yeast as the primary fermenter resulted in some interesting beers, but none that screamed fruity hazy IPA, the phenols and esters created with them was enough to dominate any subtle boost from bioflavoring via their β-glucosidase activity. So, I decided to take the experimentation a step further and ferment a hazy IPA with just 10% 71B-1122 and 90% S-04, hoping to get the needed enzyme activity from the wine yeast but keeping a neutral ale fermentation profile. I also split the batch to see how 10% of Alchemy II (the scientifically formulated blend of wine yeast designed for bioflavoring) and 90% S-04 would compare.

I again went with a grist of 60% 2-row, 20% flaked oats, and 20% malted wheat (wish I would have omitted the wheat) for this experiment, whirlpooling with chinook, which was tested as having a high amount of glycosidically-bound geraniol potential which hopefully wine yeasts can unlock. The beer was dry hopped with one of my favorite combinations of Simcoe and Citra early into fermentation to try and boost any yeast enzyme activity with the hops.

What amazed me the most about this experiment was how much different a beer can be when just 10% of the yeast pitch (measured by weight) can impact overall flavors. In this case, the S-04 and 71B-1122 had a sharp crisp flavor profile that was tropical from the Simcoe and Citra dry hops but had a noticeable lime/kiwi flavor and aroma. This green fruit flavor may have been boosted in part by the chinook bound geraniol precursors being freed by the wine yeast resulting in more geraniol available to convert to citronellol during fermentation. The Alchemy II and S-04 beer had a rounder fruit aroma, that was a bit jelly-like. I noted it reminded me a bit of the jelly inside of a donut! Apricot and candied peach aromas were the most prominent fruit characteristics. But, like with 58W3, there was a distracting plastic/peppery phenolic aroma that was a distraction to an otherwise fruity IPA.

In the case of Alchemy II, I would probably lower the amount in the blend to just 3-5% and remove the malted wheat from the grist to try and keep the phenolic character down and hopefully still get the enzyme activity to boost the fruity characteristics. I would like to see more research conducted with blends like this, but instead of just my tasting notes, they will be accompanied by lab tests to see if the enzymes from the wine yeast are increasing the fruity hop compounds or not. Ultimately, sneaking in enzyme positive wine strains as part of a blend is a better place to start experimentation than solo wine ferments based on my experience.

Copper and Thiols

Because copper can absorb thiols, it's interesting to pair this information with research discussed in Chapter 14 where we learn that α-acids from hops are effective at complexing copper ions from wort, especially in higher mash pH conditions. Research suggests that adding hops in the mash and periodically in the boil can remove copper ions. Perhaps it's worth experimenting with mash-hop additions with high α-acid hops if the goal is to push desirable, fruity thiols in American hops. Periodic bittering additions may also work to further remove copper ions. The goal would be to get the Cu levels as low as possible before a big, flavoring whirlpool addition where any copper in solution could potentially absorb the fruity hop thiols!

I reached out to Kiyoshi Takoi, who authored the study and asked his opinion on copper equipment used in the brewing process and the potential for stripping volatile thiols. For example, at the homebrew level, I typically cool my wort with a copper chiller, but wonder if is this is enough copper exposer to strip a fruity thiol like 4MMP? According to Kiyoshi Takoi, oxidized copper is a more effective absorber of thiols than non-oxidized, so it's possible that well-used copper equipment could, in fact, absorb thiols. Among various thiols, 4MMP is more sensitive to copper than 3MH. In fact, one test found that if 50 grams of copper granules were added to 250 ml of beer and hopped with Apollo and Simcoe and left overnight at around 40°F (4°C) the 4MMP content decreased by 50%. Whereas the 3MH and 3MHA remained unchanged.[275] I should point out that 50 grams of copper granules in just 250 ml of wort would be like adding 8 pounds of copper granules to a five-gallon batch, which is a crazy amount of copper.

Kiyhoshi went on to tell me that although the copper may absorb thiols generated from a hop like 4MMP in Simcoe, it's his opinion that the generation of thiols from precursors during fermentation might be more effective than those during boiling.

Although I had some assurance from Kiyhoshi that my copper chiller wasn't causing too much damage in stripping thiols from the whirlpool, I wanted to be sure. I reached out to Jaded Brewing LLC to see if they would be willing to send me two identical chillers, one copper and one stainless to test the research around thiols and copper. Luckily, Jaded agreed and sent me two chillers.

I brewed a ten-gallon batch of a hop-forward beer, split and boiled in separate kettles so one kettle could be chilled with the copper chiller and the other with the stainless-steel chiller. To help boost the thiol potential, I used a heavy dose of Citra, Columbus, and Simcoe in the whirlpool. I chose not to dry hop these beers as to not introduce another variable. The beers were fermented with 90% S-04 and 10% Alchemy II measured by weight with dry yeast.

Surprising to me, I couldn't locate a lab in the United States that does thiol testing, so I contacted a wine lab in France, Laboratoire SARCO, who agreed to do the thiol testing. As you can see from the results of the test below, the copper chiller beer had 26 ng/L more measured 3MH than the stainless-steel fermented beer. As far as these results go, there shouldn't be any reason for homebrewers to be worried about their copper chillers stripping 3MH. Although, 3MH is must less sensitive to copper than 4MMP. It was unfortunate I didn't get any 4MMP registered in these beers to see if how much the copper might be stripping. Perhaps lowering the whirlpool temperature first would have been smart in addition to adding brew day hops to try and boost 4MMP levels.

Beer	4-MMP (ng/L)	3MH (ng/L)
Copper Chiller	Not Detected	111
Stainless Steel Chiller	Not Detected	85

Looking at the thiol test results a little closer, the level of 3MH is above the stated threshold of 60 ng/L, which likely contributed to grapefruit-like character. Also interesting is the absence of any 4MMP, particularly since Simcoe was used. This could suggest volatilization of 4MMP during the whirlpool process, which is discussed in more detail below.

A study looking at how thiols are retained throughout the brewing process focused on two thiols that can potentially be found in beer. Using Simcoe hops for the testing, the authors found that during a 60-minute boil at 212°F (100°C), 4MMP content decreased 91% and 23% after heating to just 194°F (90°C). On the other hand, 3MH increased threefold at 212°F (100°C) than at 90°F (32°C), which suggests that not only is this fruity thiol preserved during the boil but enhanced!

Moving to the fermentation stage, 3MH and 4MMP both increased during fermentation and peaked in concentration around days five or six. The thiol 3MHA was not present in the wort but was in the beer after fermentation which means the yeast converted the available 3MH into 3MHA. As part of the study, multiple hop pellets were analyzed for 3MH content. Simcoe had the highest concentration, followed by Topaz, Fuggle, and Cascade.[276]

Choosing a bittering hop that is high in 3MH may be worth experimenting with because of the potential increase during the boil. This is especially true if the goal is to increase the grapefruit-like aroma of a beer or increase the levels of 3MH to be converted to the passionfruit 3MHA with an enzyme or wine yeast.

Malt-Derived Thiols

Hops may not be the only source of thiols, as Kishimoto discovered 3MH was detected in unhopped beer, but not in unhopped wort. This suggests that malt-derived 3MH precursor must be boiled to be released. So, both hops and malt are can be a source of the grapefruit-like 3MH. It's interesting that there's potential to get 3MH from malts that could be converted into 3MHA (passion fruit) with the right yeast strain selection![277]

Fascinated with the idea that there are thiol precursors in malt that could play a role in the development of fruity flavors, I investigated the literature for more information. A study was done in France where the authors investigated 3MH and G3MH thiol precursors in six-row malted and non-malted barley samples. They found that G3MH (a 3MH precursor) was higher in malted than non-malted barley, suggesting an in-situ formation during malting. This is important because it suggests that malted grains may be beneficial when trying to encourage the bioflavoring process (3MH to 3MHA). The current study hypothesizes that because of the evolution during brewing (the boil) less than 3% of thiol precursors contained in malts could potentially lead to more than 64% of 3MH in the final beer.[278]

Thiol Synergy and Hop-Derived Esters

Another reason a brewer might want to increase concentrations of thiols in beer, whether through direct addition of hops or bioflavoring by yeast, is because of thiol flavor-enhancing via synergy. A paper looking specifically at Nelson Sauvin, which is unique in that it's rich in the thiol 3-sulfanyl-4-methylpentan-1-ol (3S4MP), tested the possible synergistic effects of the thiol when dosed with other known hop compounds. Specifically, a solution with 40 ng/L (the threshold) of 3S4MP was compared to solutions with the same amount of 3S4MP in addition to other compounds (linalool, 2MIB, and geraniol), some below their thresholds.

Looking at the results for linalool and geraniol, when paired with the 3S4MP thiol, authors found that 3S4MP enhanced flavors of both terpene alcohols. Geraniol was dosed into the solution at levels lower than its taste threshold, suggesting synergistic effects with the thiol are powerful. Citronellol was also tested in combination with 3S4MP but was not found to increase in flavor.

In the case of an ester 2MIB (2-methylbutyl isobutyrate) which has green apple and apricot flavors,[279] the authors found that the presence of the Nelson Sauvin thiol 3S4MP enhanced the flavors of 2MIB, even though 2MIB was dosed below the threshold. This enhancement of flavor via synergy is interesting because it suggests that 3S4MP is acting as a flavor enhancer to 2MIB, boosting its flavor potential above the actual concentration.[280]

Although studied slightly less, various esters from hops (like with 2MIB) can also impact final beer flavors and aromas just like with thiols and terpenoids. One paper studied how these hop-derived esters are impacted during fermentation across 42 different hop varieties.[281] The study focused on green apple and apricot-like isobutyric esters (isobutyl isobutyrate, isoamyl isobutyrate, and 2-methylbutyl isobutyrate) and ethyl esters of branched-chain fatty acids (ethyl isobutyrate, ethyl isovalerate, and ethyl 2-methylbutyrate).

The authors found that all isobutyric esters gradually decreased during fermentation, however, the ethyl esters of branched-chain fatty acids were almost absent in the wort but increased during fermentation. This esterification during fermentation is another example of hop biotransformation, likely from yeast-derived esterase activity and chemical esterification.

The one hop variety that stood out in this area was Huell Melon, a variety described as having melon-forward flavors. In the tests, wort made with Huell Melon was the only one that contained ethyl isobutyrate and ethyl 2-methylbutyrate at relatively high levels. As for ethyl isobutyrate levels with Huell Melon made wort, the concentrations increased during fermentation, well above the taste threshold (even before fermentation the levels were near the taste threshold). Concentrations of ethyl 2-methylbutyrate were also above threshold after fermentation, suggesting that these two ethyl esters of branched-chain fatty acids likely contribute to the hops flavor.[282]

So, one way to potentially increase the melon-like flavor of a beer would be to use Huell Melon hops during the steep or whirlpool stage (the study dosed at a rate that corresponds to just 0.20 lbs./bbl). These flavorful hop-derived esters can survive the whirlpool and will likely increase during fermentation above taste thresholds. For what it's worth, I looked back at the one beer I've brewed using Huell Melon in the whirlpool and I described the flavor of the beer as cantaloupe-like.

The other hop variety with unique behavior in ethyl esters of branched-chain fatty acids concentrations during fermentation was Ekuanot (HBC366). All the ethyl esters were almost absent in the worts made with Ekuanot, but concentrations of all three ethyl esters were over their thresholds after a weeklong fermentation. Like with Huell Melon, these esters are likely partly responsible for the hops unique character in beer, but for Ekuanot it has more to do with the biotransformation during fermentation. The results suggest that using Ekuanot during the whirlpool could result in the precursors needed to get ethyl esters above taste thresholds.

Getting back to 2MIB, which has been determined to have a threshold at 78 ug/L, a paper brewed single-hopped beers in order to determine 2MIB concentrations (for late hop additions). Only one variety tested above the threshold, Southern Cross. Other varieties that were below the threshold, but still had relatively high levels of 2MIB, were (in order from highest) Pacific Jade, Polaris, Huell Melon, Riwaka, and Waimea.[283] It's interesting to consider pairing Nelson Sauvin (3S4MP thiol) with some of these higher 2MIB hops, to get the synergistic effect leading to flavor enhancement of this fruity isobutyric ester.

Yeast strains may also play a role in the ester potential of hops, as one study looked at 2MIB in an ale and lager fermentation. The results showed that a Pilsner fermented with a "standard lager yeast strain," resulted in slightly more 2MIB than the ale, which was fermented with an English strain. Although the increase wasn't massive, the beers had the same dry hopping and the lager strain resulted in approximately a 17% increase.[284]

Looking further at the role of individual yeast strains and thiols, a 2018 BrewingScience paper looked at the role of two different yeast strains (WLP001 California Ale and WLP029 German Ale/Kolsch) and the concentrations of terpenes, esters, and thiols paired with early fermentation dry hopping. Dry hopping with either Cascade and Hallertau Mittelfrüh on day three of fermentation, the authors found WLP001 produced beers with more of the 3MH (grapefruit) thiol and more fruity monoterpene alcohols (geraniol and citronellol) than WLP029, despite the same hopping rates.[285]

The results above suggest that WLP001 may have a greater ability than WLP029 to release more glycosidically-bound terpenes, but the hops must contain the necessary precursors. The paper found Cascade contains these terpenes and Hallertau Mittelfrüh does not. Earlier research discussed in the book also found Cascade to be a precursor-rich hop. So, although the research is only looking at two different yeast strains, it's exciting that the focus of beer research is starting to emulate wine studies to see how individual yeast strains can impact beer flavor through biotransformation. Again, in this case, American Ale yeast outperformed a German Ale/Kolsch strain, however, the lager strain in the previous study outperformed an ale strain in 2MIB concentrations suggesting there's still a lot to learn!

It's fun to step back and try to start piecing together all the research to experiment even further. We know from other research that beers made with Southern Cross, Pacific Jade, Polaris, Huell Melon, and Riwaka all tested high in 2MIB. If this potential apricot-like flavor is desirable, you could consider adding these hops and ferment with a lager strain to increase the concentration of the ester in the finished beer. You could then also pair the hop with a 3S4MP thiol-rich variety like Nelson Sauvin to get even further flavor enhancement of the ester via synergy. Sounds like a fun India Pale Lager experiment!

A fun experiment along these lines would be to brew an India Pale Lager with a small percentage of a wine strain (like Vin 7) to both boost 2MIB as well as to encourage bioflavoring from thiols and glycosides. Late hopping with high 2MIB hops like Southern Cross, Pacific Jade, or Vic Secret, and dry hopping with Nelson Sauvin to push the synergistic impact from 3S4MP and 2MIB! An added benefit to the lager co-pitch with Vin7 would be the lower fermentation temperatures as the strain likes to ferment around 58°F (14°C).

This lager/wine yeast experiment gets even more intriguing when looking at research focusing on fermentation temperatures and thiol concentrations. A paper that examined whether thiol concentrations increase or decrease based on fermentation temperature dosed test beers with Mosaic hops at the onset of fermentation (early dry hopping) and measured thiols 3MH and 3MHA. The authors found that almost twice the amount of 3MHA was measured in the beer fermented at 59°F (15°C) compared to the one at 71°F (21°C) with a wheat beer yeast (Tum 68).[286] Specifically, the tropical and desirable 3MHA (which is converted from 3MH) went from 4 ng/l to 8 ng/l at the lower temperature. This might not seem like much, but with a low threshold for 3MHA (9 ng/l), you can see why it's important. Also, because 3MHA is converted from 3MH, it's equally important that the 3MH concentration also increased when fermented at the cooler temperature going from 31 ng/l to 37 ng/l. Obviously, the more you can push the 3MH the more potential for 3MHA (especially with the right yeast strain or with a commercial enzyme).

The results above can be somewhat explained by a 2011 paper focusing on the aroma compounds in wheat beer when injected with CO2 at different temperatures (mimicking fermentation). The authors found that the polarity of the compounds played a role in the potential loss during fermentation. The more hydrophilic a compound, the more likely it will remain in the solution during fermentation and be less impacted by temperature increases.[287] This makes sense as studies have shown that in beer and wine must fermentations volatile compounds are partly transported to the surface by CO2 and released into the gas phase.[288]

Because thiols have lower boiling points and are less soluble than other solvents like alcohols, you can see why they may be more impacted by increased fermentation temperatures. This is also likely true for hydrocarbons and monoterpene alcohols from hops introduced during the whirlpool or from early dry hopping. The warmer the fermentation temperature, the more likely the hydrocarbons would be removed (woody, spicy, and resinous compounds) compared to the fruitier more soluble monoterpene alcohols.

Getting back to hop synergistic impact from thiols, a paper put 4MMP (blackcurrant) thiol to the test with monoterpene alcohols (linalool, geraniol, and β-citronellol). The results showed that 4MMP did have an additive impact with monoterpene alcohols and that only 1.2 ng/L was needed for this to take place, which is slightly higher than its threshold value. Specifically, the synergy between 4MMP and linalool, geraniol, and β-citronellol enhanced tropical characteristics. Using hops rich in both 4MMP and these monoterpene alcohols could result in a more perceived tropical flavor.

The same study also looked at the impact of blending different hop varieties and the synergistic impact between monoterpene alcohols without the presence of thiols. To do this, they chose to blend a small amount of Bravo (because of its high geraniol content) to both Simcoe (lower in geraniol) and Apollo (also high in geraniol) separately. Adding the geraniol rich Bravo to both varieties increased the citrus and flowery scores than solutions without.

You can start to see why carefully selecting a blend of hop varieties by their monoterpene and thiol levels could be beneficial. We know that by using monoterpene-rich hops, could boost the citrus qualities of beer. We also know that if we combine these same monoterpene-rich hops with thiols like 4MMP, we could enhance the fruity perceptions even further via synergy. Below are examples of hops high in 4MMP and monoterpene alcohols that you could experiment mixing together in whirlpool or dry hop to promote this flavoring enhancing effect. Again, trying to further boost both the monoterpene alcohols by unlocking glycosides and bound thiols with yeast strains tested for the appropriate enzyme (β-glucosidase for glycosides and β-lyase for thiols) is just another route to even further boost hop flavors.

Hops with high 4MMP levels - Citra, Simcoe, Eureka!, Summit, Apollo, Topaz, Mosaic, Ekuanot, Galaxy, and Nelson Sauvin.

Hops with significant 4MMP levels - Zeus, Cluster, Chinook, Cascade, Centennial, Amarillo. German Northern Brewer, Hallertau Blanc, German Cascade, Mandarina Bavaria, Polaris.[289]

Hops rich in geraniol: Brewers Gold, Centennial, Olympic, Cluster, Simcoe, Mosaic, Chinook, Crystal, Bravo, and Galena.

Hops rich in linalool: Ultra, Liberty, Nugget, Crystal, Mt. Hood, Triple Pearl, Mount Rainier, Santiam, Fuggle, Meridian, Golding, Tettnang, and Citra.[290]

Key Findings

- The main thiols studied in hops and grapes are 4MMP (blackcurrants), 3MH (grapefruit, gooseberry, guava), and 3MHA (passionfruit and guava). The thiol 3MHA is converted from 3MH.
- Thiols from hops can contribute to the fruitiness of beer because of their low taste thresholds and can be found in both free and bound forms. The liberation of bound thiols is done via an enzyme called β-lyase from yeast (certain wine strains have been found to be the most effective) or a commercial enzyme product.
- Hops high in bound thiol precursors should be added during the late hopping phase to help cleave these precursors during fermentation. On the other hand, hops that are rich in free thiols can be added to the dry hop, where enzyme activity from yeast isn't required to release the aromatic thiols.

- American grown hops tend to have more of the beneficial thiols.
- The 3MH thiol precursor was found in higher concentrations in malted barley vs. non-malted barley, suggestion all malt grist could help promote the 3MH to 3MHA conversion.
- Thiols from hops can have a positive synergistic impact on fruit-forward flavors in beer. For example, 4MMP can lower flavor perceived thresholds for monoterpene alcohols like geraniol.
- Almost twice the amount of 3MHA was measured in a beer fermented at 59°F (15°C) compared to one at 71°F (21°C). 3MH was also tested slightly higher at the cooler fermentation temperature, suggesting that thiols may benefit from cooler ferments.

Chapter 12: Concentrated Lupulin

Developed by Yakima Chief, Hopunion Cryo Hops® (LupuLN2) are designed for brewers to produce extremely aromatic beers, but with less astringent flavors. This is because Cryo hops are the concentrated lupulin of whole leaf hops that contain aromatic hop oils but with less of the vegetative material. Here is how Yakima Chief describes the Cryo making process.

> Whole hop cones are separated into concentrated lupulin and bract at extremely low temperatures, preserving each component of the hop; nothing is crushed. LupuLN2 offers brewers approximately twice the concentration of resin content of traditional T90 hop pellets and should be dosed at approximately half the amount by weight. Brewers should note that LupuLN2 will create intense hop flavor and aroma with reduced vegetal and polyphenol flavor contribution because the leafy, plant material has been removed. The flavor profile of LupuLN2 is variety specific, but more pronounced due to the concentration. LupuLN2 is available in hop powder and hop pellet form. It can be applied anywhere in the brewery, but early kettle recommendations are not recommended for risk of boiling out the intense aroma.

Brewery Experiences with Cryo

To learn more about brewing with Cryo, I asked two pro brewers in Austin, TX about their experience with the new product. Joe Mohrfeld, Director of Brewing at Pinthouse Pizza Brewpub, and formerly of Odell Brewing and Josh Hare, founder and Brewer at Hops and Grain Brewing were both given early samples of Cryo and ran their own brewing experiments, with sensory and lab results.

After several test brews, Hops and Grain have liked their results best when using 40% of the total dry hop charge in Cryo for both Citra and Mosaic varieties and a slightly higher percentage of Cryo when using Simcoe. When doing side-by-side experiments brewing with Cryo against traditional T90 pellet beers (from the same hop lot), their trained sensory panel and consumers that gave feedback preferred the Cryo beers as the one they liked the most.

Pinthouse Pizza liked their experiments with Cryo, but especially the higher yields they experienced. When Pinthouse Pizza replaced half their dry hops with Cryo compared to traditional pellets, they yielded as much as a barrel of additional beer in a 15-barrel batch. This is because the leafy material that was removed to create Cryo is no longer available to absorb beer during dry hopping. This is especially true if you use Cryo at half the amount you would typically use traditional pellets, which is recommended by Yakima Chief. This extra yield is equivalent to an additional 248 pints per batch!

Joe Mohrfeld finds that dry hopping with Cryo hops compared to traditional pellets results in a noticeably different beer. Cryo hops seems to give a more intense and truer varietal specific aroma, reminiscent of actually "being in the bail room." So, if Cryo hops are so great, why even use traditional pellets? When dry hopping with 100% Cryo, Pinthouse Pizza wasn't thrilled with the results. In these beers, the hop aroma intensity was there, but it lacked depth, meaning it was a little one note. The sweet spot for them seems to be dry hopping with 30-50% with Cryo and the rest in traditional pellets. This ratio seems to bridge the gap of softer fruit aromatics from the pellets with a brighter, more rounded, and intense aroma coming from the Cryo. They also found the Cryo seemed to lower the astringent harshness you can get with heavy pellet additions.

Brewing with Cryo Hops

Unlike pellets, which tend to sit at the top of fermenting beer for a short period but gradually fall into suspension, Cryo powder can hang around longer than most brewers are accustomed to. In my experience on a five-gallon dry hop with lupulin powder, I gave the fermenter a little swirl to encourage the powder to get into suspension after a few hours of adding it. On a commercial scale, the first time Pinthouse Pizza dry hopped with Cryo powder, they came back two days later psyched to pull a sample and found the beer didn't have any aroma. After looking in the tank, they could see the powder was still on top of the beer and hadn't fallen into suspension yet.

If you're fermenting with a top-cropping strain, the thick krausen sitting on the top of the beer may amplify this problem. To get Cryo powder into suspension, a brewery might need to recirculate the beer or blast CO2 through the cone to encourage the powder sink. Mainly for ease of use, the pellet form of Cryo seems to be what most brewers prefer, mainly because you can use them just like you would normal pellets.

The plus side, however, is once you do get the powder into the beer, it doesn't seem to want to drop out. Unlike pellets, which will slowly sink to the bottom of the fermenter, Cryo powder tends to stay in suspension. This could explain the faster extraction times that some are reporting when using Cryo powder. If the hop powder is staying in suspension, this theoretically removes the need to agitate or recirculate the beer to encourage extraction. Pinthouse Pizza found that after just 30 minutes of recirculation, they had what seemed to be nearly full extraction with the powder. Hops and Grain also mentioned that when using Cryo powder, the contact time needed for extraction was much less.

Hops and Grain found that one potential downside of using large amounts of Cryo powder without running it through their centrifuge resulted in a beer with a gritty-like mouthfeel. I didn't experience this in my beer described below, however, I did use a 300-micron filter around the dip tube in the keg which may have helped with this. On the commercial level, Sapwood Cellars has used Cryo pellets and never experienced this gritty-like mouthfeel, so it's likely only with the powder form.

To test out the advertised benefits of Cryo, I brewed a ten-gallon split batch NEIPA. One of the five-gallon was dry hopped with Mosaic Cryo powder and the other with traditional Mosaic pellets to see for myself how dry hopping differs between the two products. Specifically, the dry hopping schedule for the beers was as follows:

Dry Hops:

1-ounce Mosaic Cryo Powder at day 4 of fermentation and 1-ounce Mosaic Cryo Powder in the serving keg.

or

2-ounces Mosaic pellets at Day 4 of fermentation and 2-ounces of Mosaic pellets in the serving keg.

I didn't have a hard time telling these beers apart. To me, the powder dry hopped beer produced big aromas of pine, sap, cannabis, resin, and peppercorn, with some additional tropical notes. I was reminded of a beer I made with Eureka hops, which also had strong resinous characteristics with some cherry-like fruitiness. The Mosaic pellet dry hopped aroma was much less intense and had a softer edge. The pellets still produced a beer with some of that dank Mosaic quality but with more pronounced sweet fruit aroma.

The flavor again showed how different the powder behaves compared to traditional pellets. The Mosaic pellet dry hop was much more astringent and vegetal on the palate, which seemed to hide some hop saturated flavor. This could be explained by research indicating that the increase in bitterness and astringency found in the dry hopped beers correlates to the total polyphenol content,[291] but this assumes Cryo powder has less polyphenols because it has less vegetal material. Josh at Hops and Grain also suggested that the increased polyphenols, when using pellets, seems to "mute" the desired hop flavor. Although further lab test described later show high polyphenol content in beer made with Cryo hops.

One unexpected result in my experience was the noticeable difference in clarity between the two beers. The pellet hopped beer, which had twice the amount of hop material in weight, was significantly cloudier and had more of that murky NEIPA look where the powder beer had more of a hop sheen.

Interested if the polyphenol content in Cryo powder is actually less than traditional pellets (potentially aiding in the increased clarity), I examined Hops and Grains lab results when using Cryo. Also included in the lab results were the differences in the IBUs when using Cryo powder vs. traditional pellets. In a separate experiment, they split fifteen-barrels of beer into two seven-barrel fermenters and used the same yeast strain and pitch rate. One seven-barrel batch was dry hopped with Cryo powder and the other with pellets. Both tanks were dry hopped and recirculated with either Ekuanot™ Cryo or Ekuanot™ in pellet form and sent to a lab for IBU testing and polyphenol counts. Half of the amount of Cryo was used compared to pellets, per the Yakima Chief recommendation.

IBU Results:

Powder #1: 31.9
Powder #2: 37.86
Powder #3: 36.25
Pellet #1: 59.02
Pellet #2: 58.11
Pellet #3: 57.62

Powder AVG IBU: 35.3
Pellet AVG IBU: 58.25

As you can see from the IBU results above, the beer that was dry hopped only with pellets had roughly a 35% increase in measured IBUs compared to the Cryo hops. Although the IBU test has its downsides, like not being able to distinguish between bittering acids, the measured increase in IBUs from dry hopping with pellets compared to Cryo is substantial.

Luckily, Hops and Grain also had their beers tested via HPLC, which can also determine humulinones levels. As expected, in part because humulinones are thought to form during the pelletization process when the lupulin gland is exposed, the Cryo dry hopped beers had fewer bitter humulinones than the pellet beer. Specifically, the pellet dry hopped beer had approximately 3.5 times more humulinones.

Also interesting within the HPLC results is that the Cryo dry hopped beer had approximately 31% more iso-α-acids than the pellet dry hopped beer. The higher concentration in iso-α-acids with Cryo is most likely explained by the reduction in vegetal material, which can pull out hot-side bitterness. Ultimately, dry hopping with Cryo hops resulted in more iso-α-acids (retaining more of the original hot-side bitterness) and fewer bitter humulinones compared to dry hopping with pellets. This could mean that if dry hopping with Cryo at half of the amount pellets, you may want to slightly back down the hot-side IBUs to prevent the beer from tasting too bitter.

Also interesting from these results is the pellet hopped beer had a higher measured final beer pH (+0.07), which makes sense considering the more beer is dry hopped, the more the pH should increase. Because half the amount of Cryo was used the pH increase from dry hopping should be theoretically less.

Polyphenols and Cryo Hops

Here are Hops and Grain's lab results from a 30-barrel batch of beer where polyphenol readings were taken at the end of fermentation (before dry hopping), after a 100% Cryo powder dry hop, and after a second dry hop with 100% pellets of the same variety at twice the amount of lupulin powder used.

Total Polyphenol (Pre-Dry Hop):
#1: 227.55
#2: 134.44
#3: 166.54
AVG: 176.18

Total Polyphenol (Post-Cryo Dry Hop):
#1: 301.33
#2: 258.76
#3: 340.05
AVG: 300.05 (+123.87 from Pre-Dry Hop)

Total Polyphenol (Post-Pellet Dry-Hopping and Recirculation):
#1: 402.83
#2: 482.95
#3: 334.03
AVG: 406.6 (+106.55 from Post-Cryo Dry Hop)

Surprisingly, the increase in polyphenols from the Cryo powder dry hop was slightly higher than from the pellet dry hop. Although a small sample size, the results indicate that when it comes to polyphenols, the measured increase from using half the amount as you would in pellet form still results in substantial increases. I'd be interested in further testing where the beers were separated, and one receives Cryo powder and the other pellets (not added to the same beer which was done here). I wonder if it's possible that Cryo has better extraction of the polyphenols it has available (even if less than pellets) because they tend to stay in suspension longer (especially the powder).

To summarize the Hops and Grain findings, when dry hopping with half the volume of cryo-to-pellets:

Pellet Dry Hop - Higher measured IBUs, lower iso-α-acids, higher humulinones, higher pH, and increased polyphenols.

Cryo Dry Hop - Lower IBUs, higher iso-α-acids, lower humulinones, lower pH, and increased polyphenols

Research suggests the extraction rate of polyphenols will reduce once a threshold has been reached in whirlpool and dry hop additions. For example, in one study, fifteen commercial beers were compared pre and post-dry hop for polyphenol content.[292] The

Authors found when the starting polyphenol concentration was already high, the extraction efficiency of added polyphenols was reduced during dry hopping. The average polyphenol content of these dry hopped commercial beers was measured at 247 mg/L. As it relates to the Hops and Grain's results, this could explain why the pellet addition had about the same amount of polyphenol extraction as the Cryo, because there were already so many polyphenols in solution (from the Cryo charge) it could have reduced the pellet extraction that followed.

To put the Cryo powder results from Hops and Grain into perspective, the same study mentioned above also tested unhopped wort for polyphenols and then dry hopped five-gallon kegs at 4g/L (cited as the industry average) and 16 g/L (about 10 ounces for a five-gallon batch) with Chinook pellets, tested at dry hop durations of 24 and 72 hours without agitation. The results showed the concentration of polyphenols peaked at 211 mg/L with the higher 16g/L dry hop charge at 72-hours of contact time. Comparing these results with pellets, the increase in polyphenols was approximately 100 mg/L after dry hopping. Hops and Grain averaged an increase of approximately 124 mg/L with the Cryo powder, suggesting Cryo can still be a significant source of polyphenols. One caveat, however, is that Hops and Grain recirculated their dry hops, which could increase the overall extraction.

The Chinook pellet test above also showed that generally, the concentration of extracted hop components (including polyphenols and humulinones) increased with dose and time. However, the highest and second highest levels of increases were found in the 16 g/L six-hour dry hop and 4 g/L 24-hour dry hop. This suggests dose and time isn't necessarily a hard and fast rule for determining extraction rates. Interestingly, the humulinone concentration in the tested beers were quite low, peaking at 6.8 mg/L in a five-gallon batch. I had a beer tested with approximately ten-ounces of dry hops as well and it came back at 24.3 mg/L. The biggest difference, other than different hop varieties, was the timing of the additions. In my case, the hops had extended time on the beer in the serving keg.

Key Findings

- Cryo hops, developed by Yakima Chief, Hopunion, are designed for brewers to get approximately twice the concentration of resin content of traditional T90 hop pellets but with less leafy plant material.
- One recommendation is to replace approximately 30-50% of a dry hop charge with Cryo and the rest in traditional pellets. This ratio seems to bridge the gap of softer fruit aromatics from the pellets with brighter, more rounded, and intense aroma from Cryo.
- Cryo (especially when in powder vs pellet form) tends to float on the top of beer and should be agitated into solution via recirculation or CO_2 bursting (or fermenter agitation).
- Cryo may result in faster hop extraction times because it's more likely to stay in suspension than pellets and has less vegetal material potentially slowing extraction.
- Cryo dry hopped beers will likely result in fewer extraction of humulinones and will not strip as many iso-α-acids due to less vegetal material. In other words, Cryo dry hopped beers will leave more of the hot-side bitterness in place and not impart as much cold-side bitterness from humulinones introduced during dry hopping.
- Despite having less vegetal material, Cryo hopped beers were tested to still impart a significant number of polyphenols, comparable to a later dry hop addition with traditional pellets.

Chapter 13: What's Causing the Haze

What exactly is causing the haze in New England style IPAs? It's a question that can rile people up. Some think its poor brewing habits. Others think it's the magic of biotransformation. By looking at the literature on how heavy hopping rates, high protein grist, early dry hopping, and the interaction between polyphenols and proteins may impact turbidity, we can get a better understanding of how to create and control haze levels.

Fermentation Dry Hopping

About 80% of polyphenols in beer have been said to originate from malt, with 20% from hops. It's safe to assume the ratio of polyphenols coming from hops has gone up in recent years as whirlpool and dry hop additions have grown rapidly. Polyphenol increase in hop-forward beers is important in understanding haze because when polymerized (oxidized) polyphenols react with proteins, the bindings between protein and polyphenols are irreversible, resulting in a permanent haze.[293]

This is shown in a study where a polyphenolic extract from spent hops is dosed into beer and tested for turbidity levels. After the addition of polyphenols to the base beer, a haze would form. Sensory analysis of the higher polyphenol beers had higher marks for harsh, medicinal, and metallic tastes.[294] This research is important because we know that 50 to 60% of polyphenols are getting extracted during dry hopping and about 25% are potentially dropping out, leaving about 35% of available polyphenols from dry hops in the finished beer.[295] So, at higher dry hopping and whirlpool rates, the concentration of hop polyphenols available to proteins is high.

A common practice when brewing hazy IPAs is to dry hop early into fermentation (usually between days two and four), sometimes as soon as brew day. This is more common on the homebrew level, as most commercial breweries dry hop after primary fermentation is complete so they can harvest hop-free yeast. Early dry hopping may be important as it relates to proteins and polyphenols. A study that looked at how protein content in beer changes during active fermentation examined the impact of two different yeast strains (WLP001 and KVL011). They found that with both, protein content decreased during fermentation, likely degraded proteolytically by yeast or precipitating out with the yeast slurry. Specifically, WLP001 had a decrease of 16% and KVL001 decreased 42%.[296]

Based on the study above, I speculate that early fermentation dry hopping might expose the extracted hop-derived polyphenols from the early dry hop additions to a higher amount of available proteins in the wort, increasing the polyphenol and protein interactions and potentially leading to permanent haze. Dry hopping after fermentation is complete should be a slightly less protein rich environment, leading to less haze formation. Further testing is needed, but it's likely that as yeast flocculates (strain dependent) they can remove some haze forming proteins from the beer and make less of it available for polyphenol interaction. When these hop polyphenols are present during early fermentation and before any yeast flocculation, more haze forming complexes should be able to take place.

Haze and pH

Another factor playing a role in haze is the pH of the beer during the dry hop. Protein and polyphenols bind differently at different pHs, but a pH around 4.2 (normal final beer pH) is the most ideal for protein and polyphenol-induced haze. The changes in pH in the range of 3.7 to 4.2 are negligible as it relates to haze. However, the lower the pH, the less haze will form from protein and polyphenol reactions. The change in haze potential is because the pH impacts how the proteins behave on the net charge of the molecules.[297] This research is backed up by another study that also found the pH range of 3.8 to 4.3 resulted in the highest turbidity.[298]

In this case, post-fermentation dry hopping is likely done around the pH sweet spot for protein and polyphenol-induced haze. So, early fermentation dry hopping (where more proteins are available) combined with post-fermentation dry hopping (at the peak haze pH) should increase haze potential even more.

ABV Level and Haze

You might have noticed that some double IPAs tend to have more haze than a session IPA. The alcohol level can impact haze in part because ethanol has been shown to decrease the precipitation of proteins and polyphenols.[299] This means at higher ABVs, proteins and polyphenols are more likely to stay suspended and cause haze compared to lower strength beers.

Malted vs. Unmalted Grains

It seems one of the biggest factors in haze is the amount of proteins and the type of proteins that are finding their way into IPAs. The process of malting grains and the impact on proteins can influence polyphenol and protein interactions. A study looking at the haze of beer brewed from a control of 100% malted barley compared to two beers with either 20% and 40% of the barley replaced with unmalted wheat found that the higher the addition of unmalted wheat, the less permanent haze. The beer with 40% unmalted wheat had significantly less permanent haze than the beer with 100% barley. The authors also tested polyphenols in the beers and found that the higher the percentage of unmalted wheat in the beer, the lower number of measured polyphenols.

Protein modification during malting is a big factor in haze potential because as proteins undergo malting, the proteolysis (breakdown) of these proteins can increase haze.[300] The protein degradation in wheat malt, for example, results in less protein precipitate occurring during the brewing process. This is because malting leads to lower molecular weight proteins that are more likely to remain suspended in beer, as opposed to heavier, unmalted proteins. Generally, about a third of proteins introduced into wort find their way into the final beer.[301]

The germination step of malting is where proteins are degraded and potential for haze increases. One study found the longer the germination period in days during malting, the more permanent haze in beers made with those malts. Interestingly, this same study found that using wheat malt in more than 15 to 20% of the total grist reduced the haze.[302] Although not discussed, it's possible too many of these proteins in suspension can lead to them interacting and dropping out.

A good way of estimating how long a grain has been germinated and get a clue of its haze-inducing potential, is to look at the Kolbach index percentage. As germination time increases, so does the measured Kolbach index. Comparing wheat malts, for example, an option with a higher Kolbach percentage may impart more permanent haze in a heavily hopped beer. If you are looking to have more haze in a hoppy beer, using 10 to 20% malted wheat in the grist (even better with a high Kolbach index) may get you more permanent haze. Pair this with a lot of hops, including early dry hopping, and you could increase haze even more.

What exactly is going on during malting, specifically the germination period and protein degradation, that is encouraging haze formation? Gluten proteins (storage proteins) represent about 60% of the wheat protein content. These gluten proteins can be broken down into two main groups of gliadins and glutenins. The elasticity of proteins comes primarily from the glutenin fraction, and the viscosity comes mainly from gliadin.[303] Non-gluten proteins are about 15 to 20% of the wheat seed, are lighter in molecular weight, and include active enzymes and protease inhibitors, including lipid transfer proteins.

During malting, the biggest change that occurs to proteins is the enzymatic degradation of the cereal endosperm, and its conversion into soluble peptides and amino acids.[304] This enzymatic degradation into peptides and amino acids are critical, as it relates to haze potential from the proteins. Combinations of proteins and polyphenols are thought to result from hydrophobic bonding between hydrophobic amino acids such as proline, tryptophan, phenylalanine, tyrosine, leucine, isoleucine, and valine.[305]

A study looking at the breakdown of storage proteins into amino acids during the malting of wheat found a significant increase in the amino acids referenced above that are capable of binding to polyphenols and lead to haze. For example, tyrosine rose by a factor of 19, valine by a factor of 9, phenylalanine by a factor of 19, and leucine by a factor of 9. These potential haze forming amino acids saw a massive increase after malting. In fact, because enzymatic hydrolysis continues during germination, the amino acid concentrations increased each day the wheat spent germinating.[306]

It's also been shown that certain proteins have a higher affinity to bind with polyphenols that are rich in proline. An example of a proline-rich protein linked to polyphenol binding are hordeins (found in barley) and gliadins (found in wheat).[307] As the protein content in a grist increases, so do hordeins and gliadins, which can bind to polyphenols.

A study looking at the difference between unmalted and malted grains found that barley malt had measured proline concentration of 1,421 ppm whereas unmalted barley had just 203 ppm.[308] This suggests that malted barley has about seven times the amount of proline than unmalted barley and because the haze potential of proteins is proportional to the amount of proline, you can see why malted grains are better for inducing haze. In fact, one reference suggests that only proteins that contain proline bind polyphenols.[309]

Not related to malting of grains, but relevant to proline, is the use of lactose in IPAs. Some brewers have experimented with adding lactose to their IPAs, which can also have an impact on clarity. While haze potential of proteins from grains is proportional to the amount of their proline and amino acid, lactose contains Casein, which represents about 80% of the protein in cow's milk and has more proline than most proteins.[310] The high proline content in milk would then likely encourage the formation of haze with polyphenols.

So, the haze potential in beers is increased when grains are malted not only because of the reduction in molecular weight of the proteins, but also because of the protein changes resulting from these reductions (storage proteins to amino acids). Total protein content alone is likely not the best way to determine haze potential. For example, barley proteins are made up of a higher percentage of the hordein protein fraction (major storage protein), which also means higher proline levels.[311] Even though other grains have a higher total protein content, they could contribute less to haze because of their lower amounts of proline. For example, malted buckwheat and quinoa have higher total protein than barley malt, but half as much total proline, because their proteins are mainly globulins and albumins, whereas barley had more from the hordein protein fraction.[312]

Experiment on Haze and Malted Grains

I did an experimental brew to try and put some of this information to the test by intentionally brewing a clear NEIPA using 17% oat flour!

Oat flour is made by milling whole grain oat groats,[313] which are different from quick flaked which undergo kiln toasting and are steamed before being rolled into flakes.[314] Though oat flour hasn't been subject to the heat, you don't have to do a cereal mash as the gelatinization temperature of oat flour was found in the study below to be around 134°F (56°C).

The clearing potential of oat flour has been tested to show that when high amounts of barley was replaced with oat flour, larger amounts of unmodified, high-molecular weight proteins were brought into solution and were "extensively degraded by endogenous malt proteases or precipitated during the mashing process."[315] Essentially if heavier proteins drop out, resulting in fewer final proteins in the finished beer, should result in less protein/polyphenol reactions and ultimately less haze. It's also important to remember that when 20% of barley was replaced with oats, there was a 30% reduction in polyphenols, which should also play a role in increasing clarity. Lastly, I used 18% malted wheat in this experiment as it was found that that when wheat malt is more than 15% of the grist it can reduce haze levels (lower amounts can increase haze).

Recipe:
Original Gravity: 1.057
Final Gravity: 1.010
ABV: 6.2%
Water: 100% Reverse Osmosis treated with 1.50 grams/gallon calcium chloride

Grist:
65% Briess 2-Row
17% Bob's Red Mill Oat Flour
18% Malted Red Wheat
(Acidulated malt added as needed for mash pH of 5.35)

Hops:
10 grams Columbus @ 60 minutes
30 grams Eureka 15-minute whirlpool @185°F (85°C)
30 grams Columbus 15-minute whirlpool @185°F (85°C)

Fermentation:
WLP030 Thames Valley Ale Yeast @68°F (20°C)

Dry Hops:
Day Three of Fermentation: 56 grams Eureka and 28 grams Nelson Sauvin. On day 10 of Fermentation: 28 grams Eureka and 28 grams Nelson Sauvin. On day 14, kegged with 28 grams Eureka, 28 grams Nelson Sauvin, and 28 grams Columbus

Result:
This was the first time I've used WLP030, which is described as a very flocculant strain for all things English. Great for porters, stouts and ESBs. Lower ester production than most English strains but

creates a bigger mouthfeel than most cleaner strains.[316] For this beer, the strain was incredibly aggressive, fermentation finished in a matter of days, which meant the day three dry hop was at the tail end or end of fermentation, which potentially meant there were fewer proteins available for the dry hop polyphenols to bind to due to yeast precipitation.

Regarding clarity, it was much clearer than beers I typically make for the style. You can see pictures of the experiment on scottjanish.com. Granted, it isn't the kind of clarity you'd see in something like a Pilsner but compared to a typical hazy IPA, it was clear enough to see your finger holding the glass through the beer. In this case, it did appear that pairing an increase in undermodified proteins from the oat flour with dry hopping after fermentation led to increased clarity, which agrees with the research.

Another real-world example of a beer brewed with undermodified grains leading to a clearer beer is from Michael Tonsmeire, who documented in a Nov. 27, 2017, blog post at themadfermentationist.com results from a New England Pale Ale.[317] The grist of this particular beer consisted of 80% 2-row and 20% chit malt, which resulted in a much clearer beer than he anticipated. Although not brilliantly clear, it looked much more like an unfiltered West Coast IPA than a turbid hazy IPA, which could be in part from the decrease in haze-causing prolines from a shorter germination time of chit malt. Remember, a shorter germination would also leave more unmodified proteins in the grist, which are more likely to drop out of the beer and not be available to interact with polyphenols.

Hop Variety and Polyphenol Content

We know that polyphenols and proteins are important to beer haze, but the number of polyphenols of each hop variety contains may also play a small role. If you use large amounts of high-polyphenol varieties in the whirlpool, it seems more likely you could be increasing the chance of protein/polyphenol interactions early into fermentation.

Knowing the polyphenol content of hop varieties can also play a role in the astringency level of heavily hopped beers. For example, if you are going to dry hop with two different varieties and know one of them has higher concentrations of polyphenols, you could dry hop early into fermentation with the higher of the two and allow some of the active yeast to absorb a portion of the polyphenols (or the other way around, depending on your goal). The other variety can be dry hopped later, when fermentation has slowed or is complete.

Although I haven't come across a paper or database testing the average polyphenol content of the more than 200 hop varieties registered worldwide, I was given a guide to the various hop varieties in Germany. Included among the different hop analytics is the polyphenol content (EBC 7.14) of 22 different German varieties

Polyphenols represent a rather small portion of the hop as is seen among the following German varieties where the highest polyphenol content hops averaged 5%, the middle ground hops averaged 4.4%, and the lowest polyphenol varieties averaged just 3.6%. In general, hops with the highest content are classic aroma varieties, the middle ground ones are aroma varieties, and the lowest are bittering varieties. Although there are outliers, there is a pattern showing that hops with higher α-acid content have lower polyphenol concentration. Lower α-acid hops have more polyphenols. Below is the full data on the German hop polyphenol averages.

Hop Variety	Polyphenols (%w/w)	α-acids
Hallertau Blanc	5.4	8.5
Spalter	5.3	4.1
Saazer	5.3	3.2
Tettnanger	5.2	4
Spalter Select	4.9	5.1
Hallertauer Mfr.	4.6	4.1
Saphir	4.5	4.1
Smaragd	4.5	5.9
Hersbrucker Spat	4.4	3.1
Cascade	4.3	6
Hallertauer Maerkur	4.2	13.3
Perle	4.1	7.4
Hallertauer Tradition	4.1	6.2
Mandarina Bavaria	4.0	7.9
Polaris	4.0	18.6
Huell Melon	3.9	5.8
Northern Brewer	3.9	9.2
Herkules	3.8	16.7
Opal	3.7	7.9
Nugget	3.4	11.3
Hallertauer Taurus	3.1	15.9
Hallertauer Magnum	2.6	13.9

Fining Agents

One area worth mentioning as it relates to beer haze is the use of carrageenan (Irish moss or Whirlfloc) in the boil kettle. Carrageenan is not a moss, but is a polysaccharide found in red seaweed. Typically, carrageenan is added to the kettle with about 10-15 minutes left of the boil, which gives it enough time to dissolve in the wort (it won't dissolve below 140°F (60°C)). Speaking for myself, I have always added Irish moss to my beers only because it was considered good practice, and I didn't bother to challenge or even think much about the step. Of course, the whole reason to add Irish moss to the boil is to help remove wort-soluble proteins and beta-glucans (according to advertisements for the various products) that can later combine with polyphenols and lead to haze. Carrageenan removes protein by binding negatively-charged sulfate to positively-charged proteins, which eventually gets large enough to drop out of the beer.

Is it counterproductive to purposely create a mash high in proteins (with malted wheat or spelt) and beta-glucans (high percentage of flaked oats) and then intentionally add a supplement to remove those very two things?

Certain yeast strains like WY1318, as well as specific hop varieties high in total oil like Galaxy, seem to enhance the haze in IPAs according to interviews with brewers. Grist high in modified proteins like malted wheat will also help increase haze. In a typical NEIPA, there should be plenty of proteins available to interact with the heavy hopping rates without skipping on the Irish moss. I personally use it when brewing the style to help get proteins out that should otherwise settle and to aid in the creation of larger clumps of hot break that drop out in the kettle allowing for clearer beer going into the fermenter. On the commercial scale, this is nice because it's less gunk going through the heat exchanger.

Not only could adding Irish moss help the beer look less like gravy, it may also help reduce the harshness that excessive protein and polyphenol reactions can bring. I would like to see tests done measuring the impact of protein and polyphenol reactions with and without the use of a fining agent like Irish moss in the kettle. At the very least, if your beers are coming across astringent, it seems like a good idea to give it a shot.

What about other types of fining agents, like gelatin and Biofine Clear (a vegan alternative) potential impact on hazy IPAs? Surprising to some, we use Biofine Clear at Sapwood Cellars on some of our hazy beers, especially some that we plan on canning. In our experience, Biofine Clear doesn't impact the clarity substantially and might help to speed up the time the beer peaks. In other words, clarifiers might help drop some of the particulate in the beer that would otherwise take several days cold to drop. I would like to see lab tests in this area, but since filtering beer had more of an impact on the removal of hydrocarbons (the more woody and resinous compounds) and less so on the fruiter monoterpene alcohols, I suspect clarifying agents might have a similar result.

Key Findings

- Protein content can decrease during fermentation, likely degraded proteolytically by yeast or precipitating out with the yeast slurry. So, dry hopping early into fermentation could result in more haze via protein and polyphenol interactions.
- Dry hopping early into fermentation, when the pH is still high (like brew day dry hopping) may also slightly increase haze because the lower the pH, the less haze will form from protein and polyphenol reactions.
- Higher ABV hoppy beers may also be hazier because ethanol has been shown to decrease the precipitation of proteins and polyphenols.
- Because of higher proteolytic activity in malt (breakdown of proteins during malting) proteins are degraded, leading to smaller proteins. These smaller proteins are more likely to remain in suspension and available to bind to polyphenols to form haze. Malted grains can increase the protein and polyphenol interactions and unmalted can reduce the interaction.
- The breakdown of storage proteins into amino acids during the malting process increases the chance for haze because these new amino acids are capable of binding to polyphenols.
- In general, hops high in α-acids are lower in total polyphenol content. Likewise, hops low in α-acids are generally higher in total polyphenol content.

Chapter 14: Stability in Hazy IPAs

Brewing hazy IPAs can come with its challenges, the main one being shelf stability. I've had issues with hazy IPAs oxidizing very quickly – a common problem for many. A small amount of oxygen finding its way into a can or keg can cause darkening of color and drastic changes to the aroma and taste within days. This chapter looks at potential reasons why hazy IPAs are more susceptible to oxygen and potential methods to improve stability in the style.

Beer Oxidation

Oxygen is well known as the main enemy of fresh, delicious hoppy beer, which is why brewers will go to great lengths to avoid any pickup throughout their process. Oxygen needs to be converted to a radical activated form before it can react with other compounds in beer. This activation can be caused by trace metals in the beer, like iron or copper.[318]

One of the primary antioxidants in beer is sulfite (sulfur dioxide), which is produced by yeast during fermentation from the reduction of sulfate in water and grist material. Sulfite acts as an antioxidant by its ability to remove or scavenge the reactive oxygen species H_2O_2 (Hydrogen peroxide).[319] The recommended level for flavor stability in beer is about 8-9 mg/L. Levels of sulfur dioxide can increase in beer when fermentation is done at a high wort pH, low wort oxygenation, and low yeast pitching rates.[320] Sulphur dioxide can also be added to beer indirectly when using isinglass as a fining agent because it's used as a preservative in the production process.[321]

If iron or copper is present in small amounts in beer (for copper, levels as low 50 ppb can cause problems), it can trap oxygen introduced during brewing and packaging. This can lead to the initial formation of hydrogen peroxide, which can then initiate ethanol oxidation (1-hydroxyethyl radical). Sulfites can step in and help delay oxidation by being consumed through interaction with hydrogen peroxide. The more the sulfite level is depleted, the more iron and copper ions are likely present in the beer.[322]

The rate of beer staling significantly increases with copper, even more so than with iron, as iron is less reactive in beer. Copper can bind strongly to proteins, amino acids, and polyphenols,[323] which is why avoiding copper as much as possible seems like a good idea, especially in hazy IPAs where proteins and polyphenols are at such high levels.

Protein-Derived Thiols

Another avenue of protection from oxidation can come from protein-derived thiols acting as an antioxidant by quenching the 1-hydroxyethyl radical, which accumulate during aging.

Thiols from malts is an often overlooked variable when crafting recipes. In Chapter 11, I discuss how there is some potential for fruit-flavored thiols like 3MH (grapefruit) coming from malt that can be converted with the right yeast strain to 3MHA (passionfruit). Other than flavor impact from malt-derived thiols, there also appears to be a stability benefit to them.

How might protein thiol groups serve as antioxidants? I'll defer to the explanation by Marianne Lund and Mogens Anderson in their paper titled, *Detection of Thiol Groups in Beer and Their Correlation with Oxidative Stability:*

> Protein thiol groups are thought to react with H2O2, causing the formation of protein sulfenic acids that may react further with other protein thiol groups or small thiols to form mixed disulfides. Mixed disulfides may be reduced by either sulfite itself or other reducing compounds, resulting in the regeneration of the original protein thiol groups and thiosulfates that ultimately may be converted to sulfates. Regenerated thiol groups can participate in the new reaction cycles with H2O2 and, taken as a whole, act as a catalyst for the removal of hydrogen peroxide by sulfite.

Sulfites are the primary antioxidant in beer, and these protein-derived thiols act as a secondary antioxidant to encourage redox stability. It's difficult to know the total thiol content of your malts, but it has been found that total thiol content is highly correlated with total protein content, which makes sense.

A 2013 paper suggests that even though proteins interact with polyphenols and cause haze in beer, brewers might want to aim for higher protein content to enhance oxidative stability. The idea, of course, is that the more protein-derived thiols in the beer, the better stability.[324] But, it's not just proteins, but malts that are high in protein-derived thiols that will help with shelf life.

Looking through research on how to increase protein-derived thiols in hazy, hoppy beers to help with stability, led me to the lipid transfer protein (LTP1). Often studied for its positive role in head retention, the LTP1 protein was singled out as a possible candidate for playing a role in inhibiting oxidative reactions in beer, in part, because of its ability to withstand the various brewing conditions.[325]

To test out the antioxidative properties of the stable LTP1 protein, a paper experimented with three Australian lagers, one fresh off the production line ("fresh"), one aged for 12-weeks at 86°F (30°C) ("aged") and another for five years at 68°F (20°C) ("vintage"). The authors found that the Australian lager characteristics remained in the fresh and vintage beers but was lost in the aged beer. The flavor stability of the fresh and vintage beers was found to be correlated with the presence of the LTP1 protein. Essentially, the authors concluded that the presence of thiol-rich LTP1 indicates that the protein can play a prominent role in maintaining redox balance of beer from its free radical scavenging and antioxidant capacity in both fermentation and in packaged beer. [326] Using the results of the study, you can make a case for enhancing LTP1 proteins in hazy hoppy beers to maximize flavor stability after packaging.

Interestingly, the role of the LTP1 protein in promoting head retention may be in part because it's rich in the same free thiols that might also play a role in beer stability. Structurally, the LTP1 protein consists of 8 cysteine residues and it's likely this high content of thiol cysteine in the protein is the basis for its antioxidant effects.

So, to increase the protein-derived thiols to help with stability, we should be using grains high in the LTP1 protein. One potential way to do this is by brewing with a high percentage of undermodified grains. Like chit malt or Carapils as it was found that it's not until the LTP1 protein undergoes modifications during the germination, malting, and brewing process does it have a positive impact on beer foam.[327] Although the study was for beer foam, we are still interested in the LTP1 protein for stability. In addition, the LTP1 protein has been found to decrease in concentration during malting, which is likely decreased due to Maillard-reactions that occur during kilning.[328]

Although there is a lack of specific literature, I'm curious if the antioxidant benefits from LTP1 might also benefit from malting modifications like found above with head retention. If so, it would be interesting to put together parts of the research and speculate that if malting degrades LTP1 proteins (decreasing antioxidant potential) and germination may be required to get the beneficial effects of LTP1 (like with head retention), then under-modified malts may be ultimate sources of LTP1.

A real-life example of this theory is with an experimental beer I brewed (and discussed in Chapter 4) which consisted of a grist of 50% Briess Carapils (an undermodified malt) and 50% 2-row. Although not the focus of the experiment, I was amazed that this beer was one of the most stable hazy IPAs I had brewed. It remained consistent during dispensing in the keg, but what surprised me the most was a few bottles I filled from the keg and kept in the refrigerator for four months still showed similar characteristics to when it was fresh, except for reduced bright hop aroma. This beer was also absent of flaked oats, which may also help explain the stability (discussed later in the chapter).

This experimental beer may also have benefited in terms of stability from the lack of malted wheat. A study looking at mashes that consist of either 100% malted barley, 100% malted wheat, or 50/50% of barley/wheat found that with a grist higher in barley malt had more (LTP1) transferred into the final wort. The higher proportion of malted wheat beers had more middle molecular and haze relevant protein fractions, which aligns with the research in the haze chapter regarding the role of malted wheat and enhanced haze.[329]

If stability is an issue in your hazy beers, particularly if they are also very astringent coming from haze-inducing proteins interacting with polyphenols (likely also retaining more of the volatile green hop compounds like myrcene), it may be worth lowering the amount of malted wheat and replacing it with an undermodified grain. This may help increase LTP1 for stability (and head retention) and decrease the protein polyphenol interaction.

Mashing Conditions and Free Thiols

Another potential route to increasing free thiol content in beer is to ensure proper mashing conditions. The enzyme thiol oxidase, contained in barley malt, is activated in the presence of oxygen. This can then consume protein-derived free thiols from the malt, which are beneficial to beer stability. In other words, oxygen introduced during mashing could potentially increase free thiol oxidase activation.

Thiol oxidase is heat stable, meaning heat doesn't deactivate the enzyme at mash temperatures. It is impacted, however, by pH levels and malt storage. The higher the pH, the more active it is. It's significantly reduced when the pH is below 6.0, but the lower, the better. Even at a normal mashing pH of around 5.4, it still displayed some activity. Regarding malt storage, the longer it's stored, the lower the enzyme activity. It doesn't take much storage, however. After just one month, the thiol oxidase activity could be virtually eliminated.[330]

For most brewers, thiol oxidase shouldn't be of much concern, merely by the fact that by the time we get the malt, it is likely aged long enough to have the enzyme eliminated. However, for those using fresh malts, lowering the mash pH and avoiding oxygen uptake during the mash are good options to keep as many of the beneficial free thiols in the beer as possible.

Crystal Malts and Stability

Another potential factor in increasing the shelf life of hoppy beers is to avoid the use of crystal malts as a large percentage of the grist. The addition of such malts can reduce the oxidative stability of beer, because Maillard compounds in crystal malts are caramelized products that accelerate metal-catalyzed oxidation.[331] Any available oxygen in the beer would react quicker with any trace metals, like iron or copper. However, many professional breweries are making great hazy IPAs with a touch of crystal malt and aren't having accelerated stability issues. It's probably best to experiment with 5% or less in the grist for a touch of sweet malt character to play with fruity hop flavors but not compete for flavor or cause stability issues.

Manganese and Stability

When it comes to transition metal ions and their impact on oxidation in beer, the focus is primarily on iron and copper. But like those, manganese can also promote the staling of beer by converting ground state oxygen to reactive oxygen species (ROS).

A study that looked at metal reactions throughout the brewing process dosed wort with either copper, iron, or manganese. Copper was mainly reduced during wort boiling and lost into the trub.

Fermentation had a significant impact on the iron concentrations, removing most of the addition to levels seen in the control beer, which had no iron added. Like iron, fermentation reduced most of the copper, but not as much as with the iron. The final concentration was a quarter of the total amount of copper added. Manganese, on the other hand, resulted in almost half of the added amount still detectable after fermentation. In other words, unlike copper and iron, manganese sticks around better after fermentation.

After aging the beers with added metal additions for a month at 82°F (28°C), both the iron and copper beers had similar flavor stability to the control beer with no added minerals. The beer with added manganese had accelerated deterioration with a prominent sherry aroma after the same storage period.[332]

Another paper looking at metal concentrations in beer after fermentation confirmed that both iron and copper are significantly reduced in beer during barley fermentations. However, again, manganese was found in detectable amounts after fermentation and increased with each re-pitch of yeast. Each time yeast is harvested and pitched into another beer, it consumes less manganese content, which is also true with iron and copper. Also, for what it's worth, the study found that malted buckwheat and quinoa had much higher concentrations of manganese than barley and subsequently had higher amounts in the final beer.[333]

How much manganese is typically in beer? A study looking at manganese concentrations in fifteen different commercial beers found relatively low levels for most of the styles, but dry hopped styles had higher levels.[334] For example, an Imperial IPA had 0.21 ppm of manganese and two different pale ales had 0.23 ppm and 0.15 ppm, compared to an American light lager with just 0.05 ppm.

Because the beers with dry hop additions had higher manganese concentration, the paper then looked at the manganese content in hops themselves and found they contain a high amount of manganese. Of the hops tested, Columbus, had nearly twice the amount as the others. Pacific Jade and Galaxy had two of the lowest levels of manganese.

Hops	Manganese (ppm)
Columbus	101.9
Cluster	61.6
Fuggle	59
Cascade	56.3
Centennial	55.9
Tettnang	54.9
Citra	54.5
Saaz	54.2
Mosaic	52
Pacific Jade	38.1
Galaxy	33.1

It also appears that the duration of dry hopping can impact manganese concentrations. The same study measured the manganese level in beers over the course of a fifteen-day dry hop and found that manganese levels peak after about five to seven days. Interestingly, the warmer the dry hop temperature, the more manganese pickup into the beer. The test showed that dry hopping at 68°F (20°C) had 0.10 mg/L more manganese than the beer dry hopped cold at 38°F (3°C). The data is starting to build in this book in favor of cooler and short duration dry hopping.

The authors took the study a step further and found that of the metals that can cause oxidation (iron, copper, and manganese) there was proportionally more leaching of manganese into beer through dry hopping than the other problematic metals. For example, iron had much higher levels in the hop pellets themselves, but after dry hopping, was measured in lower concentrations than manganese. It's surprising that after dry hopping, the study found that all three metals were at high enough levels to cause stalling via the reactive oxygen species (ROS), but this was especially true for manganese.

So, dry hopping can impart problematic metals into beer which can accelerate staling, but it's the manganese in hops that are the most efficient at extracting, especially the longer and warmer the dry hop duration. Although we don't have an exhaustive list yet, certain varieties like Columbus can also cause slightly faster stalling due to higher levels of manganese and could be removed from dry hopping if you are having oxidation issues, but this could have more to do with the growing conditions than the variety of hop itself.

Malts are another potential source of manganese and were also tested in the above study. In general, malted grains have much less manganese than hops, and most of the malts tested averaged around 15 ppm (compared to around 50 ppm in most hop varieties). However, you obviously use way more malt to make beer than hops. Interestingly, the grains that showed the highest manganese potential were flaked oats, which had more than three times the amount compared to a pale 2-row variety. Another malt that had slightly greater-than-average manganese content was malted wheat with 18 ppm.

Digging a little deeper into potential sources of the pro-oxidative metal manganese, I found a paper looking at manganese as it relates to yeast health. The authors found that unmalted barley has 40% higher levels of manganese than malted barley. The decrease in manganese in malted barley is likely due to metal losses in the "roots and shoots discarded after malting." If these manganese losses are caused by the processes of malting itself, it's probably safe to assume that most malted versions of a grain will contain less manganese than the flaked version. For example, flaked wheat or spelt (or even flour) in mashes would likely increase the manganese content in beer. Remember, manganese by ingredients are much more likely to stick around throughout the brewing processes compared to other metals.

So, what does this all mean? The typical recipe for a hazy, hoppy beer often has a high percentage of flaked grains, malted wheat, and is also heavily dry hopped. It appears the hazy, hoppy style is destined to not only produce hop bombs, but manganese bombs! This may help explain why the style is so sensitive to oxygen and can have a short shelf life with the introduction (even at low levels) of oxygen at packaging.

To try and test the research, I brewed a hoppy, hazy beer high in manganese to see how quickly it might oxidize (because there's nothing more I enjoy than five-gallons of oxidized NEIPA on tap). To do this, I chose a grist of approximately 20% flaked oats, 20% sprouted spelt flour, and 60% 2-row. This grist should have a high potential for manganese with 40% of the bill consisting of unmalted grains, of which oats have high manganese content and spelt, which has over two times the amount as barley.[335] Because manganese can get extracted from hops during dry hopping, I dry hopped the beer with six ounces (170 grams) of hops.

To minimize oxygen introduction in the experiment, the beer fermented in a keg and was transferred into a purged serving keg via CO_2. The serving keg spent 24 hours at room temperature, then went into the fridge where it stayed cold at 40°F (4°C). After just three weeks in the keezer, the beer was already showing noticeable signs of oxidation, turning a few shades darker.

I sent a sample of the beer to Ward Labs to be tested for total metal concentrations to see how the combination of spelt flour, flaked oats, and heavy dry hopping played a role. The manganese content was through the roof! Below are my results compared to a sampling of commercial hoppy beers mentioned earlier in the chapter. As you can see from the results, my oxidized beer had approximately a 3.35-fold increase from the highest tested commercial beer.

Beer	**Result (ppm)**
My Hazy IPA	1.0
Commercial Pale Ale	0.23
Commercial Imperial IPA	0.21
IPA	0.11

Based on the research, it does seem logical to conclude that the manganese content in my oxidized beer likely played a significant role in its early demise. If you are having trouble with hazy, hoppy beers oxidizing, it makes sense to experiment with ways to reduce the manganese content in your beer, in addition to avoiding oxygen at every stage post-yeast pitch.

One obvious way to reduce manganese content is to avoid, or use less, non-malted grains in the grist. For example, at Sapwood

Cellars, we are hesitant to use flaked oats in beers that will be canned, opting often for malted oats where the manganese level should be less. Short dry hop durations at lower temperatures can also help avoid peak extraction (as well as reduce the chance of hop creep).

I also sent a sample of this beer to Oregon Brew Lab to be tested for total protein content via the ASBC Beer-11C method. Although this test doesn't differentiate between the types of proteins in the beer (to precisely know the LTP1 concentration), it does give a total amount in grams per twelve ounces. I also sent a sample of a hazy IPA I had on tap that had not oxidized quickly and was made with a different grist of all malted 2-row and chit malt, which should be higher in the LTP1 protein due to less modification from the malting processes. Below are the results.

Oxidized NEIPA Recipe Grist:
60% 2-Row
19% Flaked Oats
19% Sprouted Spelt Flour
2% Acidulated Malt (pH adjustment)
Measured Proteins in finished beer: 1.5 g/12oz

Non-oxidized NEIPA Grist:
62.5% 2-Row
35.5% Chit Malt
2.0% Acidulated Malt (pH adjustment)
Measured Proteins in finished beer: 2.2 g/12oz

As you can see from the results, the beer that oxidized within three weeks had approximately 47% less total protein than the hazy IPA that didn't oxidize. Although, to be fair, the experiment wasn't exactly a true side-by-side. The oxidized beer was a slightly smaller beer with about three fewer pounds of grains in the mash. However, this is only approximately 12% less total grain compared to the 47% increase in total proteins.

These results are also interesting considering the non-oxidized beer was made with just 2-row and under modified chit malt and resulted in a higher total protein content, despite oats and spelt having more protein than barley. This would align with the research discussed in Chapter 5 showing that unmalted gluten proteins are heavier in molecular weight because they are not degraded during mashing and are more likely to drop out. So, it's not just the amount of protein to consider when crafting recipes, but the type of protein.

Hot-Side Hop Timing

It's often discussed in brewing circles whether mash hopping (adding hops to the mash) or first wort hopping (hops added to the boil kettle before filling with wort) is beneficial. Some brewers argue it's a waste of hops, others claim the bitterness level is smoother or less intense. I'm going to stay out of that debate entirely, but instead look at early hot-side hopping as a potential way to increase the oxidative stability of beer.

A study released in 2016 examined the impact of different hop timing had on the pro-oxidative iron ions. [336] In the study, five different beers were brewed to have identical bitterness levels using Hallertauer Magnum CO2 hop extract (α-acid). Below is when the beers were dosed with the differing hop extract to obtain the same bitterness level:

Reference Beer - start of the boil only
Mash Hop Beer - mash-in and at start of the boil
Divided Hop Beer - start of boil, 30 minutes, end of boil, and whirlpool
First Wort Beer - first wort, 30 minutes, and end of boil
Continuous Hop Dosage Beer - start of boil, five-minute intervals starting at 30 minutes

The test showed that the beer's iron concentrations were "clearly affected" by the hop dosage. Specifically, the mash hopping beer, the divided hop dosage beer, and the continuous hop dosage beer resulted in the lowest iron concentrations. The reference beer, which only had the α-acids added, led to the highest iron level. The beers with more frequent hopping had reduced iron contents of up to ~30% and improved oxidative stabilities compared to the reference beer.

Removing pro-oxidative metal ions at these early stages via hops might be a way to prevent faster oxidation later. The authors of the study suggest that α-acids in hops can diminish oxidative reactions during wort boiling and in beer. Hops may also react with intermediates in the Maillard reaction or block or inhibit oxidative pathways of the Maillard reaction. Since specialty malts like crystal have pro-oxidative properties, mash hopping may be particularly helpful when these are incorporated into the grist. So, using small amounts of hops in the mash and early in the boil may help stability.

A study looking directly at hop acids and their ability to complex metal ions helps us to understand why the layering of hops is beneficial in promoting beer stability. In the study, hop acids (α-acids, β-acids, and iso-α-acids, and hop acid mixture) were incubated with various metal ions (iron, copper, calcium, magnesium, manganese, and zinc) and screened for changes in concentrations. The results showed that the addition of hop acids was capable of complexing iron and copper metal ions, which are both problematic in accelerating oxidation in beer. The hop acids did not have as much of an impact on the other four metals. As for the different hop acids, α-acids had more of a positive impact than β-acids and iso-α-acids, but the mixture of them all was the most effective.

Another variable tested was how the pH levels might impact the ability of hop acids to complex metals. The authors found that the higher the pH, the more efficient the hop acids were in complexing both iron and copper (reducing the problematic metals in finished beer, which should enhance stability). The pH levels tested were 4.3, 5.2, and 5.7 to mimic beer mash levels and final beer levels, with 4.3 being a common final beer pH. The effectiveness of a higher pH is likely a reason why mash hopping was found to be ideal in the previous study to promote beer stability. When hops are added to the mash (which is at a higher pH level above 5.0) the introduction of α-acids are more effective at complexing more of the iron and copper ions. As an example of how hops can complex metal ions, hop α-acids were found to be capable of complexing nearly 85% of copper available at a pH of 5.7.[337] Adding mash hops prior to adjusting for the pH may even further boost the complexing of metals since the pH is higher.

I reached out to the author, P.C. Wietstock at the Technische Universität Berlin, to learn how the research would apply to hazy hoppy beers where few bittering hops are used. For increased flavor stability, Wietstock suggested to dose hops early in the brewing process, even when only small portions are used to keep bitterness low. For a flavor-forward hoppy beer, this could mean dividing up the bittering portion of the hops and layer them into your beer. For example, small portion in the mash, again in the boil kettle, with typical hopping to follow.

I also asked Wietstock about the high concentration of manganese in oats and if early hop additions could potentially help with any oxidizing issues from the mineral element. He was unaware of data suggesting hop α-acids will react with manganese, but they are also capable of quenching organic radicals, which are formed as follow-up products of radical reactions that can arise from transition metals like manganese.

So, layering hop additions can be used as a tool in brewing to reduce the amount of metals in beer that can cause oxidation, mainly from oxygen introduction during brewing like during transfers, dry hopping, and packaging. This can be especially important for homebrewers where negative effects of oxygen introduction are magnified in comparison to large commercial brewers.

Copper and α-acid Experiment

While I was doing research on α-acids and their ability to complex metal ions, I happened to be sipping on a homebrewed mixed-fermented peach sour made with a high percentage of flaked quinoa. The beer had had a strong penny-like copper flavor which raised my suspicions about its copper levels. So, I sent it to Ward Laboratories, Inc. to get tested for metal concentrations. Below are the results.

Metal	Concentration (ppm)
Iron	0.57
Copper	4.96
Manganese	0.55

For the love of copper, this beer was tested extremely high at 4.96 ppm, which is clearly a bad thing in terms of both taste and stability. Brewers want copper levels extremely low in finished beer to both to avoid a metallic taste as well as to prevent the quick oxidation of beer. The recommended level of copper in wort is <0.25 ppm.[338] Compared to a hazy IPA I also had tested at only 0.26 ppm of copper; you can see how high this beer is in copper.

Where is the copper coming from? Looking at a study of beers made with 100% malted quinoa or barley found that copper levels were substantially higher in quinoa beers. The malted barley beer measured just 0.018 mg/L of copper, whereas the quinoa beer measured 0.075 mg/L, which is about four times the amount.[339]

It's likely that some of the copper in this beer was from using a large percentage of flaked quinoa. However, based on the research, it seems very unlikely that all the 4.96 ppm was quinoa's fault.

Where could all the copper be coming from? It makes sense to next look at peaches, the other non-traditional ingredient in the beer.

Fruit and vegetable plants can take up heavy metals by absorbing them from airborne deposits, through metal-rich soils via the root systems, and by the water used throughout the plant's life.[340] So, it seems possible some pickup of copper could have happened, but enough to explain the massive amount in this beer? Knowing nothing about growing peaches, I started researching various treatments used to control diseases when I stumbled across an article titled, "Peach Disease – Bacterial Spot Differentiation from Copper Injury" on the Penn State Extension website.

The article was written by Kari Peter an assistant professor of tree fruit pathology, who has expertise in various fruit diseases. Peter writes that copper will kill fungi and bacteria, and when a copper solution is sprayed on peach trees, copper ions are gradually released from deposits each time the plant surface becomes wet with rain. This gradual release of copper protects against plant pathogens and acts as a fumigant/bactericide treatment.

I contacted Peter and explained that I was trying to figure out the source of the high copper content in a beer which had contact with eleven pounds of peaches. I was curious if it was plausible that the treatment of the trees with a copper solution for disease prevention could be a major source of the metal. Peter said that there is a high probability the copper came from the peaches, but the variety of the peach plays a role as well as the region in which it was grown.

Peter explained that bacterial spot is a troublesome disease for East Coast peach growers and there aren't very many control options, which is why copper is often used because it's the most effective for managing the disease. Both the peaches and I are on the East Coast, so it seems we are onto something.

Since my peaches were organic, I figured all of this might not even matter. I was wrong. It turns out that copper treatment is the natural option for a lot of disease prevention. To avoid the issue, Peter recommends using peaches that are more resistant to bacterial spot. Because of the genetics of such varieties, they require fewer copper treatments.

Ok, enough about peaches, right? Bringing this all back to the important role hop acids can play in complexing problematic metals like copper, I thought this was the perfect opportunity to test the research. I wanted to try and dry hop the beer to see if the extracted α-acids might complex some of the copper.

I first bottled off a handful of bottles of the pre-dry hopped from the keg to later compare to the dry hopped beer. There are a few things to consider when adding dry hops for α-acid purposes at this point in the beer's life. For one, the low pH of the beer (3.4) should impact the α-acid solubility, as will the colder serving temperature, which could alter the amount of complex formation with copper. To try and encourage α-acid solubility, I chose to bring the keg back to room temperature for an extended dry hop of two weeks. I first purged the hops with CO2 and then added them to the keg in a fine mesh nylon bag and purged the keg to minimize oxygen after the hops were added.

I wanted to overdo the α-acid content for experimentation purposes, so I dry hopped with one ounce of Citra Cryo Hops (24-26 %AA) to what remained of the keg, which I estimated to be about two gallons.

After dry hopping for two weeks, I put the keg back in the fridge for another two weeks with the dry hops remaining in the keg. When it was time to taste test, I had no problem identifying each beer by aroma alone, which isn't unexpected after dry hopping with Citra. The Citra dry hopped beer had a softer aroma that was much more candy-like. The pre-dry hopped beer had a sharper, funky edge that still had a metallic copper aroma.

The only way to know for sure if the α-acids from the dry hop lowered measurable copper ions was to send another sample of the dry hopped version of the beer to the lab for more testing. The results showed the copper levels were dramatically reduced, all the way to below the recommended <0.25 ppm level for beer! I expected to see a reduction in copper, especially after tasting the beer, but I didn't think it would be this massive. Going from the starting copper level of 4.96 ppm to 0.23 ppm is about a 21-fold reduction.

Both the literature and my own experiment shows that the acids from hops can help lower problematic metals in beer and in turn, improve shelf life. Something as simple as layering hops early in the brewing processes can have a positive impact and seems worth experimenting with.

Packaging and Storing Hoppy Beer

What impact does beer aging have on its sensory changes? Dalgiesh studied this in detail in 1977 and developed a plot of the changes over time. In general, as beer ages, it will likely start to pick up a sweeter taste that increases or develop caramel, burnt sugar, and toffee-like aromas.[341] Also likely increasing in beer as it ages is a cardboard-like flavor, which Meilgaard found constantly increases until reaching a maximum and then can back off a touch.[342] Other factors can play a major role in how a beer ages, for example, if a beer is poorly packaged or has a great deal of headspace in a bottle it will deteriorate quickly and may see an increase in what's called a "ribes" flavor, which is described as having an odor of blackcurrant leaves.[343]

How a beer is stored after packaging also plays an important role in how well it ages. The warmer a beer is stored the quicker the original flavors (especially with hoppy beers) decrease and other oxidized cardboard-like flavors increase as one study found that lager beers stored at 86°F (30°C) compared to 68°F (20°C) had increase cardboard-like characteristics.[344] It's not just that new oxidized flavors can develop in beers, but the original qualities of a fresh beer can decrease with time. For example, desirable fruity and floral esters may decrease in intensity with time, which may be just as important as the development of the previously described stale flavors.[345]

The bitterness intensity and quality of beer can also be impacted by aging. Specifically, a study of five different commercial beers were aged in brown bottles in dark conditions for a year at 68°F (20°C) and the result was a degradation between 10-15% of initial bitter substances. Most surprising was that in these same beers, the change in linalool (often used as a marker to determine hoppiness) remained relatively constant, suggesting that the loss of the desired fresh hop aroma may be more of a result of flavor competition with other staling flavors and not the actual loss of the hop oil compounds.[346]

Another interesting result in the above study is that of the five aged commercial beers, the one with the lowest pH (3.9) also had the lowest measured levels of linalool. The authors looked at this more closely a few years later and found that the lower pH did seem to influence the linalool reduction. Specifically, they found linalool decreased about 5% from a beer pH of 4.5 to 4.0 and decreased about 17% from a pH of 4.5 to 3.5.[347] It would be interesting to see follow-up studies to see if a higher final beer pH might help retain important hop compounds, particularly fruity monoterpene alcohols.

One way to potentially increase the shelf life of hazy hoppy beers for homebrewers is to avoid bottling and upgrade to kegging. Hoppy beer sitting at room temperature for the estimated two weeks during carbonation time may be doing more harm than good when it comes to getting the fresh hop character you're striving for. Each bottle, depending on the method used, can also pick up a small amount of oxygen during filling which may lead to quicker oxidation, especially if refermentation is delayed.

Another downside to bottling hoppy beers comes from the crown liners on the inside of the caps, which can absorb some of the hop compounds. However, the compounds most impacted in this study were the more volatile green and woody compounds. For example, the sesquiterpene hydrocarbons (myrcene, humulene, and cadinene) were found only in the liners and not in the beer. The fruitier alcohols didn't migrate to the liners, but some fruit-forward esters did, especially the longer chain fatty acid esters. Of these that were found in the liner were ethyl octanoate and ethyl hexanoate. In further testing, the researchers found that within just 18 days of storage, about 80% of the hydrocarbons were present in the liners.[348] If you have a hazy IPA that's extremely astringent and green, try bottling it from a keg with a cap with a crown liner and see if it settles down a bit.

One often overlooked variable when bottling or natural keg condition (adding a priming sugar solution for carbonation), is adding fresh yeast at the same time the sugar is added. After primary fermentation, most of the yeast has flocculated to the bottom of the fermentation vessel and if cold crashed, even more of the yeast is left behind. The mass reduction of yeast could cause problems with the addition of priming sugar and the subsequent refermentation combined with the stress of the high alcohol environment and pressure (with the bottle capped or keg sealed). Also, the yeast that is still available to ferment the newly introduced sugar may be of reduced health as cell membranes may be depleted in sterols and unsaturated fatty acids which can result in a reduction in sugar uptake and delay the conditioning processes.[349]

What type of yeast should you consider when adding for quick and healthy refermentation during condition? Quick yeast conditioning activity with the addition of active dried yeast has been studied to be a more consistent choice than using cropped yeast from primary fermentation. Here you would top crop yeast around day three of fermentation and add it back during conditioning.[350] Active dried yeast are grown in the presence of air, and the cells contain a sterol-rich membranes that help with the quick assimilation of sugars and cell division.[351] The makeup of dried yeast might reduce lag time and accelerate oxygen removal. Dried yeast also benefits from the ease of use because you can easily measure out desired amounts by weight and quickly hydrate it (generally with ten times its weight in water).

So, if dried yeast it best, does it matter what strain we use to natural bottle or keg condition beer? In a study of five different dried yeast strains used to bottle condition, the authors found the strains produced different final gravities, different flavors via higher alcohols and esters, and different refermentation time frames, including the initial yeast growth. It does seem like the yeast strain used to bottle can have an impact on final flavors. The authors here also suggest that using dried yeast over harvested yeast (or no repitched yeast at all) may lead to enhanced CO_2 production just from healthier yeast.[352]

Overall, it seems like a good practice to pitch some fresh yeast into a beer that will be naturally carbonated to ensure a healthy and quick refermentation. Regarding how much yeast to pitch, a good starting place is around two grams of dried yeast for a typical five-gallon batch hydrated in twenty grams of water.

One dried yeast strain I've had success with for refermentation in hoppy beers is CBC-1 from Lallemand. This particularly strain is selected for refermentation because it is resistant to high alcohol, has a neutral flavor profile (esters and alcohols), and has quick and vigorous fermentation. The only downside is that CBC-1 is a killer yeast, which means it can kill zombies (and other yeast strains sensitive to the killer toxin).[353] The killer aspect isn't as big of a deal for refermentation because primary fermentation is over. However, it should be treated like intentional bacteria in sour beers in that careful attention should be paid to sanitation and cleaning after it's used to not contaminate future primary fermentations.

Key Findings

- Oxygen needs to be converted to a radical activated form before it can react with other species in beer. This activation can be caused by trace metals in beer, like iron, copper, or manganese.
- Sulfite is the primary antioxidant in beer, but protein-derived thiols act as a secondary antioxidant (particularly the lipid transfer protein LTP1).

- Crystal malts reduce the oxidative stability of beer by accelerating metal-catalyzed oxidation and should be kept at low levels in hazy IPAs.
- Problematic metal ions like copper, iron, and manganese are reduced during the brewing process from wort boiling, lost to trub, and during fermentation. Fermentation removes most of the copper and iron, but manganese will remain in higher amounts if present in the wort and can lead to quicker oxidation.
- Different hop varieties have varying concentration of manganese which can be extracted into beer during dry hopping. Manganese extracts more efficiently during dry hopping than iron and copper, even when it's in lower concentrations in the hop.
- Shorter dry hop durations and colder dry hop temperatures can reduce the amount of manganese extracted during dry hopping.
- Unmalted grains have more manganese than malted grains.
- Flaked oats have more than three times the amount of manganese than malted barley.
- Periodic and early hopping of the mash and wort can improve the oxidative stabilities of beer primarily by introducing α-acids which can complex iron and copper metal ions.
- When bottle or keg conditioning hoppy beers, it's best to add some fresh dried yeast to encourage healthy and quick refermentation.

Chapter 15: Tips from Commercial Breweries

Although the science of brewing hoppy beers is extremely fascinating and inspirational, sometimes the science doesn't always align with brewing results. When it comes down to it, what matters most is what the product in the glass tastes like, even if the methods used go against some of the research. To bring in some of this real-world experience into the equation, I thought it would be helpful to reach out to some of the breweries making the best (and most consistent) hoppy beers in the country to see how they are getting such great results!

Other Half Brewing

Founded by Sam Richardson, Matt Monahan, and Andrew Burman in Brooklyn, NY, Other Half has become known for producing some of the best hazy hoppy beers in the country. On release days, large lines of customers wait hours to take home a four-pack of their hop-forward beers.

Other Half has been instrumental in the quick rise of hazy IPAs by popularizing the style. They were also one of the first breweries to use the phrase and incorporate double dry hopping ("DDH"). Others in the industry have adopted the term and practice it with regularity.

Because experimentation is such a big part of the brewery (brewing a couple hundred different beers a year) I chatted with Sam in general terms on how Other Half is consistently producing such great hoppy beers.

Other Half is lucky to brew with Brooklyn water, which offers a neutral, low mineral profile allowing them to easily add additional minerals based on the style. For example, most of their hazy, hoppy beers favor calcium chloride additions to help enhance body, especially when brewing lower ABV beers. They will often mash these lower ABV beers as high as 160°F (71°C) to boost the mouthfeel. The lower alcohol beers might also get a higher percentage of protein-rich grains to compensate for the lower alcohol content (again, for mouthfeel).

Sam stressed that it's important not to over-hop smaller low ABV beers to the point they become astringent. It's been their experience that the higher ABV beers can handle larger hopping rates. Research in the book also suggests that larger whirlpool additions in lower ABV beers (preferably at reduced temperatures and with lower α-acid hops) can help boost mouthfeel and likely hop saturated flavor in low ABV beers.

Although the focus is on late whirlpool additions and heavy dry hopping in hazy IPAs, Other Half still likes to include a 60-minute bittering addition to help produce a more rounded and complex hot-side flavor profile. They have also found that just a little bit of bitterness in a hazy IPA helps to prevent a beer from becoming too flabby and one-dimensional, providing a bit of pop to a soft hop-saturated mouthfeel.

Sam shared that their higher ABV hop-forward beers benefit from early boil hop additions (for increased IBUs) to help balance out higher finishing gravities. In terms of hop usage, their whirlpool additions are smaller than their dry hop charges. Interestingly, their experience has tended to show that lower dry hopping rates can produce a beer that peaks earlier and requires less conditioning time but comes at the expense of hop flavor and aroma dropping off quicker. On the other hand, higher dry hopping rates tend to get them a beer with extended flavor and aroma but requires a little more conditioning time.

Despite the common suggestion that hoppy beers should be consumed as quickly as possible, hazy, hoppy beers tend to benefit from a bit of conditioning time. In fact, this was shared by pretty much every brewery I spoke to for the book and may be one of the biggest misconceptions of the style. Other Half, for example, suggest consumers sit on their beers for about a week or two for the best drinking experience. Its important cans are kept cold however, as warm storage or multiple temperature swings can cause the beers (and the hop aroma and flavor) to drop off sooner. In a perfect world, if tank space and time weren't a factor for Sam (it's a business after all), he would probably prefer to let his hoppy beers sit in the brite tank for about a week, rather than just a few days, to mature before canning.

Other Half is fortunate to have an advantage over homebrewers and small breweries in that each year they go to Yakima, WA for the hop harvest to select hops for the coming year. Unlike most hops that homebrewers can purchase, which are often blends of various lots, Other Half gets to pick individual hop lots to be pelletized. Citra from one lot can be very different in both measured hop compounds and sensory experience than Citra from another lot. In Other Half's case, they are looking for hops that are rich in tropical fruit-like flavors with very little to no vegetal and onion characteristics. In Sam's opinion, the annual hop selection process is one of the most important things Other Half does each year, which speaks highly to the practice.

Another key component unique to Other Half's hoppy beers is the use of a centrifuge, which helps to remove solid matter (like yeast and hops) from the beer. The use of a centrifuge makes economic sense if you are producing enough beer to justify the cost, because you can see an increase in yield with less beer loss to hops and trub (Other Half saw about a 5-10% yield increase). The use of a centrifuge may also reduce the conditioning time a hazy beer needs before peaking by removing more of the greener hydrocarbons from the beer. The centrifuge didn't change their approach to brewing hazy hoppy beers in terms of recipe or processes tweaks and certainly hasn't made a drastic difference in clarity as their beers are still plenty hazy! You can see so for yourself by checking out the beer on the back cover of this book!

Prison City Pub and Brewery

Prison City Pub and Brewery, located in Auburn, NY, didn't set out to be known as a business recognized around the country for its hazy-style IPAs. In fact, their goal was to focus on sour beer upon opening in 2014. It took Prison City about three months to even brew an IPA, which was a West Coast-style beer called Riot. Their first attempt at a hazy IPA, Mass Riot, quickly altered the course of the brewery with the help of Paste Magazine. In 2016, *Paste Magazine* ranked Mass Riot first out of a blind tasting of 247 different IPAs, an unbelievable feat considering it was their first attempt at the style! Again in 2018, Mass Riot placed sixth in the blind tasting. It didn't take long for hoppy beer lovers to start making the trip to Upstate New York to taste the winning IPA and Prison City quickly became an IPA expert, rebrewing the beer to keep up with demand. Not surprisingly, they made the top ten again in a 2018 blind tasting of 151 Pale Ales with a beer called Illusion of Knowledge.

Ben Maeso, the head brewer at Prison City, is a believer in yeast blending to try and incorporate positive characteristics that each strain might bring to a beer. For Mass Riot, Ben uses a blend measured by weight of 75% London Ale III and 25% Chico (or WLP001). Because one strain may start to dominate the blend, they will only go about three generations of re-pitches before starting over with a freshly measured blend. Ben doesn't like the lower attenuation of London Ale III, which he attributes to a beer that's "too full on the palate." The Chico blend of Mass Riot should help London Ale III attenuate the beer a little more, leaving a slightly drier beer. Despite mashing on the lower end of the range for hazy hoppy beers at 150-151°F (65°C-66°C), the blend of strains attenuates a 7% hop-forward beer to a final gravity of about 1.014-1.015, which Ben says is about the sweet spot for Prison City beers.

Regarding grist for hoppy beers, Prison City enjoys a base malt that consists of a 50/50 split of Pilsner and Vienna malt. The Vienna brings a hint of complexity to the beer without dominating like a crystal malt. The base malt is paired with the heavy use of flaked oats and wheat to help with the soft mouthfeel and the appearance. The mouthfeel is also boosted using chloride-heavy water. If they want to boost the gravity of an IPA, they might add approximately 10% of the grist total of dextrose or brewers' crystals (which are part dextrose and maltose and mimics a malt extract fermentation to maintain body and mouthfeel).

Hot-side hopping of Mass Riot consists of a small, ten IBU bittering charge with pellets at the start of boiling, followed by another small bittering charge with ten minutes left in the boil. The focus on flavor comes with heavy whirlpool additions of approximately 1 lbs./bbl. Ben has played with adjusting the whirlpool temperature to 170°F (76°C) before adding the whirlpool charge vs. adding the hops right at flameout, but he couldn't tell much of a difference with the final hop flavor in the resulting beers.

Mass Riot is dry hopped with Simcoe, Citra, and Mosaic (lighter on Mosaic and Simcoe) at a rate of about 2-3 lbs./bbl. Rarely will they dry hop over 3 lbs./bbl. They stagger their dry hop additions, which research shows could help with extraction efficiency. They also try to boost extraction by agitating the beer while it's dry hopping with one short burst of 20 PSI of CO2 (per dry hop charge) to encourage the hops to get into suspension.

The first dry hop charge is about 1 lbs./bbl and the second addition is 1-2lbs./bbl. The timing of the dry hopping depends on if they are planning to harvest the yeast or not. When harvesting, they will wait to dry hop until after terminal gravity is reached and then soft crash the beer, harvest, and add the first dry hop charge. When they aren't harvesting the yeast, they can dry hop with some active fermentation still occurring. To help with any oxygen finding its way into the beer when dry hopping after fermentation is complete, they will sometimes add simple sugars with the yeast to encourage a small amount of fermentation to scrub oxygen. Total contact time with dry hops is typically around seven days.

Prison City has experimented with recirculating dry hops with success, which research shows will increase the speed and amount of hop extraction. They have found the pump type used can make a difference, a low shear pump with soft points helps give them less "green" hop bite. When recirculating dry hops, they will do so under pressure for a short period of about two to four hours.

Prison City's heavily hopped beers spend about five to seven days in a brite tank where some of the hop astringency will settle out. Before filling the tank, they will do a long slow trickle of CO2 to purge as much oxygen as possible before adding the fermented beer. Their preference is for less headspace in the brite tank to improve aroma, which could suggest that with larger headspace volumes, while CO2 is carbonating the beer, it could also be pushing out aromatics into the empty headspace. Like Other Half, Prison City suggests that their beers are best after they have cold-conditioned for a few weeks in the can.

Reuben's Brews

Founded in 2012 by Adam and Grace Robbings, Rueben's Brews is one of the most decorated breweries I spoke with in preparation for the book (over 150 medals in five years). Known for their great execution across a variety of styles, Reuben's Brews was recommended to me by another prominent brewer saying they were making one of the best hazy IPAs in the Pacific Northwest.

I sat down with Adam at the brewery to discuss his background and general approach to brewing hoppy beers. As an NHC medal-winning homebrewer, it became clear why Adam has become such a knowledgeable professional brewer. On the homebrew level, Adam was brewing large batches using a 25-gallon system and splitting the large batch four ways to test the smallest of variables. It helped him improve his processes, recipes, and palate.

When it comes to brewing hoppy beers on the commercial scale, Adam finds one of the most important things is to "get the stage right." In other words, yeast choice and hop selection matter, but if your process isn't dialed in, you can only go so far. Recipe formulation and science are important variables to consider when brewing a hoppy beer, but if you are allowing too much oxygen in post-fermentation, for example, it can all be for nothing.

Adam has found that whirlpool additions can often come with a lot of IBUs, especially when the hops are added right at flameout and isomerization is still relatively high at the near-boiling temperatures. In fact, Adam views a whirlpool addition more like a 30-minute boil addition. Interestingly, layering whirlpool additions is often done at Reuben's, which research suggests could result in a more complex mix of hop compounds finding their way into the fermenter.

One trick Adam shared when trying to reduce isomerization from large whirlpool additions is to drop the temperature of the wort quickly after flameout by diluting the wort with filtered cold water. In other words, they will brew a beer with a higher gravity than they intend and at flameout, add cool water to the whirlpool, diluting the gravity as well as quickly reducing the temperature of the wort. This could be a good way to try and lock in aromatics from whirlpool additions, reduce the load on the chiller, and reduce bitterness from the late-stage hopping.

Before dry hopping, Adam likes to soft crash the yeast and harvest for subsequent pitches. This is another common difference I've noticed among commercial brewers and homebrewers. Homebrewers are often less concerned with harvesting yeast and will dry hop extremely early into fermentation, whereas most commercial breweries I spoke to are dry hopping after fermentation, soft crashing, and a VDK test. At Reuben's, a soft crash means dropping the temperature of the tank after primary fermentation to 62°F (17°C), which is enough to encourage the yeast to drop. Adam is suspicious of dry hopping during active fermentation as it can strip the volatile hop compounds.

Adam will often use Wyeast 1318 in their hazy, hoppy beers. He has noticed that after a soft crash, but before dry hopping, the beer is somewhat clear. However, after dry hopping, the haze level increases and is permanent. In Adam's experience, this haze from dry hopping seems to be enhanced when dry hopping with varieties that have high total oil figures and less so when only using low total oil varieties.

When it comes to dry hopping, Adam likes to encourage the hops to stay in suspension as much as possible, which research suggests is the best way to increase extraction. Like Prison City, Reuben's likes to rouse the dry hops to get them into back into suspension by pulsing CO_2 into the beer at 15 psi through the cone once a day. A process they have found has made a big difference in the aromatics of their hoppy beers. Once Adam thinks he has gotten all he can from a dry hop charge, he will drop the hops from the cone before adding another charge. Getting the older dry hops out of the tank could help reduce polyphenol concentrations, hop creep, and manganese extraction.

Post fermentation, VDK testing, yeast harvesting, and dry hopping, it's extremely important to have as low of dissolved oxygen (DO) readings as possible for hoppy beers. Adam explained that they have been working for years on dropping the DO levels in their beers and this has gone a long way to improve the quality and duration of the hop aroma and flavor of their beers. Reuben's Brews has reduced oxygen by slowly filling from the bottom of the tanks with a little top CO_2 pressure constantly hissing through. This is similar to filling a keg on the homebrew level through the dip tube (filling bottom up) while continually hitting the head space with low CO_2 purges during filling.

Another factor in the quality of the hoppy beers at Reuben's is the quality of their ingredients. Adam explained that they are lucky enough to select their hops from an individual hop yard, which not only makes a non-blended pellet unique in its flavor and aroma, but they also know when the hop was harvested and how it was treated.

Breakside Brewery

Breakside has won a healthy share of medals in recent years for hop-forward beers. In 2018, Breakside won two World Beer Cup medals for IPAs. Their flagship IPA, Breakside IPA, has won several medals including gold at the Great American Beer Festival in 2014. I spoke to head brewer Ben Edmunds about their approach to brewing award-winning hoppy beers.

Breakside starts their hop-forward beers with a strong focus on mash pH. In fact, Ben said, "you can't make a good hoppy beer if you aren't checking mash pH," and who can argue with his trophy room! Specifically, they shoot for a higher mash pH in lower ABV session beers (5.5-5.7). The higher mash pH is an attempt to coax more hop flavors into the smaller beer. In most of their bigger hoppy beers, the mash pH is lowered to around 5.3. Breakside will continue to check the pH throughout the entire mash to ensure that it's in their target range. It's not just something they do after mashing in.

Among the brewers I talked to, Breakside uses more gypsum than others for a moderately Burtonized profile. They have slowly adjusted their water in the hazy IPA era, however. Originally starting with a 10:1 sulfate-chloride ratio (favoring gypsum) they moved to 8:1, 4:1, and finally to 3:1 for their hop-forward beers. In their experience, water too high in chloride loses the "snap" that gypsum can bring.

When it comes to hoppy beers where Breakside wants more malt character ("San Diego Style"), they opt to use malt extract rather than using crystal malts. Adding the malt extract to the boil with about 15-30 minutes left has helped them with shelf-stability and preventing an oxidized malt-character taste after the beer is packaged.

Breakside is using most of their "old-school" hops in the boil. They like the classic hot-side flavor profile when using hops like Chinook, Cascade, and Simcoe. Like other breweries brewing great haze, they aren't completely ignoring early bittering additions, however, adding less than a pound of hops per 30-barrel batch at the start of the boil isn't resulting in many IBUs. Breakside isn't against using extremely old Lambic-style hops on the hot-side, which Ben described as being an underestimated hop class. The research earlier in the book found that cheesy short chain acids in aged hops can act as precursors for fruit-forward esters. As these old hops boil, Ben describes the aroma from the kettle as cheesy to start but evolving into a citrus-rind aroma. Breakside doesn't go as far as to purposely oxidize their hops, however.

Breakside chooses to add about two to three pounds of hops with ten minutes left in the boil, followed by 1-1.5 lbs./bbl of hops in the whirlpool. In terms of whirlpool temperatures, they have found that lower temperatures tend to give them a softer, fruiter hop character. They usually target a range of 180-210°F (82°C-99°C). However, the cooler whirlpool breaks apart their trub pile, which can have a negative impact on efficiency. Although Breakside has experimented with Cryo hops, they haven't been thrilled with the results, as Cryo seemed to lack the complexity of traditional pellets, something other brewers have mentioned as well.

When it comes to dry hopping, Breakside chooses to use more dank-forward hops sparingly to balance out or add depth to the fruiter American hops. Like other breweries, keeping hops in suspension is a focus to enhance the extraction rate of their dry hop additions. They do this by rousing during dry hopping with CO2 from the bottom of the tank shortly after their first dry hop addition. They will rouse the dry hops a total of two to three times during the entire dry hop duration.

Bissell Brothers

Bissell Brothers was founded in 2013 by brothers Peter and Noah Bissell in Portland, ME and has emerged as an industry leader in hop-forward hazy beers. I sat down with Noah at the brewery to discuss the different brewing techniques they have found to be the most successful in maximizing the hop aroma and flavor in their beers.

Portland's water is neutral and doesn't require a lot of doctoring. For Bissell Brother's IPAs, they add gypsum and calcium chloride after carbon filtering, aiming for a 1:2 sulfate-to-chloride ratio (favoring chloride). Typically, their final water profile will have 100 ppm of chloride and 50-75 ppm of sulfate.

Bissell Brothers varies their grist slightly among their core hazy hoppy beers. For example, The Substance (IPA) contains Crystal 20 and about 4% each flaked oats and flaked wheat. Whereas the slightly hazier and bigger Reciprocal (double IPA), has approximately 30% malted wheat. Like with other breweries, Noah Bissell indicated they have noticed that when using high oil hops (particularly Australian ones) they tend to see an increased level of haze.

To hit their desired mash pH of 5.2-5.3 in a standard 60-minute mash, they use lactic acid to adjust for different water treatments and grists. They boil slightly longer than most at 70-minutes, where they experience an evaporation rate of just 2-3%. The longer boil also helps to enhance the color of their beers a touch.

Although the focus is on hop flavor through late hot-side additions, they still bitter their beer with approximately ten calculated IBUs with an early pellet addition. Their whirlpool hops are added after a twenty-minute rest after the boil, which allows the beer to get down to about 195°F (90°C). Despite the lower temperature, they still get a large amount of IBUs from the whirlpool. The IBU pickup is largely because the total knockout (cooling) period on their system is about 40-minutes. They typically whirlpool with about 1-1.25 lbs./bbl of hops.

I asked Noah Bissell about research suggesting that lower fermentation temperatures might help preserve certain hop thiols, but in their experience (using the equivalent of Wyeast 1272), they haven't been able to tell much of a difference at lower temperatures. They generally opt to ferment around 65-70°F (18-21°C) and at these temperatures, a good healthy primary fermentation is finished in about five days. The final gravity of their hoppy beers is generally in the range of 1.012-1.017. The first generation of yeast tends to finish higher and re-pitched beers tend to finish slightly lower.

Bissell Brothers only harvests yeast from batches that don't get late-fermentation dry hops. If the yeast is going to be harvested, they will soft crash to around 60°F (15.5°C) to encourage the yeast to settle, they will then harvest and dry hop. Another technique they use to harvest yeast for highly hopped beers is to brew a small non-hoppy low ABV beer and use the harvested yeast from these batches for future heavily hopped beers. Fresh yeast pitches are sometimes combined with harvested slurry to ensure a healthy fermentation in bigger beers. They are careful not to go more than eight generations with their yeast to ensure a consistent profile.

To avoid oxygen pickup in double dry hopped beers, Bissell Brothers adds their first charge of dry hops before the beer has reached final gravity. Typically, this means their first dose of dry hops will be when the beer is down to about 1.020. After dry hopping, they will cap the fermenter, allowing CO_2 production to build up in the tank, which gets a head start on carbonation and potentially locks in aromatics from the dry hops. The final bit of fermentation that takes place might also scrub oxygen that was introduced during the dry hop.

Because avoiding oxygen during dry hopping is important to the quality of their beers, Bissell Brothers will pump CO_2 through the spray ball at four psi while adding the dry hops to the tank. This is especially important for the second dose of dry hops which occurs after fermentation has ended.

Bissell Brothers chooses to slowly crash their beers rather than quickly forcing to low temperatures overnight. They do this by gradually decreasing the temperature over the course of a week, while the beer is dry hopping. For single dry hopped beers, they will add the hops after crashing the tank to 60°F (15.5°C), after two or three days they will then incrementally lower the tank temperature down to 30°F (-1.1°C). Typically, the dry hops are on the beer above 50°F (10°C) for around four days and at 30°F (-1.1°C) for five days. They do not rouse their dry hops in anyway during the process, opting for a light touch approach with no forced hop extraction. In total, their dry hopping rates tend to be in the 2-3.5 lbs./bbl range.

Great Notion

Located in Portland, OR, Great Notion has established itself as one of the leading hazy IPA breweries in the Pacific Northwest. I sat down with James Dugan and Andy Miller in their brew pub to discuss the detailed techniques they are using to brew hazy IPAs and some of the obstacles they have had to tackle as a result of brewing such heavily hopped beers.

Great Notion is lucky in that their water source is already soft and neutral, but they do build it up favoring chloride to sulfate (1:2 sulfate-chloride ratio) to enhance mouthfeel. They also add a little pop of flavor to their beers with a small amount of sodium, which is seasoned to taste.

Brewers can experiment with sodium additions in their beer post-fermentation by dosing small amounts of salt in a glass and scaling up the desired amount to a full batch. The grist of their hoppy beers is generally Pilsner malt with a mixture of malted wheat and flaked oats. They have found that the lower ABV hoppy beers benefit from a little Crystal 15 to boost base flavor. Control of mash pH is done with phosphoric acid to hit a target of 5.3. Final beer pH for them is generally around 4.2.

On the hot-side, Great Notion is moving toward almost all whirlpool hops. The move to late hop additions is intended to enhance hop flavor and control bitterness. However, they want to be sure to get enough bitterness in their beers to support the higher finishing gravities of +1.020.

To test out new hop varieties or blends, Great Notion will pull a liter of beer from a batch prior to dry hopping and dry hop that sample with eight grams of the experimental hop or blend. This is a good way to get a sense of a varieties potential without devoting an entire batch to the experiment.

In general, Great Notion tends to increase the number of dry hops used when the total oil of the hop is lower. For example, when using a hop variety like Motueka (1.0. mL/100g of total oil) they will bump up the pellet dosage compared to a hop like Galaxy (3-5 mL/100g). Research in Chapter 7 suggests this may be a good approach when also taking into consideration the oxygenated fraction of the variety.

Fermentation for Great Notion is generally completed in about seven days, at which point they ramp up temperature from 66°F (18.8°C) to 70°F (21.1°C) to encourage the yeast to finish. After things settle down, they will do a soft crash to 62°F (16.6°C) for a couple of days to encourage the yeast to settle to the bottom of the cone so they can harvest it for future batches. They are not dry hopping their beers until after they harvest the yeast, so no early fermentation dry hopping is occurring.

A standard dry hopping rate for Great Notion is around 3-4 lbs./bbl, which is generally done over the course of a week. Great Notion shared their experience with hop creep from dry hopping, which is when enzymes from hops free up additional fermentable sugars. In their case, these newly freed fermentables (with little yeast left in the tank) would result in an unhealthy refermentation creating diacetyl. When dry hopping with Mosaic in particular, they would have to wait up to twelve days for the diacetyl created during refermentation after dry hopping to clean up.

According to research, lowering the dry hop temperature or keeping it at the soft crash temperatures, may lead to less enzyme activity from the dry hops. This is exactly what Great Notion has done, lowering dry hopping temperatures from 70°F to 65°F (21.1°C to 18.3°C). They were also burping their tanks with Co2 at the warmer dry hop temperatures to encourage hop extraction, but this was also likely encouraging hop creep by waking up any settled yeast which could then begin working on the newly freed fermentables.

Post-packaging conditioning time for Great Notion's hazy hoppy beers is an important step to allow them to reach their peak. If consumed too early, the style can come across too green and harsh, a comment I heard from multiple breweries while researching for the book. In general, they feel their beers peak around 14-21 days, after about five weeks, the hop character begins to fade. They shared a sample of a freshly-packaged hazy IPA with me compared to the same beer which had some time to condition in the serving tank and the difference was clear: the beer that was recently packaged resembled sampling a beer that was currently being dry hopped whereas the conditioned beer was much smoother with more noticeable hop saturated flavor.

It was interesting to me that Great Notion has found Citra to be one of the most versatile hops in terms of using it with good results on both the hot and cold-side of brewing. According to research, Citra is a variety that should be more versatile because it contains similar amounts of both free and bound compounds. This contrasts with Galaxy, which they find offensive on the hot-side and Mosaic, which they love on the hot-side. Interestingly, Great Notion also noted that high total oil when dry hopping with Galaxy tends to create a beer with noticeably more haze, another common finding among breweries.

Sapwood Cellars

After doing the research for this book and having had the good fortune of interviewing brewers I respect the most, it only seems right that I share the processes Michael Tonsmeire and myself employ on our ten-barrel system at Sapwood Cellars in Columbia, MD.

We start our brew day by running tap water through a carbon filter, our water is fairly neutral and is a good base to work from. We then add calcium chloride and gypsum to get us to a ratio of about 150 ppm chloride and 100 ppm sulfate for most beers. Directly after the filter, the water runs through a tankless hot water heater, which can heat up to 180°F (82°C) on the demand. The colder the ground water and the hotter the call for water, the slower the collection process is. Generally, we can fill our hot liquor tank with 170°F (77°C) water at a rate of 3-5 gallons per minute. We have an electric heating element in our hot liquor tank that can hold temperature or slightly increase it depending on the desired strike or sparge water temperatures.

We buy all our grain pre-milled but will likely move to a mill and auger system with time. This was a decision related more to reducing startup costs than anything else. We start dumping in our bags of grain into the mash tun once we have transferred enough water over from the hot liquor tank to get over the filter screens. We have electric driven rakes that we turn on while graining in to help mix everything together evenly. Generally, we reverse the rakes every four sacks of grain or so to help break up any dough balls. To avoid issues running off, we generally add about ten pounds of rice hulls per 55-pound sack of non-malted or huskless grain.

We typically use a sack or two of chit malt (representing about 8-10% of the grist) in most of our hoppy beers to help with head retention and potentially stability. We will often use malted wheat to help with body (and likely haze) at around 10% of the grist. Every recipe is a little different, however, as our intentions for each beer change.

The smaller the ABV of the beer, the more likely we might include specialty grains, like golden naked oats. As the ABV increases, we'll back that percentage down a bit to avoid too much malt character competing for hop aroma and flavor. For example, a sub 5% session IPA might have 15% golden naked oats, but an 8% double IPA would likely have much less (or none at all). We speculate that as the volume of grain increases to raise the ABV, the maltiness of the beer also increases, so smaller amounts of specialty grains go further in bigger beers.

In addition to mash hops in our hazy beers, we will add a few pounds of hops to the kettle as we are collecting wort. This helps to control boil overs as well as add a little bit of base bitterness. Generally, our whirlpool hopping rate is around 2 lbs./bbl and we use the research as much as possible to experiment with different varieties in the kettle. With no direct science to explain why, we have found Idaho 7 to be a great hot-side whirlpool hop, the flavors of which tend to stick around better than most varieties after fermentation.

To avoid picking up too much bitterness in our lower ABV hoppy beers, we lower the temperature of the wort prior to adding the whirlpool hops. We do this by adding about 1 barrel of cold water directly from the filter to the kettle. This will generally lower the wort temperature about 5-10 degrees. We will sometimes drop the temperature to about 170°F (76°C) by running wort through our heat exchanger after the boil. The higher ABV beers stand up better to higher IBUs (and more dry hops) so we won't pre-chill the wort before adding whirlpool hops to anything above 6% ABV.

We add hops carefully during the start of the whirlpool to avoid oxygen introduction (this stems from the research that found oxygen introduction during the whirlpool can lead to a green onion thiol in hop-forward beer during fermentation). After the whirlpool, we let the beer rest for 20-25 minutes to settle. We then run the beer through a glycol assisted heat exchanger with an inline oxygen stone hitting the wort with 1.5 L/m of oxygen on the way to the fermenter. Bigger double IPAs will get around 2.0 L/m of oxygen.

Almost all our hoppy beers are fermented with a strain from RVA Yeast Labs LLC located in Richmond, VA called Manchester #132 (a Boddington strain). One of my favorite strains from homebrewing, Manchester #132 has just a hint of vanilla-richness that rounds out bright tropical hop varieties. Although, we experiment with all kinds of different yeast strains. We will generally brew a lower ABV beer with a fresh pitch of Manchester and harvest enough yeast from it for another 3-4 batches (typically, one full brink). We don't dry hop our beer during active fermentation when we plan to harvest the yeast, rather, we let the beer finish fermentation and then soft crash to 58°F (14°C) for a couple days, harvest, and then dry hop.

In fact, we have found that on the commercial scale, active fermentation dry hopping results in less flavor and aroma compared to our homebrew batches. We still have some beers that we dry hop at the same time we pitch the yeast or during mid-fermentation, however. For these beers, we intentionally want the greener hydrocarbons from the hops blown off but the fruiter monoterpenes alcohols to remain, creating a subtle hop fruity base.

To avoid oxygen introduction during post-fermentation dry hop charges, we use a hop doser mounted to the hop port at the top of the tank. The hop doser is big enough to hold eleven-pounds of hops and is equipped with hardware to allow us to purge the doser and pellets with CO2 prior to dropping them into the beer. The hop doser is advantageous because it allows us to add the dry hops without having to depressurize the tank.

Our dry hopping rate is around 2 lbs./bbl for lower ABV hoppy beers and about 4 lbs./bbl for higher ABV beers. We dry hop most of our beers in stages, generally around 22 pounds per stage. We find that around two to three days is enough to get extraction of each addition. We rouse our dry hops with short bursts of CO2 (around 15 psi) through the cone once a day to encourage the hops to get into suspension to extract. All our post-fermentation dry hopping is happening below 60°F (15°C), which should help avoid hop creep. We drop the cone between dry hop stages to remove the previous addition before the new one is introduced.

After dry hopping, we crash our hoppy beers to 35°F (2°C) and hold at this temperature for at least two full days before transferring to the brite tank. We purge our brite tank with CO2 before transferring in the beer from the fermenter. We do this by running 15-20 psi of CO2 for 30 minutes through the carbonation stone which is near the bottom of the tank. We do this while also keeping the spray valve arm on the top of the tank open. After the 30-minute purge, we pressurize the brite tank to 15 psi and then release the pressure down to zero and repeat twice (like purging a homebrew keg), eventually setting the pressure in the brite tank to match the fermenter's pressure.

After transferring the beer into the brite tank, pushing with CO2 (not a pump) we carbonate with a rotameter to about 2.5 volumes of CO2. After 2-3 days in the brite tank we keg the beer, but first we purge each keg. We do this by filling the keg with 25-30 psi of Co2 and releasing down to zero (which also blasts out any remaining peracetic acid). We do this keg purge twice and then fill the keg with Co2 to match the brite tank pressure, which is usually around 10 psi at 35°F (1.6°C).

We are always experimenting with new variables at our brewery. It's possible that in a few years our process might be drastically different. Whether inspired by new research or conversations with other brewers, we are always striving to improve our process, learn as much as we can, and make the best beer possible.

Cheers!

References

[1] Chapman, A. C. (1903). LVII.—Essential oil of hops. J. Chem. Soc., Trans., 83(0), 505-513. doi:10.1039/ct9038300505

[2] Chapman, A. C. (1895). VIII.—Essential oil of hops. J. Chem. Soc., Trans., 67(0), 54-63. doi:10.1039/ct8956700054 Chapman, A. C. (1895). VIII.—Essential oil of hops. J. Chem. Soc., Trans., 67(0), 54-63. doi:10.1039/ct8956700054

[3] Chapman, A. C. (1928). CLXXII.—The higher-boiling constituents of the essential oil of hops. J. Chem. Soc., 0(0), 1303-1306. doi:10.1039/jr9280001303

[4] Howard, G. A. (1956). New Approach to The Analysis Of Hop Oil. Journal of the Institute of Brewing, 62(2), 158-159. doi:10.1002/j.2050-0416.1956.tb02841.x

[5] Jahnsen, V. J. (1963). Composition Of Hop Oil. Journal of the Institute of Brewing, 69(6), 460-466. doi:10.1002/j.2050-0416.1963.tb01953.x

[6] Tressl, R., Friese, L., Fendesack, F., & Koeppler, H. (1978). Studies of the volatile composition of hops during storage. J. Agric. Food Chem. Journal of Agricultural and Food Chemistry, 26(6), 1426-1430. doi:10.1021/jf60220a036

[7] Steinhaus, M., & Schieberle, P. (2000). Comparison of the Most Odor-Active Compounds in Fresh and Dried Hop Cones (Humulus lupulus L. Variety Spalter Select) Based on GC–Olfactometry and Odor Dilution Techniques. J. Agric. Food Chem. Journal of Agricultural and Food Chemistry, 48(5), 1776-1783. doi:10.1021/jf990514l

[8] Roberts, M. T., Dufour, J., & Lewis, A. C. (2004). Application of comprehensive multidimensional gas chromatography combined with time-of-flight mass spectrometry (GC×GC-TOFMS) for high-resolution analysis of hop essential oil. J. Sep. Science Journal of Separation Science, 27(5-6), 473-478. doi:10.1002/jssc.200301669

[9] Keukeleire, D. D. (2000). Fundamentals of beer and hop chemistry. Química Nova, 23(1), 108-112. doi:10.1590/s0100-40422000000100019

[10] Ono, M., Kakudo, Y., Yamamoto, Y., Nagami, K., and Kumada, J. Quantitative analysis of hop bittering components and its application to hop evaluation. J. Am. Soc. Brew. Chem. 42:167-172, 1984.

[11] Ting, P., & Ryder, D. (2017). The Bitter, Twisted Truth of the Hops: 50 Years of Hop Chemistry. *American Society of Brewing Chemisits, Inc.,* 161-180.

[12] Malowicki, M.G., Shellhammer, T.H., 2005. Isomerization and degradation kinetics of hop (Humulus lupulus) acids in model wort-boiling system. J. Agric. Food Chem. 53 (11), 4434–4439.

[13] Verzele, M., 1965. Practical aspects of the isomerization of α-acids. Proc. Eur. Brew. Conv. Congr. Stockholm, 398–404.

[14] Jaskula-Goiris, B., Aerts, G., & Cooman, L. D. (2010). Hop α-acids isomerization and utilization: an experimental review. Cerevisia, 35(3), 57-70. doi:10.1016/j.cervis.2010.09.004

[15] Malowicki, M. G., & Shellhammer, T. H. (2005). Isomerization and Degradation Kinetics of Hop (Humulus lupulus) Acids in a Model Wort-Boiling System. Journal of Agricultural and Food Chemistry, 53(11), 4434-4439. doi:10.1021/jf0481296

[16] Laufer, S.; Brenner, M. W. Some Practical Considerations on the Fate of Hop Resins in Brewing. Proc. 69th AnniV. ConV. Am. Soc. Brew. Chem. 1956, 18-28.

[17] Kunze, W., 2004. Technology Brewing and Malting, 3rd edition. VLB Berlin, Germany.

[18] Justus, A. (2018). Tracking IBU Through the Brewing Process: The Quest for Consistency. MBAA TQ, 55(3), 67-74.

[19] Lermusieau, G.; Collin, S. Hop Aroma Extraction and Analysis. In Analysis of Taste and Aroma; Jackson, J. F., Linskens, H. F., Eds.; Springer: Berlin, Germany, 2002; pp 69–86.

[20] Yakima Chief – Hopunion. (n.d.). Retrieved January 07, 2018, from https://ychhops.com/varieties

[21] Guadagni, D. G., Buttery, R. G., & Harris, J. (1966). Odor intensities of hop oil components. Journal of the Science of Food and Agriculture J. Sci. Food Agric., 17(3), 142-144. doi:10.1002/jsfa.2740170311

[22] Algazzali, V.; Wiesen, E.; Zunkel, M.; and Schoenberger, C. Development and implementation of hop flavor reference standards for sensory training. Presented at the American Society of Brewing Chemists Meeting at Brewing Summit 2018 [Online], San Diego, California, August 12–14, 2018; A-097. American Society of Brewing Chemists Meeting website. https://www.asbcnet.org/events/archives/2018meeting/proceedings/

[23] Rettberg, N., Thörner, S., & Garbe, L. (n.d.). Bugging Hop Analysis – on the Isomerization and Oxidation of Terpene Alcohols during Steam Distillation. BrewingScience, 65, 112-117. Retrieved 2012.

[24] Weidenhamer, J. D., Macias, F. A., Fischer, N. H., & Williamson, G. B. (1993). Just how insoluble are monoterpenes? Journal of Chemical Ecology, 19(8), 1799-1807. doi:10.1007/bf00982309

[25] Sharpe, F. R., & Laws, D. R. (1981). The Essential Oil Of Hops A Review. Journal of the Institute of Brewing, 87(2), 96-107. doi:10.1002/j.2050-0416.1981.tb03996.x

[26] Hieronymus, S. (2012). *For the Love of Hops*. Natl Book Network.

[27] Matsui, H., Inui, T., Oka, K., & Fukui, N. (2016). The influence of pruning and harvest timing on hop aroma, cone appearance, and yield. Food Chemistry

[28] Wort Bittering Extracts (Pre-isomerised hop products -

potential and practical uses. (2002). Brauwelt International Technical Feature, 20-25.

[29] Scort, R. W., Theaker, P. D., Marsh, A. S., Grimmett, C. M., Laws, D. R., & Sharpe, F. R. (1981). Use Of Extracts Prepared With Liquid Carbon Dioxide As A Substitute For Dry Hops. Journal of the Institute of Brewing, 87(4), 252-258. doi:10.1002/j.2050-0416.1981.tb04027.x

[30] Foster, R., Patino, H., & Slaughter, C. (2000). The Contribution of Post-Fermentation Bittering to Beer Composition and Stability. 37, 89-95.

[31] Opstaele, F. V., Goiris, K., Rouck, G. D., Aerts, G., & Cooman, L. D. (2012). Production of novel varietal hop aromas by supercritical fluid extraction of hop pellets—Part 1: Preparation of single variety total hop essential oils and polar hop essences. The Journal of Supercritical Fluids, 69, 45-56. doi:10.1016/j.supflu.2012.05.009

[32] (Lermusieau, G., Liégeois, C., & Collin, S. (2001). Reducing power of hop cultivars and beer ageing. Food Chemistry, 72(4), 413-418. doi:10.1016/s0308-8146(00)00247-8

[33] Taylor, D., Humphrey, P.M., Yorston, B., Wilson, R.J.H., Roberts, T., Biendl, M.: A guide to the use of pre-isomerized hop pellets, including aroma varieties, MBAA Technical Quarterly 37, 225-231, 2000.

[34] Wilson, R.J.H., Roberts, T., Smith, R.J., Biendl, M.: Improving hop utilization and flavor control through the use of pre-isomerized products in the brewery kettle: paper read at the World Brewing Congress Orlando, 2000. Published in: MBA Technical Quarterly 38, 11-21, 2001)

[35] Huvaere K, Andersen ML, Storme M, Van Bocxlaer J, Skibsted LH, De Keukeleire D. Flavin-induced photodecomposition of sulfur-containing amino acids is decisive in the formation of beer lightstruck flavor. Photochem Photobiol Sci. 2006; 5: 961-969.

[36] Irwin, A. J., Bordeleau, L., and Barker, R. L. Model studies and flavor threshold determination of 3-methyl-2-butene-l-thiol in beer.

J. Am. Soc. Brew. Chem. 51:1-3, 1993.

[37] https://www.brewersfriend.com/forum/attachments/kalsec-hop-bitter-extracts-explained-pdf.1778/

[38]https://kalsec.com/wp-content/uploads/2016/10/Isolone-Logo-6-1.pdf

[39] Nance, M., & Setzer, W. (2011). Volatile components of aroma hops (Humulus lupulus L.) commonly used in beer brewing. Journal of Brewing and Distilling, 2(2), 16-22.

[40] Praet, T., & Van Opstaele, F. (2016). Flavor Activity of Sesquiterpene Oxidation Products, Formed Upon Lab-Scale Boiling of a Hop Essential Oil-Derived Sesquiterpene Hydrocarbon Fraction (cv. Saaz). Journal of the American Society of Brewing Chemists. doi:10.1094/asbcj-2016-1205-01

[41] Praet, T., Van Opstaele, F., De Causmaecker, B., Aerts, G., & De Cooman, L. (2016). Heat-Induced Changes in the Composition of Varietal Hop Essential Oils via Wort Boiling on a Laboratory Scale. Journal of the American Society of Brewing Chemists. doi:10.1094/asbcj-2016-3257-01

[42] Questions for Advanced Brewing Book on Hops [E-mail to the author]. (17, April 21).

[43] Praet, T., Opstaele, F., Causmaecker, B., Bellaio, G., Rouck, G., Aerts, G., & Cooman, L. (2015). De novo Formation of Sesquiterpene Oxidation Products during Wort Boiling and Impact of the Kettle Hopping Regime on Sensory Characteristics of Pilot-Scale Lager Beers. BrewingScience, 68, 130-145.

[44] Haley, J., & Peppard, T. L. (1983). Differences In Utilisation Of The Essential Oil Of Hops During The Production Of Dry-Hopped And Late-Hopped Beers. Journal of the Institute of Brewing, 89(2), 87-91. doi:10.1002/j.2050-0416.1983.tb04153.x

[45] Schull, F., Forster, A., & Gahr, A. (2017). Comparison of different dosage criteria when using aroma hops for late hopping.

[46] Schüll, F., Forster, A., & Gahr, A. (2018). Aroma Description of Two Aroma Breeding Lines. *Hopfen-Rundschau International,* 46-57.

[47] Dresel, M., Praet, T., Van Opstaele, F., Van Holle, A., Naudts, D., De Keukeleire, D., . . . Aerts, G. (2015). Comparison of the Analytical Profiles of Volatiles in Single-Hopped Worts and Beers as a Function of the Hop Variety. BrewingScience, 68, 8-28.

[48] Mitter, W., & Steiner, S. (2009). Annual fluctuations in hop quality – options for adjustment in the brewhouse.
Brauwelt International, 36-37.

[49] Sharp, D., Qian, Y., Shellhammer, G., & Shellhammer, T. (2017). Contributions of Select Hopping Regimes to the Terpenoid Content and Hop Aroma Profile of Ale and Lager Beers. Journal of the American Society of Brewing Chemists. doi:10.1094/asbcj-2017-2144-01

[50] Inui, T. (n.d.). Study on the attractive hop aroma for beer. Speech presented at World Brewing Congress 2012, Portland, OR.

[51] H. (2010). Maximizing Hop Aroma and Flavor Through Process Variables. Technical Quarterly. doi:10.1094/tq-47-2-0623-01

[52] Dimethyl Sulfide – Significance, Origins, and Control. (2014). Journal of the American Society of Brewing Chemists ASBC. doi:10.1094/asbcj-2014-0610-01

[53] S. (2010). Influence of Cardiolipin on Lager Beer Dimethyl Sulfide Levels: A Possible Role Involving Mitochondria. Journal of the American Society of Brewing Chemists ASBC. doi:10.1094/asbcj-2010-0803-01

[54] Bamforth, C. W., & Anness, B. J. (1981). The Role Of Dimethyl Sulphoxide Reductase In The Formation Of Dimethyl Sulphide During Fermentations. Journal of the Institute of Brewing, 87(1), 30-34. doi:10.1002/j.2050-0416.1981.tb03981.x

[55] Anderson, R. J. & Howard, G. A., Journal of the Institute of Brewing, 1974, 80, 357.

[56] Hysert, D.W., Morrison, N.M. and Jamieson, A.M. J. Am. Soc. Brew. Chem. 37:30 (1979).

[57] Anderson, R. J., Clapperton, J. F., Crabb, D., & Hudson, J. R. (1975). Dimethyl Sulphide As A Feature Of Lager Flavour. Journal of the Institute of Brewing, 81(3), 208-213. doi:10.1002/j.2050-0416.1975.tb03679.x

[58] The Measurement of Sulfur-Containing Aroma Compounds in Samples from Production-Scale Brewery Operations. (2005). Journal of the American Society of Brewing Chemists ASBC. doi:10.1094/asbcj-63-0129

[59] Dickenson, C. J. (1983). Cambridge Prize Lecture Dimethyl Sulphide-Its Origin And Control In Brewing. Journal of the Institute of Brewing, 89(1), 41-46. doi:10.1002/j.2050-0416.1983.tb04142.x

[60] Volatile Sulfur Compounds in Hops and Residual Concentrations in Beer—A Review. (2003). Journal of the American Society of Brewing Chemists ASBC. doi:10.1094/asbcj-61-0109

[61] Hanke, S., Ditz, V., Herrmann, M., Back, W., Becker, T., & Krottenthaler, M. (2010). Infl uence of Ethyl Acetate, Isoamyl Acetate and Linalool on off-fl avour Perception in Beer. BrewingScience, 63, 94-99.

[62] Vaporization of DMS Influenced by Foam. (2015). Journal of the American Society of Brewing Chemists ASBC. doi:10.1094/asbcj-2015-0910-01

[63] Liebenow. R. and Esser, K. Erfahrungen mit der Heissbeluftung der Ausschlagwurze. Monatsschr. Brau., 20, 23-24 (1967)

[64] during the cooling down phase after boiling) and from hops. (Noba, S., et al., Search for compounds contributing to onion-like off-flavor in beer and investigation of the cause of the flavor, J.

Biosci. Bioeng., (2017), http://dx.doi.org/10.1016/j.jbiosc.2017.05.009

[65] Foster, R. T., & Nickerson, G. B. (1985). Changes in Hop Oil Content and Hoppiness Potential (Sigma) During Hop Aging. Journal of the American Society of Brewing Chemists, 43. doi:10.1094/asbcj-43-0127

[66] Kishimoto, T., Kono, K., & Aoki, K. (2007). Odorants comprising hop aroma of beer: Hop-derived odorants increased in the beer hopped with aged hops. Proceedings of the 31st European Brewery Convention Congress; Venice, Italy, 2007.

[67] Rettberg, N., Thorner, S., Labus, A., & Garbe, L. (2014). Aroma Active Monocarboxylic Acids - Origin and Analytical Characterization in Fresh and Aged Hops. BrewingScience, 67, 33-47.

[68] Lam, K. C., Foster, R. T., & Deinzer, M. L. (1986). Aging of hops and their contribution to beer flavor. Journal of Agricultural and Food Chemistry, 34(4), 763-770. doi:10.1021/jf00070a043

[69] Peacock, V., & Deinzer, M. (1981). Chemistry of Hop Aroma in Beer. Journal of the American Society of Brewing Chemists ASBCJ, 39. doi:10.1094/asbcj-39-0136

[70] Vollmer, D., Algazzali, V., & Shellhammer, T. (2017). Aroma Properties of Lager Beer Dry-Hopped with Oxidized Hops. Journal of the American Society of Brewing Chemists. doi:10.1094/asbcj-2017-1287-01

[71] Almaguer, C., Gastl, M., Arendt, K., & Becker, T. (n.d.). Contributions of Hop Hard Resins to Beer Quality. BrewingScience, 65, 118-129. Retrieved 2012.

[72] Rettberg, N., Thorner, S., Labus, A., & Garbe, L. (2014). Aroma Active Monocarboxylic Acids - Origin and Analytical Characterization in Fresh and Aged Hops. BrewingScience, 67, 33-47.

[73] Srecec, S., Rezic, T., Šantek, B., and Maric, V. (2008) Influence of hops pellets age on α-acids utilization and organoleptic quality of

beer. Agric. Consp. Sci. 73(2), 103–107.

[74] Mikyška, A., & Krofta, K. (2012). Assessment of changes in hop resins and polyphenols during long-term storage. *Journal of the Institute of Brewing, 118*(3), 269-279. doi:10.1002/jib.40

[75] Paul, J. (2016, September 22). Hop Papers [E-mail].

[76] (n.d.). Retrieved 2018, from http://brulosophy.com/2015/05/18/water-chemistry-pt-2-messing-with-minerals-exbeeriment-results/

[77] Comrie, A. A. D. Journal of the Institute of Brewing, 1967 73, 335

[78] Bruce, J. (2002). Analysis of anions in beer using ion chromatography. Journal of Automated Methods & Management in Chemistry, 24(4), 127-130.

[79] H. (2010). Maximizing Hop Aroma and Flavor Through Process Variables. Technical Quarterly TQ.

[80] Langstaff, S. A., & Lewis, M. J. (1993). The Mouthfeel Of Beer – A Review. Journal of the Institute of Brewing, 99(1), 31-37.

[81] Langstaff, S. A., Guinard, J .• x. & Lewis, M. J. Journal of the lrutilllte of Brewing, 1991, 92, 168.

[82] Narziss, L., Reichender, E. & Bub, E. Brauwelt, 1981 121 1386

[83] Huolihan, J. (n.d.). Water Chemistry – Pt. 6: Sulfate to Chloride Ratio | Exbeeriment Results! Retrieved from http://brulosophy.com/2016/10/03/water-chemistry-pt-6-sulfate-to-chloride-ratio-exbeeriment-results/

[84] Justus, A. (2017, December 11). 066: Sulfate to Chloride Ratio [Web log post]. Retrieved from http://masterbrewerspodcast.com/066-sulfate-to-chloride-ratio

[85] Beloshapka, A., Buff, P., Fahey Jr., G., & Swanson, K. (2016).

Compositional Analysis of Whole Grains, Processed Grains, Grain Co-Products, and Other Carbohydrate Sources with Applicability to Pet Animal Nutrition. Retrieved from MDPI Foods

[86] Bruce, J. (2002). Analysis of anions in beer using ion chromatography. Journal of Automated Methods & Management in Chemistry, 24(4), 127-130.

[87] Scriban, R. Petit Journal du Brasseur, 1971, 79, 537

[88] Otter, G. E., Popplewell, J. A. & Taylor, L. J. European Brewery Convention Proceedings of the 12th Congress, Interlaken, 1969, 481

[89] De Clerck, J. Cours de Brasserie, Universite de Louvain Institut Agronomique, Section de Brasserie, Heverlee-Louvain, 1962

[90] Vermeylen, J. Traite de la Fabrication du Malt et de la Biere, Association Royale des Anciens Eleves de Institute Superieur des Fermentations, Gand. 1962

[91] Bradee, L. H. "The Practical Brewer", Masters Brewers Association of the Americas, Madison, WI, 1977.

[92] Ragot, F., Guinard, J., Shoemaker, C. F., & Lewis, M. J. (1989). The Contribution Of Dextrins To Beer Sensory Properties Part I. Mouthfeel. Journal of the Institute of Brewing, 95(6), 427-430. doi:10.1002/j.2050-0416.1989.tb04650.x

[93] Langstaff, S. A., Guinard, J., & Lewis, M. J. (1991). Instrumental Evaluation Of The Mouthfeel Of Beer And Correlation With Sensory Evaluation. Journal of the Institute of Brewing, 97(6), 427-433. doi:10.1002/j.2050-0416.1991.tb01081.x

[94] De Clerck, J. A Textbook of Brewing, Vol. 1. Chapman & Hall, London, 1957

[95] Scriban, R. Petit Journal du Brasseur, 1971, 79, 537

[96] Vermeylen, J. Traite de la Fabrication du Malt et de la Biere. Association Royale desAnciens Eleves de I'Institut Superieur des Fermentations, Gand. 1963

[97] http://www.themadfermentationist.com/2017/06/23-abv-session-neipa.html

[98] http://braukaiser.com/wiki/index.php?title=The_Theory_of_Mashing

[99] Schnitzenbaumer, B., Kerpes, R., Titze, J., Jacob, F., and Arendt, E. K. (2012) Impact of various levels of unmalted oats (Avena sativa.) on the quality and processability of mashes, worts and beers, J. Am. Soc. Brew. Chem.

[100] Envoldsen, B. S., and Bathgate, G. N. Structural analysis of wort dextrins by means of Beta-amylases and the debranching enzymes pullanse. J. Inst. Brew. 75:433-443, 1969.

[101] MacGregor, A. W., Bazin, S. L., Maori, L. J., and Babb, J. C. Modeling the contribution of alpha-amylase, beta-amylase and limit dextrinase to starch degradation during mashing. J. Cereal Sci. 29:161-169,1999

[102] Lee, W., & Pyler, R. (1984). Barley Malt Limit Dextrinase: Varietal, Environmental, and Malting Effects. Journal of the American Society of Brewing Chemists, 42. doi:10.1094/asbj-42-0011

[103] The Impact of the Thermostability of alpha-Amylase, beta-Amylase, and Limit Dextrinase on Potential Wort Fermentability. (2003). Journal of the American Society of Brewing Chemists. doi:10.1094/asbcj-61-0210

[104] Lee, W., & Pyler, R. (1984). Barley Malt Limit Dextrinase: Varietal, Environmental, and Malting Effects. Journal of the American Society of Brewing Chemists, 42. doi:10.1094/asbj-42-0011

[105] Hopkins, R. H., and Wiener, S. J. Inst. Brew. 61:488,1955.

[106] Walker, J. W., Bringhurst, T. A., Broadhead, A. L., Brosnan, J. M., & Pearson, S. Y. (2001). The Survival of Limit Dextrinase during

Fermentation in the Production of Scotch Whisky. Journal of the Institute of Brewing, 107(2), 99-106. doi:10.1002/j.2050-0416.2001.tb00082.x

[107] Forster, A., & Gahr, A. (n.d.). Hopping of Low Alcohol Beers. BrewingScience, 65, 72-82. Retrieved 2012

[108] Forster, A., & Gahr, A. (n.d.). Hopping of Low Alcohol Beers. BrewingScience, 65, 72-82. Retrieved 2012

[109] Amerine, M. A.; Pangborn, R. M.; Roessler, E. B. "Principles of Sensory Evaluation of Food"; Academic Press: New York, 1965.

[110] American Society of Brewing Chemists J. Am. SOC. Brew. Chem. 1980, 38, 99.

[111] Meilgaard, M. C. (1982). Prediction of Flavor Differences between Beers from Their Chemical Composition. J. Agric. Food Chem., 1009-1017.

[112] O'neill, T. E. (1996). Flavor Binding by Food Proteins: An Overview. ACS Symposium Series Flavor-Food Interactions, 59-74. doi:10.1021/bk-1996-0633.ch006

[113] Castro, L. F., & Ross, C. F. (2013). The Effect of Protein and Carbohydrate Levels on the Chemical and Sensory Properties of Beer. Journal of the American Society of Brewing Chemists. doi:10.1094/asbcj-2013-0913-01

[114] Buckee, G. K. & Hargitt, R., Journal of the Institute of Brewing, 1977, 83, 275.

[115] Enari, T.-M., and T.Sopanen: J. Inst. Brew. 92 (1986), 25.

[116] Forrest, I. S. & Wainwright, T., European Brewery Convention Proceedings of the 16th Congress, Amerstadam, 1977, 401.

[117] Schnitzenbaumer, B., Kerpes, R., Titze, J., Jacob, F., and Arendt, E. K. (2012) Impact of various levels of unmalted oats (Avena sativa.) on the quality and processability of mashes, worts and beers, J. Am. Soc. Brew. Chem.

[118] Hertirich, J. (n.d.). Topics in Brewing: Malting Barley. MBAA TQ, 50(1), 29-41.

[119] Bettenhausen, Harmonie M., et al. "Influence of Barley Source on Beer Chemistry, Flavor, and Flavor Stability." *Food Research International*, 2018, doi:10.1016/j.foodres.2018.07.024.

[120] Dong, L., Hou, Y., Li, F., Piao, Y., Zhang, X., Zhang, X., Zhao, C. (2015). Characterization of volatile aroma compounds in different brewing barley cultivars. J Sci Food Agric, 95(5), 915-921. doi:10.1002/jsfa.6759

[121] Haslbeck, K., Bub, S., Schönberger, C., Zarnkow, M., Jacob, F., & Coelhan, M. (2017). On the Fate of B-Myrcene during Fermentation - The Role of Stripping and Uptake of Hop Oil Compounds by Brewer's Yeast in Dry-Hopped Wort and Beer. BrewingScience, 70, 159-169.

[122] Suomalainen, H., Journal of the Institute of Brewing, 1981, 87, 296.

[123]Meilgaard, M. C. Flavor chemistry of beer; Part I: flavor interaction between principal volatiles. MBAA Tech. Q. 1975, 12, 107-117.

[124] Hough, J.S., and Stevens, R. (1967) Beer flavor: IV. Factors affecting the production of fusel oil, J. Inst. Brew. 67, 488-494.

[125] Zhang, C., Liu, Y., Qi, Y., Zhang, J., Dai, L., Lin, X., & Xiao, D. (2013). Increased esters and decreased higher alcohols production by engineered brewer's yeast strains. Eur Food Res Technol European Food Research and Technology, 236(6), 1009-1014. doi:10.1007/s00217-013-1966-1

[126] Ramos-Jeunehomme, C., Laub, R., and Masschelein, C. A. Why is ester formation in brewery fermentations yeast strain dependent? Proc. Congr. Eur. Brew. Conv. 23:257-264, 1991

[127] Enari, T., Makinen, V., & Haikara, A. (n.d.). The Formation of Flavor Compounds During Fermentation. Technical Quarterly, 7(1).

[128] Landaud, S., Latrille, E., & Corrieu, G. (2001). Top Pressure and Temperature Control the Fusel Alcohol/Ester Ratio through Yeast Growth in Beer Fermentation. Journal of the Institute of Brewing, 107(2), 107-117. doi:10.1002/j.2050-0416.2001.tb00083.x

[129] Pires, E. J., Teixeira, J. A., Brányik, T., & Vicente, A. A. (2014). Yeast: The soul of beer's aroma—a review of flavour-active esters and higher alcohols produced by the brewing yeast. Applied Microbiology and Biotechnology, 98(5), 1937-1949. doi:10.1007/s00253-013-5470-0

[130] Influence of Higher Alcohol Availability on Ester Formation by Yeast. (1994). Journal of the American Society of Brewing Chemists ASBCJ, 52. doi:10.1094/asbcj-52-0084

[131] Fermentation Kinetics and the Production of Volatiles During Alcoholic Fermentation. (1995). Journal of the American Society of Brewing Chemists ASBCJ, 53. doi:10.1094/asbcj-53-0072

[132] Scanes KT, Hohmann S, Prior BA (1998) Glycerol production by the yeast Saccharomyces cerevisiae and its relevance to wine: a review. S Afr J Enol Vitic 19:17–24

[133] Arroyo-López FN, Pérez-Torrado R, Querol A, Barrio E (2010)Modulation of the glycerol and ethanol syntheses in the yeast Saccharomyces kudriavzevii differs from that exhibited by Saccharomyces cerevisiae and their hybrid. Food Microbiol 27: 628–637

[134] Freeman, G., & Donald, G. (1956, June). Fermentation Process Leading to Glycerol. Imperial Chemical Industries Limited, 5, 197-210.

[135] Wort Trub Content and Its Effects on Fermentation and Beer Flavor. (1982). Journal of the American Society of Brewing Chemists ASBCJ, 40. doi:10.1094/asbcj-40-0057

[136] Wort Trub Content and Its Effects on Fermentation and Beer Flavor. (1982). Journal of the American Society of Brewing Chemists ASBCJ, 40. doi:10.1094/asbcj-40-0057

[137] Kinetic Analysis of Ester Formation During Beer Fermentation. (1991). Journal of the American Society of Brewing Chemists ASBCJ, 49. doi:10.1094/asbcj-49-0152

[138] Hiralal, L., Olaniran, A. O., & Pillay, B. (2014). Aroma-active ester profile of ale beer produced under different fermentation and nutritional conditions. Journal of Bioscience and Bioengineering, 117(1), 57-64. doi:10.1016/j.jbiosc.2013.06.002

[139] Fermentation Kinetics and the Production of Volatiles During Alcoholic Fermentation. (1995). Journal of the American Society of Brewing Chemists ASBCJ, 53. doi:10.1094/asbcj-53-0072

[140] High-Gravity Brewing: Production of High Levels of Ethanol Without Excessive Concentrations of Esters and Fusel Alcohols. (1985). Journal of the American Society of Brewing Chemists ASBCJ, 43. doi:10.1094/asbcj-43-0179

[141] Anderson, R. G., & Kirsop, B. H. (1975). Oxygen As A Regulator Of Ester Accumulation During The Fermentation Of Wort Of High Specific Gravity. Journal of the Institute of Brewing, 81(2), 111-115. doi:10.1002/j.2050-0416.1975.tb03671.x

[142] Hiralal, L., Olaniran, A. O., & Pillay, B. (2014). Aroma-active ester profile of ale beer produced under different fermentation and nutritional conditions. Journal of Bioscience and Bioengineering, 117(1), 57-64. doi:10.1016/j.jbiosc.2013.06.002

[143] P. H. (2012, August 7). A Study of Factors Affecting the Extraction of Flavor When Dry Hopping Beer. Retrieved from http://ir.library.oregonstate.edu/xmlui/bitstream/handle/1957/34093/Wolfe_thesis.pdf

[144] Dry Hopping on a Small Scale: Considerations for Achieving Reproducibility. (2016). Technical Quarterly. doi:10.1094/tq-53-3-0814-01

[145] P. H. (2012, August 7). A Study of Factors Affecting the Extraction of Flavor When Dry Hopping Beer. Retrieved from http://ir.library.oregonstate.edu/xmlui/bitstream/handle/1957/34

093/Wolfe_thesis.pdf

[146] https://www.reddit.com/r/beer/comments/2hj15k/beer_and_brewing_science_ama_professional_brewing/

[147] Wolfe, P., Qian, M. C., & Shellhammer, T. H. (2012). The Effect of Pellet Processing and Exposure Time on Dry Hop Aroma Extraction. ACS Symposium Series Flavor Chemistry of Wine and Other Alcoholic Beverages, 203-215. doi:10.1021/bk-2012-1104.ch013

[148] W. M., & S. C. (2013). Dry Hopping – A Study of Various Parameters. Retrieved from http://hopsteiner.com/wp-content/uploads/2014/03/Dry-Hopping-A-Study-of-Various-Parameters.pdf

[149] Humulinone Formation in Hops and Hop Pellets and Its Implications for Dry Hopped Beers. (2016). Technical Quarterly TQ. doi:10.1094/tq-53-1-0227-01

[150] W. M., & S. C. (2013). Dry Hopping – A Study of Various Parameters. Retrieved from http://hopsteiner.com/wp-content/uploads/2014/03/Dry-Hopping-A-Study-of-Various-Parameters.pdf

[151] Lagemann, A., Dixius, D., Hanke, S., & Stettner, G. (n.d.). Improved HS Trap GC-MS analysis of hop aroma compounds in dry hopped beer. EBC 2017. Retrieved from http://www.ebc2017.com/inhalt/uploads/P003_Lagemann.pdf

[152] S. (2008). Bitterness-Modifying Properties of Hop Polyphenols Extracted from Spent Hop Material. Journal of the American Society of Brewing Chemists. doi:10.1094/asbcj-2008-0619-01

[153] Forster, A., & Gahr, A. (2013). On the fate of certain hop substances during dry hopping. Brewing Science, 66, 93-103

[154] Maye, J. P., Ph.D. (2018). Hidden Secrets of The New England IPA a.k.a. Hazy IPA a.k.a Juicy IPA. Lecture presented at Hopsteiner.

[155] Oladokun, O., Tarrega, A., James, S., Smart, K., Hort, J., & Cook, D. (2016). The impact of hop bitter acid and polyphenol profiles on the perceived bitterness of beer. Food Chemistry, 205, 212-220. doi:10.1016/j.foodchem.2016.03.023

[156] Haslam, E., Lilley, T. H., Warminski, E., Liao, H., Cai, Y., Martin, R., et al. (1992). Polyphenol complexation. In C. T. Ho, C. Y. Lee, & M. T. Huang (Eds.), Phenolic compounds in food and their effects on health (pp. 8–50). Washington, DC: American Chemists Society.)

[157] Deutscher HOPFEN. (2016). Pocket Guide 2016 [Brochure].

[158] Oladokun, O., James, S., Cowley, T., Smart, K., Hort, J., & Cook, D. (2017). Dry-Hopping: the Effects of Temperature and Hop Variety on the Bittering Profiles and Properties of Resultant Beers. BrewingScience, 70, 187-196.

[159] Oladokun, O., James, S., Cowley, T., Smart, K., Hort, J., & Cook, D. (2017). Dry-Hopping: the Effects of Temperature and Hop Variety on the Bittering Profiles and Properties of Resultant Beers. BrewingScience, 70, 187-196.

[160] Mikyška, A., Hrabák, M., Hašková, D., & Šrogl, J. (2002). The Role of Malt and Hop Polyphenols in Beer Quality, Flavour and Haze Stability. Journal of the Institute of Brewing, 108(1), 78-85. doi:10.1002/j.2050-0416.2002.tb00128.x

[161] Forster, A., Beck, B., and Schmidt R. Investigation on hop polyphenols. In: Proc. Congr. Eur. Brew. Conv. Brussels, Oxford University Press, Oxford. Pp. 143-150, 1995

[162] Engstle, J., Kuhn, M., Kohles, M., Briesen, H., & Forst, P. (n.d.). Disintegration of Hop Pellets during Dry Hopping. BrewingScience, 69, 123-127.

[163] Lafontaine, S., & Shellhammer, T. (n.d.). Understanding the Impact Hopping Rate Has on the Aroma Quality and Intensity of Dry Hopped Beers. Retrieved from

http://www.ebc2017.com/inhalt/uploads/TUEL18-LAFONTAINE.pdf

[164] Schnaitter, M., Kell, A., Kollmannsberger, H., Schüll, F., Gastl, M., & Becker, T. (2016). Scale-up of Dry Hopping Trials: Importance of Scale for Aroma and Taste Perceptions. Chemie Ingenieur Technik, 88(12), 1955-1965. doi:10.1002/cite.201600040

[165] Marriott, R., & Wilson, C. (2017). Dry Hopping - a new look at techniques, utilization, and economics. EBC 2017 Presentation.

[166] Vollmer, D. M., & Shellhammer, T. H. (2016). Influence of Hop Oil Content and Composition on Hop Aroma Intensity in Dry-Hopped Beer. Journal of the American Society of Brewing Chemists. doi:10.1094/asbcj-2016-4123-01

[167] Lafontaine, S., Pereira, C., Vollmer, D., & Shellhammer, T. (2018). The Effectiveness of Hop Volatile Markers for Forecasting Dry-hop Aroma Intensity and Quality of Cascade and Centennial Hops. BrewingScience, 71, 116-140.

[168] Schmidt, C., & Biendl, M. (2016). Headspace Trap GC-MS analysis of hop aroma compounds in beer. BrewingScience, 69, 9-15.

[169] Smith, R. J.; Davidson, D.; Wilson, R. J. H. Natural foam stabilizing and bittering compounds derived from hops. J. Am. Soc. Brew. Chem. 1998, 56 (2), 52–57.

[170] Siebert, K., Modeling beer foam behavior. Oral presentation at the 73rd Annual Meeting of the ASBC as part of the Brewing Summit, Providence, USA, June, 2010.

[171] Wilson, R., Schwarz, H., & Maye, J. (n.d.). A Natural Foam Enhancer From Hops. Speech presented at World Brewing Congress 2012, Portland, OR.

[172] Maye, D. P. (n.d.). Dry Hopping And Its Effects On Beer Bitterness, The IBU Test And Beer Foam. Speech presented at 2017 Craft Brewer's Conference, Washington, DC.

[173] Thurston, P. A., Quain, D. E., and Tubb, R. S. Lipid metabolism and the regulation of volatile ester synthesis in

Saccharomyces cerevisiae. J. Inst. Brew. 88:90-94, 1982.

[174] Ohno, T. & Takahashi, R., Journal of tire Institute of Brewing, 1986, 92, 88.

[175] Clark, D. C., Wilde, P. J., Bergink-Martens, D., Kokelaar, A., and Prins, A. Surface dilational behaviour of aqueous solutions of -lactoglobulin and Tween 20. In: Food Colloids and Polymers: Struc ture and Dynamics. E. Dickinson and P. Walstra, Eds. Royal Society of Chemistry, London. Pp. 354-364, 1993.

[176] Wolf, P., Husband, F., Cooper, D., & Ridout, M. (2003). Destabilization of Beer Foam by Lipids: Structural and Interfacial Effects. Journal of the American Society of Brewing Chemists. doi:10.1094/asbcj-61-0196

[177] Segawa, S., Yamashita, S., Mitani, Y., and Takashio, M. Analysis of detrimental effect on head retention by low molecular weight surface-active substances using surface excess. J. Am. Soc. Brew. Chem.60:31-36, 2002.

[178] Isolation and Characterization of Foaming Proteins of Beer. (1980). Journal of the American Society of Brewing Chemists, 38. doi:10.1094/asbj-38-0129

[179] Buiatti, S., Bertoli, S., & Passaghe, P. (2017). Potential effect of "Chit" malt on beer foam stability. *EBC, 36th Congress.*

[180] ASBC Methods of Analysis. Beer Method 23A. Bitterness units (International Method). Approved 1968, rev. 1975. American Society of Brewing Chemists: St. Paul, MN.

[181] Intelmann, D.; Batram, C,;Kuhn, Ch.;Haseleu, G.;Meyerhof, M.;Hofmann, T. Three TAS2R bitter taste receptors mediate the psychophysical responses to bitter compounds of hops (Humulus lupulus L.) and beer. Chem. Percept. 2009

[182] P. H., M. Q., & T. S. (2012, August 7). Brewery Scale Dry Hopping: Aroma, Hop Acids, and Polyphenols. Retrieved from http://ir.library.oregonstate.edu/xmlui/bitstream/handle/1957/34

093/Wolfe_thesis.pdf

[183] Dusek, M., Olsovksa, J., Krofta, K., Jurkova, M., and Mikyska, A. Qualitative determination of B-acids and their transformation production in beer and hop using HR/AM-LC-MS/MS. J. Agric. Food Chem. 2014

[184] Dusek, M., Olsovksa, J., Krofta, K., Jurkova, M., and Mikyska, A. Qualitative determination of B-acids and their transformation production in beer and hop using HR/AM-LC-MS/MS. J. Agric. Food Chem. 2014

[185] Cook, A. H., Howard G.A., and Slater, C.A. The chemistry of hop constituents VIII. Oxidation of humulone and cohumulone. J. Inst. Brew. 1955

[186] Hudson, J. R. (1965). The Rationalization Of Hop Utilization- A Review. Journal of the Institute of Brewing, 71(6), 482-489. doi:10.1002/j.2050-0416.1965.tb02076.x

[187] Hudson, J. R. (1965). The Rationalization Of Hop Utilization- A Review. Journal of the Institute of Brewing, 71(6), 482-489. doi:10.1002/j.2050-0416.1965.tb02076.x

[188] Algazzali, V., and Shellhammer, T. Bitterness intensity of oxidized hop acids: Humulinones and hulupones. J. Am. Soc. Brew. Chem. 2016

[189] Applications of High-Performance Liquid Chromatography in the Control of Beer Bitterness. (1986). Journal of the American Society of Brewing Chemists ASBCJ, 44. doi:10.1094/asbcj-44-0101

[190] Peacock, V. Fundamentals of Hop Chemistry. 35 (1) 4-8 1998

[191] Stevens, R., & Wright, D. (1961). headspace Of Hops. X. Hulupones and the Significance of β-Acids in Brewing. Journal of the Institute of Brewing, 67(6), 496-501. doi:10.1002/j.2050-0416.1961.tb01830.x

[192] Hop Storage Index. (1979). Journal of the American Society of Brewing Chemists ASBCJ, 37. doi:10.1094/asbcj-37-0184

[193] Humulinone Formation in Hops and Hop Pellets and Its Implications for Dry Hopped Beers. (2016). Technical Quarterly TQ. doi:10.1094/tq-53-1-0227-01

[194] Yoshimasa, T. (2017). Chemical studies on bitter acid oxides derived from hops (Humulus lupulus L.) in beer brewing and storage. Retrieved from https://dx.doi.org/10.14989/doctor.r13104.

[195] Oladokun, O., James, S., Cowley, T., Smart, K., Hort, J., & Cook, D. (2017). Dry-Hopping: the Effects of Temperature and Hop Variety on the Bittering Profiles and Properties of Resultant Beers. BrewingScience, 70, 187-196.

[196] Meilgaard, M., and Trolle, B. The utilization of hops in the brewhouse. Proc. 6th Congr. Eur. Brew. Conve., Copenhagane. 1957

[197] Schmick, M. (2014). Dry Hopping and its Effect on Beer pH. University of Wisconsin-Stout, Graduate School

[198] Oladokun, O., James, S., Cowley, T., Smart, K., Hort, J., & Cook, D. (2017). Dry-Hopping: the Effects of Temperature and Hop Variety on the Bittering Profiles and Properties of Resultant Beers. BrewingScience, 70, 187-196.

[199] Oladokun, O., Tarrega, A., James, S., Cowley, T., Dehrmann, F., Smart, K., . . . Hort, J. (2016). Modification of perceived beer bitterness intensity, character and temporal profile by hop aroma extract. Food Research International, 86, 104-111. doi:10.1016/j.foodres.2016.05.018

[200] Kaltner, D., Forster, C., Flieher, M., & Pinto, T. (2013). The influence of dry hopping on three different beer styles. Brauwelt International, 355-359.

[201] Hop Acids and their Minimum Inhibitory Concentrations. (n.d.). HOPSTEINER. Retrieved from http://www.hopsteiner.de/fileadmin/redeakteur/pdf/hopfenprodukte/antibakterielle-produkte/bacteriostaticeffects.pdf

202 Maye, J. P., Ph.D. (2018). Hidden Secrets of The New England IPA a.k.a. Hazy IPA a.k.a Juicy IPA. Lecture presented at Hopsteiner.

203 Brown, H. T., & Morris, G. H. (1893). On Certain Functions of Hops Used in the Dry-Hopping of Beers. The Brewers Guardian, 107-109.

204 Janicki, J., Kotasthane, W. V., Parker, A., & Walker, T. K. (1941). The Diastatic Activity Of Hops, Together With A Note On Maltase In Hops. Journal of the Institute of Brewing, 47(1), 24-36. doi:10.1002/j.2050-0416.1941.tb06070.x

205 Kirkpatrick, K., & Shellhammer, T. (2017, June 7). Investigating Enzymatic Power of Hops. Lecture presented at 2017 ASBC Annual Meeting in FL, Fort Myers.

206 Baillo, A. (n.d.). Dry Hopping and Stirring Pellets Increases Vicinal Diketones and Lowers Apparent Extract. Lecture presented at 2017 ASBC Annual Meeting in Florida, Fort Myers.

207 Vanderhaegen, B., Neven, H., Coghe, S., Verstrepen, K. J., Derdelinckx, G., & Verachtert, H. (2003). Bioflavoring and beer refermentation. Applied Microbiology and Biotechnology, 62(2-3), 140-150. doi:10.1007/s00253-003-1340-5

208 Ting, Patrick L., Kay, Susan, and Ryder, David. The Occurrence and Nature of Kettle Hop Flavor. In: Shellhammer, Thomas H. ed., 2009, HOP FLAVOR AND AROMA Poceedings of the 1st International Brewers Symposium, Master Brewers Association of the Americas, St. Paul, MN. Pg 25-26

209 Sarry, J., & Gunata, Z. (2004). Plant and microbial glycoside hydrolases: Volatile release from glycosidic aroma precursors. Food Chemistry, 87(4), 509-521. doi:10.1016/j.foodchem.2004.01.003

210 Lecas, M., Gunata, Z. Y., Sapis, J., & Bayonove, C. L. (1991). Purification and partial characterization of β-glucosidase from grape. Phytochemistry, 30(2), 451-454. doi:10.1016/0031-9422(91)83702-m

211 Sarry, J., & Gunata, Z. (2004). Plant and microbial glycoside

hydrolases: Volatile release from glycosidic aroma precursors. Food Chemistry, 87(4), 509-521. doi:10.1016/j.foodchem.2004.01.003

[212] Goldstein, H., TingP., Schulze, W.G., Murakami, A.A., Lusk, L.T., Young, V.D., 1999b. Methods of making and using purified kettle hop flavorants.

[213] Wang, Y., Zhang, C., Li, J., & Xu, Y. (2013). Different influences of β-glucosidases on volatile compounds and anthocyanins of Cabernet Gernischt and possible reason. Food Chemistry, 140(1-2), 245-254. doi:10.1016/j.foodchem.2013.02.044

[214] The Yeast Bay, METSCHNIKOWIA REUKAUFII. Retrieved May 1, 2019, from https://www.theyeastbay.com/beta-release-cultures/metschnikowia-reukaufii

[215] Rosi, I., Vinella, M., & Domizio, P. (1994). Characterization of β-glucosidaseactivity in yeasts of oenological origin. Journal of Applied Bacteriology, 77(5), 519-527. doi:10.1111/j.1365-2672.1994.tb04396.x

[216] Daenen, L., Saison, D., Sterckx, F., Delvaux, F., Verachtert, H., & Derdelinckx, G. (2007). Screening and evaluation of the glucoside hydrolase activity in Saccharomyces and Brettanomyces brewing yeasts. J Appl Microbiol Journal of Applied Microbiology, 0(0). doi:10.1111/j.1365-2672.2007.03566.x

[217] Vervoort, Y., Herrera-Malaver, B., Mertens, S., Medina, V. G., Duitama, J., Michiels, L., . . . Verstrepen, K. J. (2016). Characterization of the recombinant Brettanomyces anomalus β-glucosidaseand its potential for bioflavoring. J Appl Microbiol Journal of Applied Microbiology. doi:10.1111/jam.13200

[218] Rodriguez, M., Lopes, C., Broock, M., Valles, S., Ramon, D., & Caballero, A. (2004). Screening and typing of Patagonian wine yeasts for glycosidase activities. Journal of Applied Microbiology, 96(1), 84-95. doi:10.1046/j.1365-2672.2003.02032.x

[219] Haslbeck, K., Jerebic, S., & Zarnkow, M. (2017). Characterization of the Unfertilized and Fertilized Hop Varieties Progress and

Hallertauer Tradition - Analysis of Free and Glycosidic-Bound Flavor Compounds and B-Glucosidase Activity. BrewingScience, 70, 148-158.

[220] Wanapu, C., Sripunya, P., & Boonkerd, N. (2012). Selection of Yeast Strains Containing -Glucosidase for Improving Wine Aroma. Journal of Agricultural Science and Technology, 691-702.)

[221] Steyer, D., Tristram, P., Clayeux, C., Heitz, F., & Laugel, B. (2017). Yeast Strains and Hop Varieties Synergy on Beer Volatile Compounds. BrewingScience, 70, 131-141.

[222] Inui, T. (n.d.). Study on the attractive hop aroma for beer. Speech presented at World Brewing Congress 2012, Portland, OR.

[223] Sharp, D., Qian, Y., Shellhammer, G., & Shellhammer, T. (2017). Contributions of Select Hopping Regimes to the Terpenoid Content and Hop Aroma Profile of Ale and Lager Beers. Journal of the American Society of Brewing Chemists. doi:10.1094/asbcj-2017-2144-01

[224] Swangkeaw, J., ViChitphan, S., Butzke, C. E., & ViChitphan, K. (2009). The characterisation of a novel Pichia anomala β-glucosidasewith potentially aroma-enhancing capabilities in wine. Ann. Microbiol. Annals of Microbiology, 59(2), 335-343. doi:10.1007/bf03178336

[225] Lei, H., Xu, H., Feng, L., Yu, Z., Zhao, H., & Zhao, M. (2016). Fermentation performance of lager yeast in high gravity beer fermentations with different sugar supplementations. Journal of Bioscience and Bioengineering. doi:10.1016/j.jbiosc.2016.05.004

[226] Wang, Y., Zhang, C., Li, J., & Xu, Y. (2013). Different influences of β-glucosidases on volatile compounds and anthocyanins of Cabernet Gernischt and possible reason. Food Chemistry, 140(1-2), 245-254. doi:10.1016/j.foodchem.2013.02.044

[227] Vervoort, Y., Herrera-Malaver, B., Mertens, S., Medina, V. G., Duitama, J., Michiels, L., . . . Verstrepen, K. J. (2016). Characterization of the recombinant Brettanomyces anomalus β-glucosidaseand its potential for bioflavoring. J Appl Microbiol Journal of Applied Microbiology. doi:10.1111/jam.13200

[228] Swangkeaw, J., Vichitphan, S., Butzke, C. E., & Vichitphan, K. (2009). The characterisation of a novel Pichia anomala β-glucosidasewith potentially aroma-enhancing capabilities in wine. Ann. Microbiol. Annals of Microbiology, 59(2), 335-343. doi:10.1007/bf03178336

[229] "The Sour Hour – Episode 37." Audio blog post. Ed. Scott Moskowitz. The Brewing Network, 21 June 2016. Web

[230] Gil, J., Manzanares, P., Genoves, S., Valles, S., & Gonzalezcandelas, L. (2005). Over-production of the major exoglucanase of leads to an increase in the aroma of wine. International Journal of Food Microbiology, 103(1), 57-68. doi:10.1016/j.ijfoodmicro.2004.11.026

[231] Andrew King, Richard Dickinson (2003, March). Biotransformation of hop aroma terpenoids by ale and lager yeasts. Retrieved from http://onlinelibrary.wiley.com/doi/10.1111/j.1567-1364.2003.tb00138.x/full

[232] Sharp, D., Vollmer, D., Qian, Y., & Shellhammer, T. (2017). Examination of Glycoside Hydrolysis Methods for the Determination of Terpenyl Glycoside Contents of Different Hop Cultivars. Journal of the American Society of Brewing Chemists. doi:10.1094/asbcj-2017-2071-01

[233] Takoi, K., Itoga, Y., Koie, K., Kosugi, T., Shimase, M., Katayama, Y., . . . Watari, J. (2010). The Contribution of Geraniol Metabolism to the Citrus Flavour of Beer: Synergy of Geraniol and β-Citronellol Under Coexistence with Excess Linalool. Journal of the Institute of Brewing, 116(3), 251-260. doi:10.1002/j.2050-0416.2010.tb00428.x

[234] https://ychhops.com/varieties

[235] Screening of Geraniol-rich Flavor Hop and Interesting Behavior of β-citronellol During Fermentation under Various Hop-Addition Timings. Journal of the American Society of Brewing

Chemists. doi:10.1094/asbcj-2014-0116-01

[236] Takoi, K., Itoga, Y., Koie, K., Takayanagi, J., Kaneko, T., Watanabe, T., . . . Nomura, M. (2017). Systematic Analysis of Behavior of Hop-Derived Monoterpene Alcohols During Fermentation and New Classification of Geraniol-Rich Flavour Hops. BrewingScience, 70, 177-186.

[237] Schmidt, C., & Biendl, M. (2016). Headspace Trap GC-MS analysis of hop aroma compounds in beer. BrewingScience, 69, 9-15.

[238] Takoi, K., Itoga, Y., Koie, K., Kosugi, T., Shimase, M., Katayama, Y., . . . Watari, J. (2010). The Contribution of Geraniol Metabolism to the Citrus Flavour of Beer: Synergy of Geraniol and β-Citronellol Under Coexistence with Excess Linalool. Journal of the Institute of Brewing, 116(3), 251-260. doi:10.1002/j.2050-0416.2010.tb00428.x

[239] http://www.themadfermentationist.com/2017/02/gose-neipa-principles-for-coriander.html

[240] Tominaga, T., Baltweck-Guyot, R., Peyrot des Gachons, C. & Dubourdieu, D., 2000. Contribution of volatile thiols to the aromas of white wines made from several Vitis vinifera grape varieties. Am. J. Enol. Vitic. 57, 178-181.]

[241] Kammhuber, K., Hundhammer, M., & Weihrauch, S. (2017). Influence of the Date of Harvest on the Sulphur Compounds of the "Special Flavour Hop" Varieties Cascade, Mandarina Bavaria, Hallertau Blanc, Huell Melon and Polaris. BrewingScience, 70, 124-130.

[242] Wakabayashi, H., Wakabayashi, M., Eisenreich, W., and Engel, K. H. Stereochemical course of the generation of 3-mercaptohexanal and 3-mercaptohexanol by B-lyase-catalyzed cleave of cysteine conjugates. J. Agric. Food Chem. 52:110-116, 2004

[243] Wust, M.: Wein - Qualitat entscheidet sich in Nanogramm, chemie in unserer Zeit, 37 (2003), pp. 8-17.

[244] Tominaga T, Furrer A, Henry R & Dubourdieu D (1998a) Identification of new volatile thiols in the aroma of Vitis vinifera L.

var. Sauvignon blanc wines. Flavour Fragr J. 13: 152-162.

[245] Steinhaus, M.;Schieberle, P. Transfer of the potent hop odorants linalool, geraniol and 4-methyl-4-sulfanyl-2-pentanone from hops into beer. In European Brewery Convention, Proceedings of the 31st EBC Congress, Venice 2007; Fachverlag Hans Carl: Nuremberg, Germany, 2007; 112.

[246] Steinhaus, M.; Fritsch, H.T.; Schieberle, P. Quantitation of (R)- and (S)-linalool in beer using solid phase microextraction (SPME) in combination with a stable isotope dilution assay (SIDA). J. Agric. Food Chem. 2003, 51, 7100-7105

[247] Reglitz, K., & Steinhaus, M. (2017). Quantitation of 4-Methyl-4-sulfanylpentan-2-one (4MSP) in Hops by a Stable Isotope Dilution Assay in Combination with GC×GC-TOFMS: Method Development and Application To Study the Influence of Variety, Provenance, Harvest Year, and Processing on 4MSP Concentrations. Journal of Agricultural and Food Chemistry, 65(11), 2364-2372. doi:10.1021/acs.jafc.7b00455

[248] Kishimoto, T.; Kobayashi, M.; Yako, N.; Iida, A.; Wanikawa, A. Comparison of 4-mercapto-4-methylpentan-2-one contents in hop cultivars from different growing regions. J. Agric. Food Chem. 2008, 56, 1051-1057

[249] Hieronymus, S. (2017, August 17). Hop Queries: Keeping our 4MMP list up to date. Hop Queries.

[250] Reglitz, K., N. L., S. H., & M. S. (2018). On the Behavior of the Important Hop Odorant 4-Mercapto-4methylpentan-2-one (4MMP) during Dry Hopping and during Storage of Dry Hopped Beer. *BrewingScience,71*, 96-99.

[251] Roland, A., Delpech, S., & Dagan, L. (2017). A Powerful Analytical Indicator to Drive Varietal Thiols Release in Beers: The "Thiol Potency". BrewingScience, 70, 170-175.

[252] Polyfunctional Thiols in Fresh and Aged Belgian Special Beers: Fate of Hop S-Cysteine Conjugates. (2015). Journal of the

American Society of Brewing Chemists. doi:10.1094/asbcj-2015-0130-01

[253] C. (2013). First Evidence of the Production of Odorant Polyfunctional Thols by Bottle Refermentation. Journal of the American Society of Brewing Chemists. doi:10.1094/asbcj-2013-0117-01

[254] Masneuf-Pomarede I, Mansour C, Murat ML, Tominaga T & Dubourdieu D (2006) Influence of fermentation temperature on volatile thiols concentrations in Sauvigon Blanc wines. Int J Food Microbiol 108: 385-390.

[255] Subileau, M., Schneider, R., Salmon, J., & Degryse, E. (2008). Nitrogen catabolite repression modulates the production of aromatic thiols characteristic of Sauvignon Blanc at the level of precursor transport. FEMS Yeast Research, 8(5), 771-780. doi:10.1111/j.1567-1364.2008.00400.x

[256] Dubourdieu D.; Lavigne; 1990: Incidence de l'hyperoxygénation sur la composition chimique et les qualités organoleptiques des vins blancs secs du bordelais. Rev. Fr. Oenol. 124, 58-61.

[257] Gros, J., Nizet, S., and Collin, S. (2011) Occurrence of odorant polyfunctional thiols in the super alpha Tomahawk hop cultivar. Comparison with the thiol-rich Nelson Sauvin bitter variety. J. Agric. Food Chem., 59, 8853-8865.

[258] Grant-Preece, P.A., Pardon, K.H., Capone, D.L., Cordente, A. G., Sefton, M.A., Jeffery, D.W., and Elsey, G. M. Synthesis of wine thiol conjugates and labeled analogues: Fermentation of the glutathione conjugate of 3-mercaptohexan-1-ol yields the corresponding cysteine conjugate and free thiol. J. Agric. Food Chem. 58:1383-1389,2010

[259] Roland, A., Schneider, R., Le Guerneve, C., Razungles, A., and Cavelier, F. Identification and quantification by LC-MS/MS of a new precursor of 3-mercaptohexan-1-ol (3MH) using stable isotope dilution assay: Elements for understanding the 3MH production in wine. Food Chem. 121:847855, 2010

[260] Swiegers JH & Pretorius IS (2007) Modulation of volatile sulfur compounds by wine yeast. Appl Microbiol Biotechnol 74: 954-960.

[261] Gros, J., Tran, T. T., & Collin, S. (2013). Enzymatic release of odourant polyfunctional thiols from cysteine conjugates in hop. Journal of the Institute of Brewing, 119(4), 221-227. doi:10.1002/jib.80

[262] Tominaga, T., R. Baltenweck-Guyot, C. Peyrot de Gachons, and D. Dubour-dieu. 2000. Contribution of volatile thiols to the aromas of white wines made from several Vitis vinifera grape varieties. Am. J. Enol. Vitic. 51:178–181

[263] Howell, K. S., J. H. Swiegers, G. Elsey, T. E. Siebert, E. J. Bartowsky, G. H. Fleet, Pretorius, I. S., and M. de Barros Lopes. 2004. Variation in 4-mercapto-4-methyl-pentan-2-one release by different wine strains. FEMS Microbiol. Lett. 240:125-129

[264] Murat ML, Masneuf I, Darriet P, Lavigne V, Tominaga T, DubourdieuD (2001) Effect of Saccharomyces cerevisiae yeast strains on the liberation of volatile thiols in Sauvignon Blanc wine. Am J Enol Vitic 52:136–139

[265] Swiegers, J. H., & Pretorius, I. S. (2007). Modulation of volatile sulfur compounds by wine yeast. Applied Microbiology and Biotechnology, 74(5), 954-960. doi:10.1007/s00253-006-0828-1

[266] Howell, K. S., Klein, M., Swiegers, J. H., Hayasaka, Y., Elsey, G. M., Fleet, G. H., . . . Lopes, M. A. (2005). Genetic Determinants of Volatile-Thiol Release by Saccharomyces cerevisiae during Wine Fermentation. Applied and Environmental Microbiology, 71(9), 5420-5426. doi:10.1128/aem.71.9.5420-5426.2005

[267] Murat, M.L.; Masneuf, I.; Darriet, P.; Lavigne, V.; Tominga, T.;Dubourdieu, D. (2001a) Effect of Saccharomyces cerevisiae yeast strains on the liberation of volatile thiols in Sauvignon blanc wine. Am. J. Enol. Vitic.52:136-139.

[268] Swiegers, J., Francis, I., Herderich, M., & Pretorius, I. (2006).

[269] http://www.oenobrands.com/en/our-brands/anchor/new-world-wine-yeasts/product-data-sheets/vin-7

[270] http://www.oenobrands.com/en/our-brands/anchor/alchemy-yeast-blends/anchor-alchemy-ii

[271] King, E. S., Swiegers, J. H., Travis, B., Francis, I. L., Bastian, S. E., & Pretorius, I. S. (2008). Coinoculated Fermentations Using Saccharomyces Yeasts Affect the Volatile Composition and Sensory Properties ofVitis viniferaL. cv. Sauvignon Blanc Wines. Journal of Agricultural and Food Chemistry, 56(22), 10829-10837. doi:10.1021/jf801695h

[272] https://www.chr-hansen.com/en/food-cultures-and-enzymes/wine/cards/product-cards/frootzen-first-ever-pichia-kluyveri-yeast

[273] Holt, S., Mukherjee, V., Lievens, B., Verstrepen, K. J., & Thevelein, J. M. (2018). Bioflavoring by non-conventional yeasts in sequential beer fermentations. Food Microbiology, 72, 55-66. doi:10.1016/j.fm.2017.11.008

[274] Zuchowski, J.; Jonczyk, K.; Pecio, L.; Oleszek, W. Phenolic acid concentrations in organically and conventionally cultivated spring and winter wheat. J. Sci. Food Agric. 2011, 91, 1089-1095.

[275] Kishimoto, Toru. “Hop-Derived Odorants Contributing to the Aroma Characteristics of Beer.” Journal Of The Brewing Society Of Japan, vol. 104, no. 3, 2009, pp. 157–169., doi:10.6013/jbrewsocjapan.104.157.

[276] K. (2008). Behaviors of 3-Mercaptohexan-1-ol and 3-Mercaptohexyl Acetate During Brewing Processes. Journal of the American Society of Brewing Chemists. doi:10.1094/asbcj-2008-0702-01

[277] Kishimoto, T., Morimoto, M., Kobaysashi, M., Yako, N., & Wanikawa, A. (n.d.). Behaviors of 3-Mercaptohexan-1-ol and 3-Mercaptohexyl Acetate During Brewing Processes. American Society of Brewing Chemists, 192-196.)

[278] Roland, A., Delpech, S., Reillon, F., Viel, C., & Dagan, L. (n.d.). First Identification of Cysteinylated and Glutathionylated Precursors of 3-Mercaptohexan-1-ol in Barley. EBC 2017 Presentation

[279] Takoi, K.; Tominaga, T.; Degueil, M.; Sakata, D.; Kurihara, T.; Shinkaruk, S.; Nakamura, T.; Maeda, K.; Akiyama, H.; Watari, J.; Bennetau, B. and Dubourdieu, D.: Identifi cation of novel unique flavor compounds derived from Nelson Sauvin hop and development of new product using this hop. Proc. 31st EBC Congr., (2007)

[280] Takoi, K., Degueil, M., Shinkaruk, S., Thibon, C., Kurihara, T., Toyoshima, K., . . . Tominaga, T. (2009). Specific Flavor Compounds Derived from Nelson Sauvin Hop and Synergy of these Compounds. BrewingScience, 62, 108-118.

[281] Takoi, K., Itoga, Y., Koie, K., Takayanagi, J., Watanabe, T., Matsumoto, I., & Nomura, M. (2018). Behaviour of Hop-derived Branched-chain Esters During Fermentation and Unique Characteristics of Huell Melon and Ekuanot (HBC366) Hops. *BrewingScience,71*, 100-109.

[282] http://scottjanish.com/toasted-oat-hull-melon-pale-ale/

[283] Takoi, K., Sanekata, A., Itoga, Y., Koie, K., Matsumoto, I., & Nakayama, Y. (2016). Varietal Difference of Hop-Derived Flavour Compounds in Late-Hopped/Dry-Hopped Beers. BrewingScience, 69, 1-7.

[284] Schmidt, C., & Biendl, M. (2016). Headspace Trap GC-MS analysis of hop aroma compounds in beer. BrewingScience, 69, 9-15.

[285] Matsche, B., Muñoz, A., Wiesen, E., Schönberger, C., & Krottenthaler, M. (2018). *The Influence of Yeast Strains and Hop Varieties on the Aroma of Beer* (Vol. 71). BrewingScience.

[286] Haslbeck, K., Bub, S., Schönberger, C., Zarnkow, M., Jacob, F., & Coelhan, M. (2017). On the Fate of B-Myrcene during Fermentation - The Role of Stripping and Uptake of Hop Oil

Compounds by Brewer's Yeast in Dry-Hopped Wort and Beer. BrewingScience, 70, 159-169.

[287] S. (2011). Volatilization of Aroma Compounds Relevant for Wheat Beer in Water Under Conditions Simulating Alcoholic Fermentation. Journal of the American Society of Brewing Chemists. doi:10.1094/asbcj-2011-0822-01

[288] Ferreira, V., Peña, C., Escudero, A., & Cacho, J. (1996). Losses of volatile compounds during fermentation. Zeitschrift für Lebensmittel-Untersuchung und -Forschung, 202(4), 318-323. doi:10.1007/bf01206104

[289] Hieronymus, S. (2017, August 17). Hop Queries [E-mail].

[290] https://ychhops.com/varieties

[291] Kaltner, D., Forster, C., Flieher, M., & Pinto, T. (2013). The influence of dry hopping on three different beer styles. Brauwelt International, 355-359

[292] Parkin, E., & Shellhammer, T. (n.d.). Toward Understanding the Bitterness of Dry-Hopped Beer. American Society of Brewing Chemists, Inc. 75(4):363-368,2017

[293] L. Mélotte, INBR, UcL, XIIIth J. DE CLERCK CHAIR, September 2008

[294] Bitterness-Modifying Properties of Hop Polyphenols Extracted from Spent Hop Material. Journal of the American Society of Brewing Chemists. doi:10.1094/asbcj-2008-0619-01

[295] Forster, A., & Gahr, A. (2013) On the fate of certain hop substances during dry hopping. Brewing Science, 66, 93-103.

[296] Berner, T., Jacobsen, S., & Arneborg, N. (2013). The impact of different ale brewer's yeast strains on the proteome of immature beer. BMC Microbiology, 13(1), 215. doi:10.1186/1471-2180-13-215

[297] Siebert KJ (1999) Effects of protein-polyphenol interactions on beverage haze, stabilization, and analysis. J Agric Food Chem 47:353-362

[298] Siebert, K. and Lynn, P. Y.: Effect of protein-polyphenol ratio on the size of haze particles, Journal of the American Society of Brewing Chemists 58 (2000), no. 3, pp. 117 - 123.

[299] Hagerman, A. E., Rice, M. E., and Ritchard, N. T. (1998). Mechanisms of protein precipitation for two tannins, pentagalloyl glucose and epicatechin16 (4→8) catechin (procyanidin). J. Agric. Food Chem. 46, 2590–2595.

[300] Delvaux, F., Combes, F., and Delvaux, F. The effect of wheat malting on the colloidal haze of white beers. Tech. Q. Master Brew. Assoc. Am. 41:27-32, 2004.

[301] (Klose, C., Schehl, B., & Arendt, E. (2008). Protein Changes during Malting of Barley using Novel Lab-on-a-Chip Technology in Comparison to two-dimensional Gel Electrophoresis. BrewingScience, 56.

[302] Delvaux, F., Combes, F., and Delvaux, F. The effect of wheat malting on the colloidal haze of white beers. Tech. Q. Master Brew. Assoc. Am. 41:27-32, 2004.

[303] Shewry, P. R., Tatham, A. S., Fido R., Jones, H., Bercelo, P., and Lazzeri, P. A. Improving the end use properties of wheat by manipulating the grain protein composition. In: Wheat in Global Enviroment. 6th International Wheat Conference, Budapest, Hungary, 2000.

[304] Narziss, L., and Black, W. Die Technologie der Malzbereitung. Ferdinand Enke Verlag, Stuttgart, Germany, 2009.

[305] Asano, K., Shinagawa, K., & Hashimoto, N. (1982). Characterization of Haze-Forming Proteins of Beer and Their Roles in Chill Haze Formation. Journal of the American Society of Brewing Chemists, 40. doi:10.1094/asbj-40-0147) In other words, during germination, storage proteins (gluten proteins

[306] Faltermaier, A., Waters, D., Becker, T., Arendt, E., & Gastl, M. (2013). Protein Modifications and Metabolic Changes Taking Place

During the Malting of Common Wheat (Triticum aestivum L.). American Society of Brewing Chemists, Inc., 71, 153-160.

[307] Asano K, Shinagawa K, Hashimoto N (1982) Characterization of haze forming proteins of beer and their roles in chill haze formation. J AM Soc Brew Chem 40:147-154

[308] The Effect of Germination Time on the Final Malt Quality of Buckwheat. (2006). Journal of the American Society of Brewing Chemists. doi:10.1094/asbcj-64-0214

[309] Asano, K., Shinagawa, K., and Hashimoto, N. (1982). Characterization of haze-forming proteins of beer and their roles in chill haze formation. J. Am. Soc. Brew. Chem. 40, 147–154

[310] Siebert KJ (2006) Haze formation in beverages. LWT-Food Sci Technol 39:987-994

[311] Fontana, M., and Buiatti, S. (2009) Amino acids in beer, in Health and Disease Prevention (Preedy, V. R., Ed.), pp. 273 284, Elsevier Academic Press, London.

[312] Deželak, M., Zarnkow, M., Becker, T., & Košir, I. J. (2014). Processing of bottom-fermented gluten-free beer-like beverages based on buckwheat and quinoa malt with chemical and sensory characterization. Journal of the Institute of Brewing. doi:10.1002/jib.166

[313] http://www.bobsredmill.com/whole-grain-oat-flour.html

[314] https://en.wikipedia.org/wiki/Rolled_oats

[315] Schnitzenbaumer, B., Kaspar, J., Titze, J., & Arendt, E. K. (2013). Implementation of commercial oat and sorghum flours in brewing. European Food Research and Technology, 238(3), 515-525. doi:10.1007/s00217-013-2129-0

[316] https://www.whitelabs.com/yeast-vault

[317] https://www.themadfermentationist.com/2017/11/new-england-pale-ale-brewing-video.html

[318] Oxygen and Oxygen Radicals in Malting and Brewing: A Review. (1993). Journal of the American Society of Brewing Chemists, 51. doi:10.1094/asbj-51-0079

[319] Kaneda, H., Takashio, M., Osawa, T., Kawakishi, S., and Tamaki, T. Behavior of sulfites during fermentation and storage of beer. J. Am. Soc. Brew. Chem. 54:115-120, 1996.

[320] Ilett, D.R. 1995. Aspects of the analysis, role, and fate of sulfur dioxide in beer: a review. MBAA Technical Quarterly 32: 213-221.)

[321] Harding, D., "Finings," Chemistry and Industry. 1979,895.

[322] Lund, M. N., Krämer, A. C., & Andersen, M. L. (2015). Antioxidative Mechanisms of Sulfite and Protein-Derived Thiols during Early Stages of Metal Induced Oxidative Reactions in Beer. Journal of Agricultural and Food Chemistry, 63(37), 8254-8261. doi:10.1021/acs.jafc.5b02617

[323] The Role of Copper, Oxygen, and Polyphenols in Beer Flavor Instability. (1991). Journal of the American Society of Brewing Chemists, 49. doi:10.1094/asbj-49-0140

[324] Almeida, N. E., Lund, M. N., Andersen, M. L., & Cardoso, D. R. (2013). Beer Thiol-Containing Compounds and Redox Stability: Kinetic Study of 1-Hydroxyethyl Radical Scavenging Ability. Journal of Agricultural and Food Chemistry, 61(39), 9444-9452. doi:10.1021/jf402159a

[325] Lindoff-Larsen, K., and Winther, J. R. Surprisingly high stability of barley lipid transfer protein, LTP1, towards denaturant, heat and proteases. FEBSLett. 488:145-148, 2001

[326] Wu, M., Clarke, F., Rogers, P., Young, P., Sales, N., O'Doherty, P., & Higgins, V. (2011). Identification of a Protein with Antioxidant Activity that is Important for the Protection against Beer Ageing. International Journal of Molecular Sciences.

[327] Sorensen, S.B., Bech, L./ M., Muldbjerg, M., Beenfeldt, T. and Breddam, K., Barley lipid transfer protein 1 is involved in beer foam

formation. Tech. Q. Master Brew. Assoc. Am., 1993, 30, 136-145

[328] Klose, C., Schehl, B., & Arendt, E. (2008). Protein Changes during Malting of Barley using Novel Lab-on-a-Chip Technology in Comparison to two-dimensional Gel Electrophoresis. BrewingScience, 56.

[329] Faltermaier, A., Negele, J., Becker, T., Gastl, M., & Arendt, E. (2015). Evaluation of Mashing Attributes and Protein Profile Using Different Grist Composition of Barley and Wheat Malt. BrewingScience, 68, 67-77.)

[330] B. (2009). Storage of Malt, Thiol Oxidase, and Brewhouse Performance. Journal of the American Society of Brewing Chemists. doi:10.1094/asbcj-2009-0219-01

[331] A. (2007). Effects of Maillard and Caramelization Products on Oxidative Reactions in Lager Beer. Journal of the American Society of Brewing Chemists. doi:10.1094/asbcj-2007-0112-02

[332] Zufall, C., & Tyrell, T. (2008). The Influence of Heavy Metal Ions on Beer Flavour Stability. Journal of the Institute of Brewing, 114(2), 134-142. doi:10.1002/j.2050-0416.2008.tb00318.x

[333] Deželak, M., Gebremariam, M. M., Zarnkow, M., Becker, T., & Košir, I. J. (2015). Part I: the influence of serial repitching ofSaccharomyces pastorianuson the uptake dynamics of metal ions and fermentable carbohydrates during the fermentation of barley and gluten-free buckwheat and quinoa wort. Journal of the Institute of Brewing, 121(3), 356-369. doi:10.1002/jib.244

[334] Porter, J., & Bamforth, C. (2016). NOTE: Manganese in Brewing Raw Materials, Disposition During the Brewing Process, and Impact on the Flavor Instability of Beer. Journal of the American Society of Brewing Chemists. doi:10.1094/asbcj-2016-2638-01

[335]

https://en.wikipedia.org/wiki/Spelt)(https://en.wikipedia.org/wiki/Barley

[336] Wietstock, P., Kunz, T., & Methner, F. (2016). Influence of

Hopping Technology on Oxidative Stability and Staling-Related Carbonyls in Pale Lager Beer. BrewingScience, 69, 73-84.)

337 Wietstock, P., Kunz, T., Pereira, F., & Methner, F. (2016). Metal Chelation Behavior of Hop Acids in Buffered Model Solutions. BrewingScience, 69, 56-63.

338 http://www.craftbrewersconference.com/wp-content/uploads/2015_presentations/R0900_Ruth_Martin.pdf

339 Deželak, M., Zarnkow, M., Becker, T., & Košir, I. J. (2014). Processing of bottom-fermented gluten-free beer-like beverages based on buckwheat and quinoa malt with chemical and sensory characterization. Journal of the Institute of Brewing. doi:10.1002/jib.166

340 Elbagermi, M. A., et al. “Monitoring of Heavy Metal Content in Fruits and Vegetables Collected from Production and Market Sites in the Misurata Area of Libya.” ISRN Analytical Chemistry, vol. 2012, 2012, pp. 1–5., doi:10.5402/2012/827645.

341 Dalgliesh, C. E. (1977). Flavour stability. Proceedings of the European Brewery Convention Congress, 623–659.

342 Meilgaard, M. (1972). Stale flavor carbonyls in brewing. Brewers Digest, 47, 48–57.

343 Clapperton, J. F. (1976). Ribes flavour in beer. Journal of the Institute of Brewing, 82, 175–176.)

344 Furusho, S., Kobayashi, N., Nakae, N., Takashio, M., Tamaki, T., & Shinotsuka, K. (1999). A developed descriptive sensory test reveals beer flavor changes during storage. MBAA Technical Quarterly, 36, 163–166

345 Bamforth, C. W. (1999b). The science and understanding of the flavour stability of beer: a critical assessment. Brauwelt International, 98–110

346 Fritsch, H., and Schieberle, P. (2003). Changes in key aroma compounds during boiling of unhopped and hopped wort. In: 29th

European Brewery Convention Congress, Dublin, pp. 259-267. Fachverlag Hans Carl, Nürnberg, Germany.

[347] Kaltner, D., Steinhaus, M., Mitter, W., Biendl, M., and Schieberle, P. (2003). R-linalool as key flavor for hop aroma in beer and its behavior during beer staling (in German). Monatsschr. Brauwiss. 56(11/12):192-196.

[348] Peacock, V., & Deinzer, M. (1988). Fate of Hop Oil Components in Beer. Journal of the American Society of Brewing Chemists ASBCJ, 46. doi:10.1094/asbj-46-0104

[349] Vanderhagen, B., Coghe, S., Verachtert, H. and Derdelinckx, G. (2002). Microbiology and biochemical aspects of refermentation. Cerevisia 28:48-58.

[350] Van den Berg, S., Demeyere, K. and Van Landschoot, A. (2001). The use of dried yeast for the bottle refermentation of beer. Cervisia 26:102-108.)

[351] Quain, D. (2006). Active dry yeast - on the rise? Brew. Guardian 135:31-35

[352] Z. (2011). The Use of Dry Yeast for Bottle Conditioning. Technical Quarterly. doi:10.1094/tq-48-1-0225-01

[353] www.lallemandbrewing.com/wp-content/uploads/.../lallemand-tds-cbc1-022817-1.pdf

Index

Made in the USA
Las Vegas, NV
11 May 2021

22833033R00157